Method Marketing

Books by Denison (Denny) Hatch:

Statuary Rape
Statues of Limitations
Cedarhurst Alley
The Fingered City
The Stork
Million Dollar Mailing$
2,239 Tested Secrets for Direct Marketing Success
   (co-authored with Don Jackson)

Method Marketing

How to Make a Fortune by Getting
Inside the Heads of Your Customers

Denny Hatch

Bonus Books, Inc.
Chicago, IL

Cover image: Masterfile/Aitch/(TC)
Cover design: Karen Sheets

Library of Congress Cataloging-in-Publication Data

Hatch, Denny.
  Method marketing : how to make a fortune by getting inside the
 heads of your customers / by Denny Hatch.
    p. cm.
  ISBN 1-56625-115-X
  1. Target marketing. 2. Direct marketing. I. Title.
HF5415.127.H38 1999
658.8′4—dc21   98-31376
                 CIP

To Peggy
With thanks and love for everything, including
coming up with the term "Method Marketing"

CONTENTS

1
About Marketing

Marketing is the business of acquiring customers and continually delighting them.

Note, I did not use the terms "customer satisfaction," "customer retention" or "customer service."

Customer delight.

Example: When you are on the road and staying in a hotel, what do you miss most from your daily routine? I'll tell you what I miss: *The New York Times* and *The Wall Street Journal* waiting by the front door when I get up, and a pot of fresh coffee to accompany my reading.

One afternoon in early June, I checked into the Sheraton New York for a direct marketing conference. At the reception desk, I handed the young man my credit card and asked for a nonsmoking room. Upon completing the paperwork and presenting me with the plastic card-key, the young man asked which newspaper I would like delivered to my door in the morning. My choices: *The New York Times* or *USA Today*. In my opinion, *USA Today* is pop crap with absolutely no reason to be published (unless you are in Montgomery, Alabama, where it looks pretty good). I asked for the *Times*.

In my room I found a Mr. Coffee with a sealed foil packet of Starbucks. With my morning coffee and *The New York Times,* I was prepared to be delighted with Sheraton Hotels. Clearly, Sheraton management was inside the heads of its guests.

The next morning when I opened the door of my room, guess what was awaiting me.

USA Today.

In *The Wall Street Journal,* Herbert Klein wrote:

> I forgot what my college professor Frank Knight said. People want their wants satisfied. They want better wants.

Yes and no.

The Sheraton New York room clerk had created a better want. Had he said nothing, I would have been happy with *USA Today.*

"Ah, how nice," I would have thought, "a free newspaper."

Instead, the New York Sheraton had set itself up for failure and set me up for disappointment.

If you you don't deliver what you promise, you're better off making no promise in the first place. If you can't deliver on a customer loyalty program, scrap the program.

Perhaps the true secret of great marketing is summed up in the words of consultant Marilyn Black:

Underpromise and overdeliver.

Textbook-Correct Marketing

A couple of years ago, I met the manager of Philadelphia's great hotel, The Rittenhouse. He told me about a corporate titan from Spain who had bought a company in the area and was staying at the Rittenhouse on his first visit. If he liked the hotel, presumably he would be back and would steer other executives from his various companies there.

On the morning after his arrival, he opened the door of his suite and at his feet were two newspapers — the European edition of *The Wall Street Journal* and that morning's Madrid daily.

He was promised nothing; the Rittenhouse had overdelivered.

Customer delight.

Herein lies the difference between a marketer and a product manager. Product managers manage products. Marketers acquire and delight customers.

That's why marketers make a lot more money than product managers.

America: A Marketer's Dream

The United States is unlike any other country in the world. We are made up of 100 million households and 11 million businesses; the individuals in these households and businesses are relatively affluent; all speak the same language and are literate. They are reachable via some 25,000 lists and delivery systems; split those lists into various segments and you're looking at more like 250,000 different lists to choose from.

Add into the mix the fact that the United States has the world's most efficient postal system, one that delivers the mail six days a week to every address in the country — and at a fraction of the cost of any comparable service in the industrialized world.

If you prefer not to use mail, you can reach the 97 million households with television sets where an average of 50 hours a week is spent watching programs broadcast by nearly 10,000 television and cable stations. Or you can interact with Americans via 91 million telephone lines and persuade 40 million of them to respond to you via the Internet. In the world of low-tech communications (e.g., space advertising), the United States boasts a vast array of weekly and daily newspapers with a combined circulation of 60 million and a several thousand magazines serving every conceivable niche.

Billions of Electronic Dossiers

Today, a consumer's name, address and ZIP code found in the white pages represent the bare bones beginning of the information accessible on an individual basis. Vast amounts of public data are available: make and model of automobile; driver's license details (height, weight, date of birth, use of glasses, poor driving record); home ownership, value of home and amount of mortgage; arrest records; bankruptcy filings.

In addition, tens of millions of Americans buy appliances every year and dutifully fill out "warranty cards," volunteering all kinds of personal information: marital status, hobbies and interests, income, presence of children and their ages. These are mailed to data collection services where the data are entered and individual electronic dossiers are compiled and maintained on computers. The Polk company processes 25 million of these a year, roughly one-quarter of all households in America; Metromail and Donnelley Marketing process many millions more.

Plus, mail order transactional data are available. Buyers of women's clothes, electronic gizmos, shoes, children's wear, business books and any of a thousand other specific "selects" are available from various list-owners and database companies.

What's more, many of the questions on surveys include matters of family health. (Does anyone in your family have allergies, back problems, cancer, eye problems, etc.?) Drug companies access the data and start mailing pitches for their drugs.

Add to this the actual health secrets — folks who take prescription drugs for AIDS, cancer, osteoporosis, allergies, depression. This information resides in numerous databases: the computers of the primary care physician and specialist, the hospital and/or HMO and the pharmacy where the prescriptions are filled.

If you wanted to, you could data enter the names from a local phone book and then import information from a host of databases until you have a vast electronic dossier on every individual in your neighborhood, your ZIP code. You could do the same for all the white pages in America and create highly detailed electronic dossiers on all 100 million households in the United States.

In fact, many marketers do just that.

2

Method Marketing: What Is It?

You're David Oreck.

You manufacture and sell the best, lightest, most rugged and efficient vacuum cleaner ever designed.

It is in use by more than 50,000 hotels worldwide — from the elegant Windsor Court in New Orleans to the Holiday Inn in Seattle. It's a truly great product; every home and office in America should have one.

Your message to the consumer:

> Take the Oreck challenge. Send for my Oreck-XL for a 15-day free trial. When it arrives, clean all your rugs and carpets with your current vacuum cleaner. Then go over them again with my Oreck-XL, look in the bag and see how much dirt your old vacuum cleaner left behind. If for any reason you feel my Oreck-XL fails to live up to my promise or your expectations, return it. I'll pay shipping both ways. You owe nothing. This is an entirely risk-free offer.

Your key copy drivers: fear and salvation:

Fear of disgusting dirt and leftover dust in your carpets; salvation with an Oreck vacuum cleaner.

In the words of the great 1920s advertising practitioner Claude Hopkins:

> The right offer should be so attractive that only a lunatic would say 'no.'

Oreck has done this.

Or has he?

Where Oreck's Message
Will Totally Bomb

You're a homeowner.

You have had chronic allergies all your life. You don't have a single carpet or rug anywhere. Instead, your entire house has exposed hardwood floors. You won't have a vacuum cleaner because it blows dust around.

How does Oreck's message resonate with you?

It doesn't.

If Oreck knows this about you, he has two choices:

(1) Spend no money promoting his product to you, because you don't have carpets and don't believe in vacuum cleaners.

(2) Offer you the deluxe "hypo-allergenic" vacuum with a filtration system that eliminates 99.7 percent of all the irritants from the air.

The point is, unless your message is specifically tailored to the individual's interests, cares and fears, you will not create a market for your product or service.

Department store mogul John Wanamaker once said, "Half my advertising is wasted." He added, "Trouble is, I don't know which half."

With the precision of database marketing — and the sophisticated arithmetic associated with it — no reason in the world exists for a marketer to waste half his advertising.

Method Marketing:
It All Began with Stanislavsky

A number of buzzwords and phrases have been coined and are in current use — and all of them have spawned excellent books: *MaxiMarketing, 1:1 Marketing, Relationship Marketing, Guerrilla Marketing, Database Marketing.*

So why "Method Marketing?"

I believe the most important text from which to learn the essentials of marketing is *An Actor Prepares*, by Konstantin Stanislavsky, for 40 years director and acting teacher at the Moscow Art Theatre.

Stanislavsky's premise: that only by thoroughly understanding how the human mind works — what causes the emotions of exclusivity, flattery, fear, greed, guilt, anger, salvation — can an actor actually get inside the head of the character in a play and *become that person* so convincingly that the audience will undergo the necessary suspension of disbelief to make the play real.

For example, Dustin Hoffman is legendary for the intensity with which he studies the characters he portrays. When he was signed to star in a television production of Arthur Miller's *Death of a Salesman,* Hoffman apparently drove the entire cast and crew nuts in rehearsals with his long discussions and debates with the playwright — and himself — as to why Willy Loman said this or did that; these dialogues were followed by endless different readings until Hoffman was satisfied that they were completely right for the character.

Hoffman didn't simply memorize the lines and recite them; *he became* Willy Loman.

This is the guts of Method Acting — formulated by Stanislavsky and, later, articulated by Lee Strasberg, who founded the famous Actor's Studio in New York, which produced many great performers from Eli Wallach and Marlon Brando to Marilyn Monroe.

In an interview actress Nicole McEwan said:

> The greatest thing about acting is that you get a chance to live in the skin of a character for two or three months, and it's never boring.

Same thing in marketing.

You cannot write copy or make a live sales pitch without getting inside the head of the person to whom you are communicating and *becoming that person.*

This is Method Marketing.

In the words of freelancer Bill Jayme:

> In the marketplace, as in theater, there is indeed a factor at work called "the willing suspension of disbelief."

What Happens When You Don't Get Inside the Head

Marketers and actors alike can be suckered into thinking they have gotten inside someone's head and really gotten the message across. In *A Dream of Passion: The Development of the Method,* Lee Strasberg quotes an article written by the great actor Walter Huston (father of director/actor/screenwriter John Huston) for Huntington Hartford's short-lived *Stage* magazine. Huston describes his elation after his opening-night performance in the title role of *Othello* on Broadway: "We earnestly believed, as deep down as a man can, that we had given a hell of a performance, as fine a piece of work as our lives ever fashioned."

The following morning, he was excoriated by critics Burns Mantle of the *Daily News* and Brooks Atkinson of *The New York Times*. Huston wrote:

> I could hardly believe it. After all those months of work, after all that fond care, after all that had been said, after hundreds of changes and experiments — after we had patted down every minute detail, could it be that we had produced such a poor thing?
>
> The brunt of all this criticism fell on me. No matter how I deluded myself, I could not escape the clear cry against my performance. I tried to tell myself that the trouble with the critics was that they did not want me, whom they considered to be a very homespun fellow, to try to put on airs. I refused to see any truth in the adverse criticism I read, but instead turned it around and used it to criticize the critics. Did they know that I had studied the role longer, had given it more thought than any role I had ever played? Couldn't they accept my conception rather than dictate to me from their ignorance? But then I knew this argument would not hold water either. All they knew about my performance, I was slow to admit, was that it did not move them; that it did not grasp and hold their interest; that it did not entertain them, did not ring their approbative bells.
>
> On the contrary, their stomachs ached for me. But then I knew that even if I had encompassed the character of the Einstein Theory so that it made plain and good sense to me, it need not necessarily therefore appeal to the public. That was a hard and large lump to swallow.

Interestingly, the same thing happened to Stanislavsky — in the same role. As Strasberg tells it:

> Stanislavsky gave what he thought was a great performance.
> He was convinced that the audience was entirely in his power. At the end of the play he was surprised to find that the other actors avoided him. His performance had been a failure, al-

though he himself felt a real satisfaction in what he was doing on the stage.

Stanislavsky's awareness of what he had experienced was remarkably perceptive. He noted that the actor's state of mind is not always a true indication of what he is doing, nor of the impression he is creating on the audience. This self-awareness and the ability to determine the truthfulness of expression are fundamental demands of the actor's art and craft, since they must function at the very moment when he is actually creating. The moment of the creation must go hand in hand with the moment of evaluation. This is one of the most difficult problems for the actor to solve. Yet at this very early stage in his creative life, Stanislavsky was beginning to come to grips with this fundamental aspect of the actor's problem.

Stanislavsky himself suggested that his failure as Othello was really a failure to find the truth in his character.

There is not a direct response copywriter in the world who has not felt this gamut of emotions when the actual results of a promotional effort were tallied, and he or she was soundly beaten. God knows, I have, more times than I care to remember.

What happens? Just as Huston and Stanislavsky failed to *become* Othello, I failed to get inside the head and under the skin of the person to whom I was writing and *become* that person.

Stanislavsky's most elementary point about the nature of creative work is the need for absolute concentration. As Strasberg explains it:

He emphasized that it is impossible to concentrate without first having practiced the exercises with imaginary objects. Imaginary objects are precisely that — objects which human beings deal with literally in life, and which the actor has to learn to recreate without the presence of the actual object. Before the actor starts work on the actual play with visual or living objects, he must devote some time to exercises on "concentrated attention with imaginary objects"; the actor must note every physical action and every sensation associated with the object. Stanislavsky stressed that for the actor to "know" means only to be able "to do"; and that one is able to do a thing only if one can control one's will, imagination, attention, and energy . . . .

For the actor to achieve this, training had to begin with the five senses — sight, hearing, touch, taste and smell — plus the kinesic, or motor, senses. The training of the senses was a vital part of the conscious training of the actor. All human responses are the result of sensory experience. If we do not see the lion behind us, we will not react. If we do not hear the approaching train, we will not get off the tracks. If we do not hear an explosion, we are not startled. For any reaction to occur, the sense must function. The form that the reaction takes is differentiated by additional elements that shape the behavior. But without the senses, there is no life. . . .

One of my chief discoveries as the director of the Group Theater was a reformulation of Stanislavsky's "creative if." As I mentioned earlier, Stanislavsky's formulation of the "creative if" consists of the proposition, given the particular circumstance of the play, how would you behave, what would you do, how would you feel, how would you react?

Getting Inside Heads

Under the Stanislavsky and Strasberg method, student actors spend a great deal of time in improvisation — being told what characters they are and given situations to deal with as those characters. Done well, improvisation is exhausting mental and physical exercise, especially if you are to convince an audience to believe what is going on before them.

In terms of marketing, the analogy holds. Using Stanislavsky's "creative if," here are two examples of what marketer must go through when creating an offer:

Example A

My mailing is going to an executive in the office. Many large corporations (Kodak, First Bank Systems) refuse to deliver Standard (Bulk) Mail, so my envelope must either travel First Class at great expense or it must look like a First Class mailing to fool the mailroom.

We've gotten the package through the mailroom, and it is now delivered to the outer office where the gatekeeper — known as Whitefang — screens the mail. How to get the mailing past Whitefang? Will Whitefang open the envelope, remove the contents and make a judgment as to whether it goes into the "A" pile, the "B" pile or the trash?

Should it be personalized — with the executive's name and address on the outer envelope and repeated on the letter with a per-

sonal salutation? According to the U.S. Postal Service, business lists go out of date at the rate of one percent a week (50 percent a year). That's because people change jobs, change titles, change departments, change mailing addresses. So, before I decide on personalization, I have to know how current the list is; after all, time and money expended to personalize a mailing only to have it go to the wrong person are wasted. In the words of consultant James Rosenfield: "A personalized mailing to the wrong person — or with the person's name misspelled — does more harm than if the mailing made no pretense of being personal."

Should it be a letter? A self-mailer? Or should the client spring for a lumpy letter or a box that has a higher perceived value than a piece of junk mail and will most certainly be on the top of the morning mail pile?

Who is the ultimate buyer? Unlike the consumer arena, business purchases are often a group decision. If it's passed on, how will it appeal to a higher-up?

What should be the key copy drivers: fear, greed, anger, guilt, exclusivity, flattery or salvation?

Example B

The product I am marketing is a book club for very young children. The person who will be reading my copy is the parent of a very young child. If I were that parent, what would make me respond to this offer? What are my concerns? What are my fears? What is it about this offer that would represent salvation in terms of bringing up my child?

What would I respond to most eagerly — a terrific free premium or a great product? Guru Axel Andersson has said, "If you want to dramatically increase your response, dramatically improve your offer."

Is the premium I am offering the best I can come up with? If one premium works well, won't two work better?

At the same time, is the offer too good? Will it result in a lot of orders from tire kickers who have no intention of paying — those mail order shoppers consultant Bob Doscher disdainfully refers to as "premium bandits?"

What do I put on the envelope?

What is my lead for the letter?

• Is it flattery ("Because you are a smart parent . . . ") ?

• Is it greed ("Yours Free when you respond . . . ")?

> • *Is it exclusivity ("This offer is limited to a very few truly caring parents . . . ")?*
> • *Is it guilt ("If you don't help your child acquire good reading skills, you will be party to a failure — in school and in life . . . ")?*
> • *Is it salvation: ("Now, be guaranteed your child will surge to the head of the class because reading is the key to success, and with your free books, your child will start to* love *reading. . . . ")?*
> • *Is it anger ("Will your child be one of those left to fall through the cracks in terms of reading skills because school systems have too many bureaucrats and not enough teachers. . . . ")?*
> • *Is it fear ("If your child fails to become a good reader, it can mean larger failures later on — in high school, in college, in life; will a failed child be able to take care of you in your old age?")?*

Understand, this is not the actual copy, but rather the possible copy approaches. Presumably all these emotions should show up somewhere in the mailing, but which is the most powerful lead?

Only after putting yourself inside the head and under the skin of a parent with young children can you begin to think about what to say to that person (who, by now, is yourself). In effect, you are exchanging your thoughts and feelings with yourself and persuading yourself that you absolutely, positively need your product. You can raise all the objections that the young parent would raise — because, mentally, you're the young parent — and you can overcome them in the course of your argument. Stanislavsky:

> "If you want to exchange your thoughts and feelings with someone you must offer something that you have experienced yourself. "Under ordinary circumstances life provides these. This material grows in us spontaneously and derives from surrounding conditions.
> "In the theatre it is different, and this presents a new difficulty. We are supposed to use the feelings and thoughts created by the playwright."

In the business of marketing, it is the list or the magazine or TV show that is the equivalent of the play.

The people on that list, the readers of the magazine or the viewers of the broadcast are the audience; they have been assembled for you and your job is to make them react.

In the case of the theater, you want them to believe you; in the case of marketing, you want them not only to believe you, but to go one step further and take action.

The same principle holds when creating a space advertisement. The first thing to do is buy a copy of the publication in which your ad will appear and see what you are up against. Remember, all advertising is in direct competition with all other advertising. Then put yourself inside the head and under the skin of the reader and *become* the reader. In the context of that publication, what ads jump out and grab you by the throat? What ads interrupt you and make you stop reading them?

> I do not regard advertising as entertainment or an art form, but as a medium of information. When I write an advertisement, I don't want you to tell me that you find it "creative." I want you to find it so interesting that you buy the product. When Aeschines spoke, they said, "How well he speaks." But when Demosthenes spoke, they said, "Let us march against Philip."
>
> — David Ogilvy

Method Marketing: It Doesn't Stop with Marketing

The notion of getting inside the head and under the skin of the person you are reaching with your message is not confined to marketing.

Writing in *The New Yorker,* Malcolm Gladwell made the distinction between the internal and external audience. The internal audience is made up of your superiors, your co-workers and your industry peers; the external audience equals customers and prospects.

The internal-audience effect can be seen in all sorts of businesses. The reason so many magazines look alike, Gladwell said, is that their Manhattan-based editors and writers end up trying to impress not readers but other Manhattan-based editors and writers. It was an effort to avoid this syndrome that Lincoln Mercury recently decided to move its headquarters from Detroit to California. The company said that the purpose was to get closer to its customers; more precisely, the purpose was to get away from people who *weren't* its customers. Why do you think it took so long to get Detroit to install seat belts? Because to the internal audience a seat belt is a cost center. It is only to the external audience that it is a lifesaver.

To be successful in a job interview, you must get inside the head and under the skin of your external audience — the interviewer. What does the interviewer see, hear and feel about the person on the other side of the desk (yourself)?

In any direct selling situation, the sales representative must be inside the head of the prospect.

For successful Point-of-Purchase promotions, you have to put yourself inside the head — and behind the shopping cart — of the shopper.

To win a battle or a war, a general must get inside the head of his foe and think like he thinks. For example, in World War II, the British High Command had a resident astrologer because it was well known that Hitler frequently consulted an astrologer.

The public relations practitioner has to get inside the head of the magazine editor and create copy that will be used. "Editors are basically lazy," publicist Evelyn Lawson used to say. "If you give them something they can use, they'll run it rather than taking the trouble to create something on their own."

In chess, tennis, baseball or any of a thousand games, you have to be inside the heads of your opponents.

At the bridge or poker table, partners must be inside each other's heads as well as figure out what their opponents are holding and thinking.

To make a successful speech, you have to get inside the heads and under the skin of the audience so you can see yourself from their point of view.

The master orator of the 1960s was John F. Kennedy. His biographers all marveled at his ability to stand outside himself mentally and watch his own performance. Like the great mass leaders of history — Hitler, Mussolini, Roosevelt, Churchill, Billy Graham, Senator Huey Long of Louisiana — Kennedy was able to charm and persuade an audience of any size. To Kennedy, the television lens was an audience of one, and he was intimate. In a room of five to 50, his eyes would sweep the room, making contact with his rapt listeners. At a giant rally of thousands, he would read the faces of the people in front and project to the very back of the hall or stadium. All the while, he would be mentally standing outside himself — or hovering overhead like a helicopter — analyzing his performance and the audience reaction.

A sidelight to this: The American artist Jamie Wyeth did an oil portrait of Kennedy in contemplation, his hand on chin, index finger on mouth. Kennedy's right eye was focused intently and directly on the viewer; his left eye was gazing over the viewer's shoulder, perhaps contemplating his current performance, perhaps rehearsing a scene yet to be played. When Jacqueline Kennedy first saw this portrait, it blew her away; *this was Jack Kennedy!*

Think about it: to be successful, every human interaction must begin by getting inside the head and under the skin of the other person — whether it's running a meeting, firing an employee, reporting to your boss or your shareholders, playing tennis or asking for someone's hand in marriage.

The Thoroughbred Analogy

I first became aware of this concept when off-track betting came to New York State. I bought Tom Ainsley's book on thoroughbred racing and carefully typed up hundreds of rules and kept them in a three-ring binder (which I still have). Every Saturday, I would buy *The Racing Form* and try to make sense out of the avalanche of data that described the past performances of the various nags.

First you have to memorize the rules (e.g., Horses for courses; eliminate a distance horse in a sprint; cheap horses know it). Once the rules are in your head, you can begin to get into the Zen of handicapping — which means getting inside three sets of heads:

• The owner or trainer. Why is this horse being entered in this race? To win? To be claimed? To get some exercise in order to be prepped for an upcoming, more winnable race? Or is the owner doing a favor for the stewards who need entries for a specific race?

• The horse players. The betting favorite is not necessarily the best horse; rather it is what the crowd *thinks* is the best horse. What do the bettors see in this past performance data that leads them to bet on this horse? What are they missing? Since you'll never make money at the track betting on favorites which go off at very low odds, you always must bet *against* the crowd.

• The horse. What kind of shape is he in? Has he had a workout or a race recently? What were his times? How did he do his last four times out? In what company? Did he show early foot? Was he gaining in the stretch?

In a card of nine or 10 races, you might find one reasonable bet or two — maybe three at best. In those few races, you'll discover the numbers can click into place as you eliminate the various contestants, and you find yourself staring at one obvious winner that is a nonfavorite (and thus will pay a decent price).

But only by knowing the rules and then understanding what's inside the heads of the crowd, the owner/trainer and the horse can you win.

Plus, you need the discipline *not* to bet on races where the numbers don't make sense; and you need the discipline to place one big bet on the nose of a horse you think will win rather than try to hedge your risk with a lot of little bets.

If you can win at track by getting into the heads of others, shouldn't you be able to win at everything else?

Only one thrill matches that of placing a big bet on a horse to win and then watching the horse perform just as you predicted and flash across the finish line by a nose or a head or a length.

That other thrill is writing and designing a mailing and then going into the mailroom four weeks later to see huge sacks of mail, all containing responses to your sales pitch.

A Quick Primer on Direct Mail

The businesses described in *Method Marketing* were all built by direct mail — either traditional direct mail envelope packages or — in the case of the J. Peterman Company — by catalog.

Direct mail is the largest advertising medium — bigger than television, bigger than print, bigger even than telemarketing. It's true that more money is spent on telephone marketing. However, half of those expenditures represents money spent on outbound calls. The other half is spent on inbound telemarketing, which is generally an order-taking function — the result of an offer made via direct mail or space or television. Inbound telemarketing is the equivalent of business reply mail or an order received over the Web.

By the year 2000, some $80 billion will be spent by advertisers on direct mail — lists, postage, printing, creative, database processing. If marketing costs represent 20 percent of revenues, then this $80 billion spent on direct mail will generate $400 billion in sales. Add the amount spent ($80 billion) and the amount generated ($400 billion), and direct mail in the United States is bigger than the entire gross domestic product of Australia. And this doesn't include television, space advertising, alternative print media.

In contrast, by the year 2000, the vaunted Internet will represent a paltry $8 billion spent by marketers.

Conversations with Ourselves

Psychologists have found that we — all of us — walk around carrying on endless conversations with ourselves. These conversations are frequently interrupted: a baby crying, a kitchen timer going off, a dog barking, someone at the door, a fire engine going by, a piece of direct mail, a catalog, a TV infomercial or a telemarketing call.

If the marketing effort is dull — if it does not interrupt and keep on interrupting — we resume the conversation with ourselves and the marketer has lost money. Once the proposition is laid aside, chances are it will not be picked up again, and no action will be taken. It's even more likely that the pieces of the mail will languish where they were left, only to be tossed into the recycling bin.

Direct marketing is action advertising. If you do not make an offer, there is no reason for a response — no reason to march against Philip. This is not a business of awareness, of shooting out warm fuzzies in hopes they will be remembered somewhere down the line. Direct marketing is accountable advertising, measurable within tenths and hundredths of a percent. You can't measure anything if you don't get a response. You won't get a response if you don't make an offer.

The Elements of a Direct Mail Package

Seattle agency head Bob Hacker has said, "Direct mail is the art, science and arithmetic of manipulating people from a distance using paper." He also said, "Direct mail is not advertising in an envelope." Here's why:

• **Envelope.** In the words of freelancer Herschell Gordon Lewis:

> The only purpose of the carrier envelope, other than keeping its contents from spilling out onto the street, is to get itself opened.

Consider Lea Pierce's dictum, "All mail gets sorted over the trash can." It's imperative to spend time on the envelope — actually imagining what goes through the mind of the person receiving it and remembering that there are — at most — three seconds between your outside envelope and the wastebasket.

• **Letter.** What makes direct mail different from other media is the ability to include a letter — that highly intimate, personal, me-to-you correspondence of any length that allows you to fire your message point-blank at your prospect in the privacy of the home or office.

Bob Hacker has pointed out that people process information two ways: rationally and analytically as well as irrationally and emotionally. Right-brain people — who rely primarily on the emotional and irrational approach — will read the letter first. This is the emotional copy, the "what-this-proposition-will-do-for-you" piece that talks benefits, benefits and more benefits. In direct mail, the letter is the main salesperson. With three kinds of copy — "you" copy, "me" copy and "it" copy — the letter contains the "you" copy. For all these reasons, as guru Dick Benson has said, "A letter should look like a letter"; that means typewriter type and no illustrations. If it looks too much like a circular, both right-brain and left-brain people will not know which piece to look at first and will lay the mailing aside.

• **Circular or Brochure.** This element is for the left-brain reader — who is rational and analytical. It is what Malcolm Decker calls the second member of the sales team who acts as the demonstrator who points to various features and says, in effect, "See, everything the letter (main salesperson) says is true." He shows and describes the features of the product with photos and drawings, charts and graphs and any other devices to make the product or service come alive. This is the place for the "it" copy.

• **Order Device.** The "turn-around-document," usually with the person's name and address imprinted on it so that it can show through the window of an envelope as the addressing piece and, when the decision to respond is made, the name and address are already filled in. As Decker points out, after the letter and the circular have had their say, it is now the respondent's turn. The order form reprises the offer in the simplest terms possible *in the respondent's own voice.* (Yes, please rush *me* the whatever plus *my* first issue of the the product. If for any reason *I* am dissatisfied, *I* will return your invoice marked "cancel" . . . ."). This is the "me" copy. In Decker's words,

> The order form should be so simple, an idiot can understand it.

• **Reply Envelope.** This brings the order home. Other methods of ordering might include an 800 number, invitation to a Web site or a fax number.

• **Lift Piece.** An extra flier or note from someone other than the signer of the letter that makes a different point and, it is hoped, "lifts" response.

About the Chapters That Follow

Here are the stories of eight marketers who built huge businesses.

Five of them — Fr. Bruce Ritter, Martin Edelston, John Peterman, Bill Bonner and Bob Shnayerson — actually created businesses entirely on the power of their copy.

These are the ultimate Method Marketers who got inside the heads and under the skin of the target audience and created such persuasive messages that people sent in their money, and businesses were created.

You'll discover not only the ups and downs of starting their businesses, but be able to read the actual copy that put them in business.

The power of these messages was derived from the calculated use of the seven key copy drivers identified by Bob Hacker and direct-marketing guru Axel Andersson:

> fear — greed — anger — guilt — exclusivity — flattery — salvation

One of the businesses — the J. Peterman Company — was started as a catalog with highly evocative, imaginative copy.

The other four were started as the result of magnificent sales letters. A brochure may have been included with the letter; all, of course, had order devices. But it was the sales letters — those intimate, me-to-you messages — that created the businesses.

(Incidentally, in some cases the letters may actually have been better than the products they describe.)

Two other stories — of Curt Strohacker and David Oreck — are about men who built businesses by being totally in communion with their customers and prospects.

And one story — that of silver-tongued silver salesman William R. Kennedy — is a fascinating tale of old-fashioned greed and stupidity.

Sprinkled among the main feature stories are what my editor Bob Scott calls short palate cleansers. The exception: "The Catch-22 of Privacy," a subject that is germane to every person in marketing — direct or otherwise.

Finally, in "My Day in Court," you'll discover how the knowledge of Method Marketing can be transferred not only into another arena, but in another country.

1:1 Marketing

Don Peppers and Martha Rogers have come up with the concept of *1:1 Marketing* — the individual talking directly to the individual. Stan Rapp calls it "intimate advertising."

What is really happening in the field of direct marketing is nothing like what Peppers and Rogers are suggesting. Consider the following scenario:

Recently I wrote and designed a subscription acquisition mailing for one of the major financial magazines. (Its name begins with the letter "F.") I dreamed up a new premium — a special report using attention-getting articles from back issues of the magazine. Bill Gates and Paul Allen were pictured on the cover of this special report with the article title, "How We Did It." Other stories included: "What to Do When Your Boss Asks You to Lie" and "Are You Being Paid Enough?"

The mailing went out and beat the control by 30 percent. Pay up was only 50 percent of control, so the net-net was 65 percent of control. The package was never used again.

When the dust settled, I called the circulation manager who had hired me.

"My package beat control by 30 percent, is that right?" I asked him.

"Yes."

"But pay up was 50 percent of control for a net-net of 65 percent of control, correct?"

"That's right."

"Tell me," I said. "What did you send the folks who responded to my mailing package?"

"What do you mean?"

"Did you send them new fulfillment material that reflected my tone of voice in my mailing and referred to the new premium? Or did you send them the same thing you send everybody, whether they come in via TV, a bind-in or blow-in card, a sweepstakes, Publishers Clearing House or whatever?"

The circ manager's one-sentence reply was loaded with layers of meaning.

"I think the retention people sent the same thing they send to everybody."

Let's parse that reply.

(1) "I think . . ."

He doesn't really know. His job is to get new subscribers. Everything beyond that is out of his control.

(2) ". . . the retention people . . ."

At this publication are two groups: acquisition and retention.

ACQUISITION: "Why can't you get these turkeys to pay?"

RETENTION: "Why do you bring in all these useless tire-kickers?"

This enables the two to blame each other, which means their jobs are safe.

The point of this is, *Nobody owns the customer. Nobody's in charge of the product.*

(3) ". . . sent the same thing they send to everybody."

The subscriber responded to my package — with my premium, with my voice — and then promptly received communications that bore no resemblance to the original offer. I had gotten inside the new subscriber's head and under the skin and landed a trial subscription.

The "retention people" wrote back in an entirely different voice.

Disconnect.

Add to this a billing series, a renewal series and probably some 40 other product managers within the mother organization blitzing the new subscriber with offers in many different voices, and you emphatically do not have Method Marketing.

You emphatically don't have 1:1 Marketing.

What's going on is: *Mass Marketing to One Person.*

This is epidemic in the direct marketing business.

For 1:1 Marketing — or any kind of Method Marketing — to be successful, it is imperative to reach the customer or client or donor with the same voice. Imagine seeing a play with Dustin Hoffman in Act One being replaced by George C. Scott in Act Two, who is then replaced by Denzel Washington in Act Three. It simply *would not compute!*

The renowned Lester Wunderman gave a luncheon speech at the 1997 Asian Direct Marketing Symposium in Hong Kong. Buried deep in his remarks was a line he practically threw away:

> In the future, product managers must learn to be customer managers.

The current buzz phrase is "integrated marketing" — which, as I understand it, is the same message going out to the individual customer or prospect whether it be by mail, space, telephone or TV.

This can only work if one person — the Method Marketer — is in charge. A committee made up of representatives from space, TV, direct mail and telemarketing thrashing out a common voice will fail.

Committees design camels, not thoroughbreds.

Why Size Matters

The companies I describe in the chapters that follow are not huge. They have revenues of eight and (low) nine figures.

When multibillion dollar conglomerates — American Express, Time-Warner, Disney, or CNN, with all their books, book clubs, videos, CDs, magazines, collectibles, toys and catalogs — start hammering the individual customer with myriad offers in myriad voices from myriad addresses, intimacy and the suspension of disbelief are impossible.

The magic is dead.

This is a book about creating magic and keeping it alive.

3

Covenant House:

The Yin and Yang of
Father Bruce Ritter

High drama, tragedy, resurrection

I am profoundly saddened by the allegations against me and
the need to deny them constantly. I have no way of proving my
innocence. My accusers cannot establish my guilt. I devoutly hope
the inquiries under way will bring an end to this incredibly
painful chapter in my life.

— Fr. Bruce Ritter, Founder
Covenant House

This is the absolutely true story of how a huge direct marketing organization — built on powerful, evocative copy — came within a
whisker of losing its credibility and its revenue, and how it scratched
its way back to viability and gained the trust it had lost.

In 1990, Covenant House, a shelter for homeless children, was an
enterprise made up of 17 centers in the United States, Canada and
Latin America with a donor file of 1.2 million people and an annual
budget of $87 million; *The New York Times* pointed out that this was
three times what the federal government was spending on similar programs.

The secret of the amazing success of Covenant House was entirely
due to the genius of 62-year-old Franciscan Father Bruce Ritter, a
highly compassionate — yet, at the same time a very dangerous —
human being.

Arguably, Bruce Ritter was one of the three or four greatest direct
mail copywriters of the late twentieth century.

What follows is one of Ritter's early letters that was mailed over and over again for years. It arrived in a plain white #10 window envelope with a nonprofit metered indicia. Inside was a two-page letter, a brochure, order card and courtesy reply envelope (with "PLACE STAMP HERE" as opposed to Business Reply Mail for which the mailer pays the postage).

The letter was on Covenant House letterhead and written in Courier type:

```
                                  Friday, 10:40 PM

Dear Friend,

   A lady should never get this dirty, she
said.

   She stood there with a quiet, proud dignity.
She was incomparably dirty — her face and hands
smeared, her clothes torn and soiled. The lady
was 11.

   My brothers are hungry, she said. The two
little boys she hugged protectively were 8 and
9. They were three of the most beautiful chil-
dren I'd ever seen.

   Our parents beat us a lot, she said. We had
to leave. The boys nodded mutely. We had to
leave, one of them echoed. The children did not
cry. I struggled to manage part of a smile. It
didn't come off very well. The littlest kid
looked back at me, with a quick, dubious grin.
I gave him a surreptitious hug. I was all
choked up.

   I would like to take a shower, the lady
said.

   Seventeen years ago, I did not know that
there were thousands of runaway, abused and
abandoned children like these in this country.
```

Father Bruce Ritter, founder of Covenant House and the greatest intuitive fund raising copywriter. (Photo: Kenneth Siegel)

I learned the hard way.

One night, in the winter of 1968, six teenage runaways knocked on the door of my apartment where I was living to serve the poor of New York's Lower East Side. Their junkie pimp had burned them out of the abandoned tenement they called "home." They asked if they could sleep on my floor. I took them in. I didn't have the guts not to.

Word of mouth traveled fast. (It does among street kids). The next day four more came. And kids have been coming ever since. It was these kids — with no place else to go — homeless, hungry, lacking skills, jobs resources — that compelled me to start Covenant House over seventeen years ago. Today our crisis centers help tens of thousands of kids from all over the country — and save them from a life of degradation and horror on the streets.

Kids like the eleven-year-old lady and her very brave little brothers. They were easy to help: to place in a foster home where beautiful kids are wanted and loved, and made more beautiful precisely because they are wanted and loved.

But sadly, not all of the more than 20,000 kids who will come to Covenant House this year will be that lucky. These kids have very few options. Many of them will have fallen victim to the predators of the sex-for-sale and pornography "industry."

One of them put it to me very simply and very directly:

"Bruce, I've got two choices: I can go with a john (a customer) and do what he wants, or I

can rip somebody off and go to jail. I'm afraid
to go to jail, Bruce. I can't get a job . . .
I've got no skills. I've go no place to live."

This child is 16. I do not know what I
would have done if I were 16 and faced with
that impossible choice.

<u>They are good kids.</u> You shouldn't think
they're not good kids. Most of them are simply
trying to survive. When you are on the street,
and you are cold and hungry and scared and you
have nothing to sell except yourself, you sell
yourself.

There was a time when I was forced to turn
these kids away simply because there was no
room. I can't do that any more. I know only too
well what the street holds in store for a kid
all alone. That is why we run Covenant House,
and that is why we keep it open 24 hours a day,
seven days a week — to give these kids an alternative, an option that leads to life and not
death.

These kids come to us in need, from every
kind of family background. Boys and girls.
White, Black and Hispanic. Children — sometimes
with children of their own. Innocent and
streetwise. They are your kids and mine. Their
number is increasing at a frightening rate.

We are here for them because of you. Almost
all of the money that we need to help these
kids comes from people like you.

A lady should never get that dirty. And <u>a
good kid should not be allowed to fall victim
to the terror of street life.</u> As more good kids
come to us, we need more help. We need yours.

Won't you send whatever contribution you can in
the enclosed envelope today?

Thanks from my (no, <u>our</u>) kids.

Peace,

/s/　Fr. Bruce Ritter

Father Bruce Ritter

P.S. I'm enclosing a brochure that will tell
you a little bit more about the thousands of
kids who come to us each year. I hope you will
read it, and give our kids whatever you can.
Thanks!

The Interruptive Techniques

Freelance direct mail writer Harry B. Walsh suggests this double prescription for a successful letter:

> The tone of a good direct mail letter is as direct and per-
> sonal as the writer's skill can make it.
> Even though it may go to millions of people, it never orates
> to a crowd but rather murmurs into a single ear. It's a message
> from one letter writer to one letter reader.
> Tell a story if possible. Everybody loves a good story, be it
> about Peter Rabbit or King Lear. And the direct mail letter with its
> unique person-to-person format, is the perfect vehicle for a story.
> Stories get read. The letter I wrote to launch the Cousteau Society
> 20-some years ago has survived hundreds of tests against it. . . .
> The original of this direct mail Methuselah started out with the
> lead: "A friend once told me a curious story I would like to share
> with you. . . ."
> Most consultants and writers teach that a letter should
> begin with offer and benefits that should be restated at least three
> times in the course of the letter along with several calls to action.
> However, in the fund-raising arena, all bets are off.

Direct mail is also an interruptive medium. To be successful, a letter must interrupt and keep on interrupting until some action is taken.

Chances are, if an interruption to the interruption occurs — and the reader lays aside the letter for any reason — the sale will be lost. Unlike a novel, it's hard to pick up a direct mail letter and have the fire rekindled; more likely, it will be covered by the sports pages and the whole thing will end up in the recycling bin. As the late Elsworth Howell, founder of Grolier Enterprises, pointed out: "Direct mail is basically an impulse sale."

In order to be interruptive, direct mail letters purposely break the rules of English we learned in school. You will see short paragraphs — never more than seven lines long — the use of ellipses, underlined subheads, indented paragraphs, bullets, check marks and even handwritten notes in the margins.

All of these tricks are designed to avoid the gray wall of type that you find in a book or magazine and, instead, keep the reader's eye moving.

Bruce Ritter invented some techniques of his own. For example, look at his lead sentence:

A lady should never get this dirty, she said.

Where are the quotation marks? Doesn't this violate the grammar we were taught in grade school. Ah . . . but wouldn't little black flecks dotted around the words mar this hard diamond of prose reminiscent of James Joyce or the early Hemingway?

And what of his use of big words like "incomparably" and "surreptitious!" Shouldn't direct mail should be written at a sixth grade level, like *Time* and *Newsweek*?

You cannot quarrel with any facet of this letter; it brought in too much money over too long a time.

We can't judge good direct mail; it judges us.

The Seeds of Tragedy

So much for Ritter's copywriting technique. Hemingway once said the greatest asset a writer could have was a shock-proof, built-in shit detector. When I first read the "dirty lady" letter, the red flag of my detector gave a feeble wave, as though a faint, cold breeze blew on the back of my neck and should have been a premonition the whirlwind to follow.

No one word or phrase jumped out. But the letter has an undercurrent of sensuality. Isn't he really ogling these children? For example, he refers to the children as "beautiful" — not once, not twice, but three times and talks of hugs twice including a "surreptitious" hug. Why surreptitious? If you hug a kid, you hug a kid. The first definition of surreptitious in Webster's *Third* is "marked or accomplished by fraud or suppression of truth."

What Bill Clinton and Monica Lewinsky did to each other in the Oval office was surreptitious.

Catastrophe!

On December 12, 1989, *The New York Post* — a tabloid that feeds on the sensational — broke the story of Kevin Lee Kite, described as a 25-year-old drifter and former male prostitute, who alleged that Fr. Ritter brought him to New York the previous February, and shortly thereafter they began a sexual relationship. Ritter claimed he was Kite's "mentor," and nothing more. At the same time New York State Attorney General Robert Abrams began an investigation into financial improprieties at the shelter. In addition, Manhattan District Attorney Robert M. Morgenthau was looking into allegations that Fr. Ritter had spent Covenant House funds on Kite for his personal benefit and, more sensationally, that someone at Covenant House obtained a false ID for Kite in the name of a Jamestown, N.Y., boy who had died in 1980.

The story took over the New York media. Nightly, it was the lead story on the local TV news and got continuing front-page coverage in all the papers. National media picked it up and sensationalized it.

Response to Covenant House mailings took a dive. Mailers canceled orders for the rental of Covenant House names, which put another dent in the organization's income. Other mailers refused Covenant House access to their lists, which meant no new mailings could go out. Even if mailings went out, they would have lost big money during this controversy, because regular donors were reserving judgment; they were holding back to see what how the story played out.

Revenues slowed to a trickle. It was the holiday season which would ordinarily account for a huge proportion of the year's income. One list broker who handled the account told a friend, "I wake up every morning with a renewed sense of dread."

At Covenant House, a siege mentality set in. Ritter hung tough. He had always run the organization autocratically as his private fiefdom and this was no different. He was still in charge, and, most important, he controlled the mailing lists. On December 18th — less than a week after the story broke, he attempted damage control with a letter to his contributors; too long for the usual 8-1/2" × 11" paper, the final version went out on an 8-1/2" by 14" sheet printed front and back. As always, he used the Covenant House letterhead; his salutation was one he frequently used to contributors:

December 18, 1980

Hello, my friends,

Please, it's vital that you read this letter. Vital to me, to our kids, to Covenant House.

"It's been the worst week of my life . . ." That's how I began the press conference I called to deal with the swirling controversy that threatens me and Covenant House.

I don't think anybody could have missed the sensational coverage in the New York Post, and then in the newspapers and on all the radio and TV stations for the past week. It's why I'm writing to you today.

A young man who convinced us that he had close ties to organized crime, prostitution and drug rings came to Covenant House for help. He was scared to death. We put him in the safe house in New York — an apartment we had available for that purpose in a building filled with nuns and priests, and owned by Covenant House. We arranged for a college scholarship and provided all the help we could.

Because of the need to protect the young man we provided a new identity and an instant family of friends to give him the emotional support he needed — most of them drawn from my personal

staff and the staff of our Youth Advocacy
Institute that operates the safe-house program.

The young man has accused me and Covenant
House of financial improprieties in providing
that care, in order to have a sexual relationship with him.

I categorically deny both allegations.

They are not true. I will be totally and
completely exonerated and vindicated when
Manhattan District Attorney, Robert Morgenthau,
completes his investigation. Mr. Morgenthau has
warned the press that serious inaccuracies and
misinformation in the press reports have dam-
aged Covenant House and my reputation.

We pray that the investigation proceeds
swiftly and that the results be published as
widely as the scurrilous attacks on me.

It has been a time of extraordinary pain and
grief for me. I have said many times that I do
not really care what happens to me. I decided
that long ago.

What happens to the kids is important. What
happens to Covenant House is important. Sadly,
attacks on me hurt both immeasurably.

As I said to the dozens of reporters at the
press conference where I attempted to answer
every question put to me as completely and honestly as I could: what hurts me more than anything else is the thought that the millions of
people who have cared about my kids and helped
them may have their faith in me, and the
Church, shattered because of these vicious allegations.

The pain is almost more than I can bear.

Were it not for the unwavering support of my family, Cardinal O'Connor and my fellow Franciscan Friars, the members of my Board, my incredibly loyal staff, many friends in the media, hundreds of faithful supporters, and most of all, my kids at Covenant House, I'm not sure I could have gotten through it. Once again, I am humbled to know that so many people love me.

And yet, the cloud of suspicion will inevitably, in the minds of some, hang over me and Covenant House until the investigation is completed. Mr. Morgenthau has promised to proceed as quickly as a complete and diligent examination can permit. I beg for your faith, and your patience.

Please do not judge harshly this troubled young man who brought this firestorm of grief and controversy on me. I would welcome him if he came back. His own suffering, throughout most of his incredibly exploited life, has been immense, and I and my staff were unable to reach him.

How I wish I could have helped him more. I trusted my own ability and experience too much. I should have taken more exacting care to avoid even the appearance of impropriety. But, after years of caring about and living with thousands of kids — cooking their meals, doing their laundry, cleaning the toilets . . .

I misread the agony and pain in his life, and the anger. Please pray for him, as I do.

Pray for me too. Only my absolute faith that God would not and could not abandon His kids whom He loves so much, has gotten me through so

far — that and the faith and support and love
of my friends.

Peace,

/s/ Fr. Bruce Ritter

Father Bruce Ritter

P.S. We have made an unedited videotape of the
entire press conference and would like to make
it available to you. If you want a copy, please
call 1-800-388-3888. We have a limited number
of copies and would appreciate your sending it
back when you are through.

You might also be interested in what one
local columnist had to say about these most
difficult times at Covenant House.

Please do not abandon our kids — they are
good and brave and beautiful young people who
need your prayers and support now more than
ever.

Like the surreptitious hug in the "dirty lady" letter, Ritter dropped
a clue in this one as to what the final outcome inexorably would be:
*I should have taken more exacting care to avoid even the appearance
of impropriety.*
It was obviously written hurriedly and was hardly vintage Ritter
copy. Enclosed with the letter was the reprint of a *Newsday* article by
columnist Dennis Duggan titled, "A Good Man Smeared With Rumor's
Mud." He still had supporters, but, like Covenant House receipts, they
were dwindling down to a precious few.
The controversy raged on for weeks as the investigations contin-
ued. Contributitons continued to plummet. The viability of the entire
Covenant House organization was in question.
On January 24th, *The Village Voice* reported that a 33-year-old
Seattle man and former Covenant House resident, John P. Melican,
had accused Ritter of having a sexual relationship with him.

On February 6th, *The New York Times* reported on allegations made by Darryl J. Bassile, 31, of Ithaca, New York, who claimed he had been lured into a sexual relationship with Fr. Ritter when he was at Covenant House in his mid-teens. Kite, Bassile and Melican did not know each other, yet their descriptions of Ritter's predatory practices jibed.

The following day, February 7, 1990, Ritter was forced out.

Picking Up the Pieces

This is as much a story about public relations and crisis management as it is about great direct mail copy. Ritter had founded a vast organization with an $87 million budget and then used it to cruise for underage sexual partners. Ritter was gone. But, clearly, decisive action had to be taken *immediately,* or Covenant House would be toast and thousands of kids back out on the streets.

As a temporary replacement for Ritter, New York City Schools Chancellor Frank J. Macchiarola agreed to step in. The organization struggled to stay in business. Not until six months later was a modicum of closure achieved. Again, a plain white #10 envelope was mailed. This time, the Covenant House logo was missing from the cornercard. Instead, it read simply:

346 West 17th Street
New York, New York 10011

The envelope went out First-Class Presort, which meant the organization did not take advantage of the nonprofit mailing rate to which it was entitled. Clearly, the Board of Directors wanted this letter out fast:

```
        RALPH A. PFEIFFER, JR.
           COVENANT HOUSE
        346 West 17th Street
        New York, NY 10011-5002
```

Chairman of the Board   August 6, 1990

Dear Friend,

    Just a few days ago, we released the findings of the special five-month investigations into Covenant House which were initiated at the request of the Board of Directors. You may have already seen or heard portions of these reports in the media.

In keeping with the promise I made to you last March, I'm writing to present a detailed synopsis of the investigations.

Good and bad, I want to share the findings with you. As someone who's generously supported Covenant House, you deserve nothing less.

Let me explain the investigative process. In March, 1990, the Covenant House Board of Directors authorized the following reviews of our operations:

• We retained a new General Counsel, Cravath, Swaine & Moore and Robert McGuire, former New York City Police Commissioner and his firm, Kroll Associates, to investigate any and all allegations of misconduct or impropriety at Covenant House.

• Richard Shinn, the former Chairman and CEO of Metropolitan Life, examined the Covenant House compensation program salary administration and related personnel issues.

• The public accounting firm of Ernst and Young conducted an independent review of financial controls and procedures at Covenant House.

• The Child Welfare League was appointed to review Covenant House's New York childcare program.

• An Oversight Committee was established to oversee the investigations, evaluate the results and to make recommendations to the Board of Directors.

The investigations centered on two broad areas: First, allegations of misconduct against Father Ritter and other staff. Second, into Covenant House, itself.

The first allegations against Father Ritter centered on charges of sexual and financial improprieties. Let me share with you the exact wording of some of the conclusions of the investigations.

"The cumulative evidence discovered by Kroll in the course of its investigation that Father Ritter engaged in sexual activities with certain residents and made sexual advances toward certain members of the Faith Community is extensive . . . Moreover, all of the allegations taken together show a generally consistent pattern of conduct."

I can only imagine what you're feeling right now. All of us — the kids, the volunteers, our counselors and staff — share those feelings.

The report also discusses the Franciscan Charitable Trust established by Father Ritter, to which Covenant House made contributions. While we expect the assets of the Trust will be donated to Covenant House, the Report finds that the contributions should not have been made without the Board's knowledge.

Please know that over the past several months the Board has adopted a policy which ensures that this will never happen again.

You should also know that since the beginning of the year, the Board has added eight new directors, while eight other directors have resigned. In addition, the Board has adopted new by-laws and a number of policy and procedural reforms including a prohibition on loans to officers and directors and a requirement that the Board approve any other loans.

A controversy which was given much prominence in the media, centered on contracts that Father Ritter awarded to his niece and her husband, for decorating and construction projects at Covenant House.

Even though the Report concludes that there was no abuse of funds in this matter, we have taken steps to ensure that this kind of conflict of interest will never occur again. Specifically, new provisions have been adopted ensuring that no such transaction can occur unless approved by the Board of Directors.

Now let me address the investigations into Covenant House programs and practices.

The Kroll investigation *"uncovered no evidence of any irregularities or operational deficiencies relating to Covenant House's collection and safeguarding of donor contributions."*

Moreover, Ernst and Young found that *"there was an adequate level of control consciousness, that financial accounting and reporting systems were designed to provide management with sufficient, accurate and timely information to manage the organization and that further improvements were planned."* Some minor deficiencies in the petty cash, cash disbursements and payroll systems were also found.

As for the use of salary compensation, Mr. Richard Shinn concluded that:

"In developing a salary structure, the management of Covenant House has been very thor-

ough and detailed in its analysis." His report concluded by saying *"simply stated, the approach and implementation of management has been professional and reflects fair compensation."*

The final investigation centered around the independent review of our programs conducted by the Child Welfare League. In summary, it was found that *"such programs are generally well-conceived, appropriately structured"* and are *"an irreplaceable resource to the City of New York and a sound model for delivering critically needed services to a population that is otherwise seriously underserved."*

I've enclosed a statement from the Oversight Committee and a summary of the Report. I hope you'll read them.

In closing, I just want to thank you for your prayers and continued support. I know only too well how difficult this has been over the past several months.

I know we've said this to you many times before, but Covenant House wouldn't be here without the help of good people like you.

I hope you will join me in reaffirming our commitment to the care of street kids who so desperately need our help.

Sincerely,

/s/ Ralph A. Pfeiffer, Jr.

Ralph A. Pfeiffer, Jr
Chairman of the Board.

Also included in the mailing:

SUMMARY OF THE REPORT

The Report describes the structure of Covenant House and the governance and management changes made since Father Bruce Ritter's resignation. Covenant House was reorganized so that full control of the organization reverted to the Board of Directors. Since March 1990, the Board of Directors has been reconstituted; eight members have resigned and eight new members have been elected. A new President, Sister Mary Rose McGeady, was chosen on July 10, 1990, and will start on September 1, 1990. New By-laws have been adopted as have a number of procedural and policy reforms concerning conflicts of interest, financial transactions and other matters.

With respect to allegations of sexual misconduct on the part of Father Ritter, the Report states that the evidence of sexual misconduct discovered by Kroll is extensive. The Report concludes that in view of the cumulative evidence found by Kroll supporting the allegations, if Father Ritter had not resigned from Covenant House, the termination of his relationship with Covenant House would have been required. The Report further states that even if one were to accept Father Ritter's explanation of the events, the same conclusion would have been justified solely on the basis that Father Ritter exercised unacceptable poor judgment in his relations with certain residents.

The Report discusses the Franciscan Charitable Trust, a trust established by Father Ritter in 1983 from surplus funds available to him from compensation paid by Covenant House to his Franciscan Order in respect of his services. At Father Ritter's direction, Covenant House made a $60,000 annual contribution to the trust for five years and the trust made loans to two Covenant House directors, Father Ritter's sister and one former Covenant House resident. The Report finds that the Covenant House contribution should not have been made without the Board's knowledge and approval, if at all. The report notes that the trust funds are reported to have a value of approximately $1 million and are expected to be contributed to Covenant House.

The Report also finds that Covenant House made loans to Father Ritter and to two other senior staff members. The loan to Father Ritter, in the form of a salary advance that was repaid, was not permitted by New York law because he was a corporate officer. The other loans should have been brought to the attention of the Board. Likewise, Covenant House's contract with companies owned by Father Ritter's niece and her husband should not have been made without Board knowledge or approval and competitive bidding.

The review of Covenant House's financial systems revealed no irregularities or improprieties with respect to Covenant House's collection and safeguarding of donor contributions. Kroll did find some operational deficiencies with Dove Services, Inc., a small subsidiary that had been discontinued, and with the payroll in the Security Department of another subsidiary, Under 21, which Covenant House reported to the proper authorities. Kroll found no other evidence of any material financial impropriety. The report addresses several other miscellaneous allegations that were found to be unfounded or relatively minor.

The last section of the Report sets forth the overall conclusion that the investigators found far more right with Covenant House than they found wrong with it. They concluded that Covenant House is sound and its work is essential and effective, and that it must survive to serve these young people who so desperately need its services.

STATEMENT OF THE OVERSIGHT COMMITTEE OF COVENANT HOUSE

On March 7, 1990, The Board of Directors of Covenant House appointed us to serve as an Oversight Committee. Our function has been to oversee and evaluate the results, conclusions and recommendations of the several investigations that the Board commissioned Cravath, Swaine & Moore, Robert J. McGuire of Kroll Associates, Ernst & Young and Richard Shinn, former President of New York Metropolitan Life Insurance Co., to perform. During the past five months, we have met several times and we have received an discussed with the investigative teams their oral and written reports.

We have examined carefully the Report to the Board of Directors and the Oversight Committee by Cravath, Swaine & Moore and Kroll Associates concerning the results of the investigations. We endorse its conclusions and recommendations.

We find the excellent Report to be a thorough, careful, and honest appraisal of Covenant House and the problems it has encountered. We are convinced the investigations have been complete and impartial. Allegations of misconduct have been fully explored, and assessed with candor as well as sensitivity. The Report identifies a number of areas in which, in the past, overall surveillance and control by the Board of Directors was weak, reflecting in part the unusual organizational structure that did not provide the usual and necessary checks and balances.

Clearly, mistakes were made. Some corrective measures have been taken and others have been recommended and will be put in place. We are convinced the recommended measures appropriately address past weaknesses and should assure a firm foundation for the future work of this unique and important organization. We recommend that there be systems for monitoring the implementation of these measures over time, and we understand these are being put in place as well.

Based upon our examination of the materials before us, we agree with the conclusion of the Report that there is far more right with Covenant House than there was wrong with it. The investigators report that, wherever they went, they found dedicated, honest and good people doing difficult, often thankless work under extraordinarily trying conditions. They conclude that the work of Covenant House is essential and extremely important and so do we.

We came away from our work convinced that Covenant House provides vital services, for which there are no practical alternatives, to large numbers of troubled young people. We believe that Covenant House, under its new and energetic leadership and with the changes put in place in recent months, deserves the public's confidence and support.

William Ellinghaus, Chairman
Rev. Theodore M. Hesburgh
Rabbi Marc Tanenbaum
Cyrus Vance
Paul Volcker

August 3, 1990

Doing Everything Right

Once Ritter and his Board of puppets were gone, Covenant House did everything as right as right could be. For example, look at the blue ribbon board of overseers: two of the most respected religious figures in the country — one Catholic, one Jewish, a former Secretary of State and the Chairman of the Federal Reserve.

When men of this caliber say: "We believe that Covenant House, under its new and energetic leadership and with the changes put in place in recent months, deserves the public's confidence and support," the media and donors have to listen.

Covenant House Today

In the 1980s, Bruce Ritter realized that he could not run both Covenant House and do all the fund raising, so he contracted with Epsilon of Burlington, Massachusetts, to handle the direct marketing. Epsilon, under the very capable direction of John E. Groman, maintained the database, executed the mailings and even had some of its creative people go up against Father Ritter. While Ritter continued to write many of the letters, Epsilon had some winners, too; one in particular that I remember was a rule-breaking card deck — a series of 3" x 5" cards with photos of some of the kids on the front and their story on the back, along with a letter, a tiny reply envelope and, of course, an order card.

With Ritter's departure, Epsilon — together with Sister Mary Rose, herself a brilliantly intuitive direct marketer — picked up the fallen torch and fanned the flame back to viability.

Replacing Ritter as chief copywriter was Epsilon's Tom Gaffney who, in chatting with Sister Mary Rose, jotted down notes about one of the Covenant House residents. The result was this masterpiece that rivals Ritter for effect — and effectiveness, since it was control for a number of years. It was printed in black-and-white on Covenant House letterhead:

You're going to have trouble believing this
letter. I mean, what I'm about to tell you is
so strange and incredible, you'll never forget
it. But please understand that EVERY SINGLE
WORD OF THIS STORY IS TRUE!!! I'm really praying you'll take a few minutes to read it.
Thank you.

Dear Friend

   She came to our front door Tuesday morning,
dressed in dirty rags, holding a little alu-
minum paint can in her arms.

   From the second she stepped inside our shelter, she mystified us. Whatever she did, wherever she went, the paint can never left her
hands.

   When Kathy sat in the crisis shelter, the can
sat in her arms. She took the can with her to
the cafeteria that first morning she ate, and to
bed with her that first night she slept.

   When she stepped into the shower, the can
was only a few feet away. When the tiny homeless girl dressed, the can rested alongside her
feet.

   "I'm sorry, this is mine," she told our
counselors, whenever we asked her about it.
"This can belongs to me."

   "Do you want to tell me what's in it,
Kathy?" I'd ask her? "Um, not today," she said,
"not today."

   When Kathy was sad, or angry or hurt —
which happened a lot — she took her paint can
to a quiet dorm room on the 3rd floor. Many
times on Tuesday and Wednesday and Thursday,
I'd pass by her room, and watch her rock gently

back and forth, the can in her arms. Sometimes she'd talk to the paint can in low whispers.

I've been around troubled kids all my life, (over 41,000 homeless kids will come to our shelters this year!). I'm used to seeing them carry stuffed animals (some of the roughest, toughest kids at Covenant House have a stuffed animal). Every kid has something — needs something — to hold.

But a paint can? I could feel alarm bells ringing in my head.

Early this morning, I decided to "accidentally" run into her again. "Would you like to join me for breakfast?" I said. "That would be great," she said.

For a few minutes we sat in a corner of our cafeteria, talking quietly over the din of 150 ravenous homeless kids. Then I took a deep breath, and plunged into it . . . .

"Kathy, that's a really nice can. What's in it?"

For a long time, Kathy didn't answer. She rocked back and forth, her hair swaying across her shoulders. Then she looked over at me, tears in her eyes.

"It's my mother," she said.

"Oh," I said. "What do you mean it's your mother?" I asked.

"It's my mother's ashes," she said.

"I went and got them from the funeral home. See, I even asked them to put a label right here on the side. It has her name on it."

Kathy held the can up before my eyes. A
little label on the side chronicled all that
remained of her mother: date of birth, date of
death, name. That was it. Then Kathy pulled the
can close, and hugged it.

"I never really knew my mother, Sister,"
Kathy told me. "I mean, she threw me in the
garbage two days after I was born." (We checked
Kathy's story. Sure enough the year Kathy was
born, the New York newspapers ran a story, saying that the police had found a little infant
girl in a dumpster . . . and yes, it was two
days after Kathy was born.)

"I ended up living in a lot of foster
homes, mad at my mother," Kathy said. "But
then, I decided I was going to try to find her.
I got lucky — someone knew where she was living. I went to her house."

"She wasn't there, Sister," she said. "My
mother was in the hospital. She had AIDS. She
was dying."

"I went to the hospital, and I got to
meet her the day before she died. My mother
told me she loved me, Sister," Kathy said crying. "She told me she loved me." (We double-
checked Kathy's story . . . every word of it
was true.)

I reached out and hugged Kathy, and she
cried in my arms for a long, long time. It was
tough getting my arms around her, because she
just wouldn't put the paint can down. But she
didn't seem to mind. I know I didn't . . .

I saw Kathy again, a couple hours ago, eating dinner in our cafeteria. She made a point

Sister Mary Rose McGeady, whose integrity and brilliant management saved Covenant House — and thousands of wayward children — from oblivion.

to come up and say hi. I made a point to give her an extra hug . . . .

I've felt like crying tonight. I can't seem to stop feeling this way. I guess this story — the whole horrible, sad, unreal mess — has gotten to me tonight.

I guess that's why I just had to write you this letter.

Please — I know you and I have never met before. But I need to ask you something very important, and I'm praying you'll consider it, if you can.

Do you think you could help Kathy . . . and our other kids at Covenant House? Please?

There's one very important thing you need to know about Covenant House and our kids and it is this — A DONATION TO COVENANT HOUSE IS THE AB-SOLUTE BEST WAY YOU CAN HELP THE TERRIFIED AND HELPLESS HOMELESS KIDS ON OUR STREETS!

This year more than 41,000 homeless kids . . . kids who are 12, 16, 17 years old . . . will come to our doors.

We'll give these kids food, and a safe bed to sleep in (the streets are incredibly danger-ous!) and medicine, and counseling if they need it (most kids do).

But most of all, we'll give these kids love. For thousands of these kids, the love we give them tonight will be the first love they've ever known!

We are here for kids like Kathy 24 hours a day, in 9 cities across America, 365 days a year. No kid — no kid! — is ever turned away ever!

Thanks to the love and help of thousands of caring people — people just like you — Covenant House spends MORE than the entire federal government to help these kids. (That's what I meant when I said that giving to us is THE best way to help these kids.)

But so much more needs to be done. And we can't do it alone.

Do you think maybe you could help? Please? Any donation you can send — $15, $25, $50 — any amount, will be a godsend to our kids. Please do it today if you can.

Please.

I want to assure you of one very important thing. We're going to do all we can to help Kathy, to let her know she is loved. And I know, with your help, we are going to reach Kathy, and help her in a way no one has ever done before. You have my promise on that. . . .

And when we do reach her, it will be because of you. It will be because people like you haven't stopped caring, and haven't stopped loving. Yes, it will be possible because of you. It will be possible because of you.

Thanks so much for reading this long letter. And please, pray for us if you can. Your prayers really help a lot.

In God's love,
/s/ Sister Mary Rose
President

P.S. Our financial need is really urgent right now. Please help, if you can. (Thanks for caring . . . .)

Tom Gaffney, Epsilon's ace copywriter, whose high intensity letters for Covenant House rival those of his predecessor, Fr. Bruce Ritter.

Covenant House bounced back from near oblivion to where it takes in some $60 million a year; but revenues have never quite matched the halcyon days before Ritter's fall, when the priest's powerful copy brought in nearly $90 million a year from a donor base of over one million contributors vs. the current 400,000 12-month donors.

And what of Ritter? He was ousted from the priesthood, but was never prosecuted and never did jail time. Sources report he bought a small house somewhere in upstate New York. He turned one room into a private chapel, grew a beard and has become a recluse.

Points for Marketers to Consider

1.

When I got out of the Army in 1960 and moved to a $60-a-month walk-up railroad flat on East 71st Street in Manhattan, my bathtub was in the kitchen and the toilet was in a closet down the hall by the stairs. One Saturday, I heard a knock on my door, and I answered it. On the floor in a portable crib was a newborn baby. My brain and my heart did a series of flip-flops. "No," I said to myself. "Oh, no! Not me. This is not happening to me!"

I stepped into the hall and on the stairs were the parents, my friends Shell and Edie Henry, laughing with glee at their joke.

Yet, don't all of us wonder how we would react if the doorbell rang and on the front stoop were two or three battered children? What would we do? Turn them over to a shelter? Call the police?

Bruce Ritter was an intuitive Method Marketer who tapped into that fear lurking deep within us and built a vast enterprise on our collective guilt.

2.

Is your message to your prospects, customers or donors *emotional* enough? Ritter's letter — and later, Tom Gaffney's letter — were not *New York Times* reports analyzing the statistics of runaway children on the streets and the cost to society of dealing with them. Rather, they are highly charged stories about individual kids that play upon three of Bob Hacker's copy drivers: guilt, guilt and more guilt.

3.

Ritter's prose (and Gaffney's) paint graphic pictures in the mind's eye. Is your descriptive copy *visual?* Or do you have to rely on brochures and photos to make your product or service come alive?

4.

You cannot bore people into buying.
— David Ogilvy

5.

Probably well over half of our buying choices are based on emotion.
— Jack Maxson

6.

Are you prepared to deal with a public relations disaster? Covenant House was bopping along, doing good works, enjoying a fine reputation. Suddenly Bruce Ritter was exposed as a pederast. The media had a field day. Anger and outrage coupled with old-fashioned sex and embarrassment to the Catholic Church is a reporter's dream, guaranteed to make everyone squirm — protagonists, antagonists, readers and viewers. You bet it sold newspapers and guaranteed high ratings for television news.

7.

What if you find yourself with an executive who is accused of committing a heinous act and who absolutely maintains innocence?

In the public relations field, the new buzzphrase is "reputation management." A nasty fight that is allowed to spill out and fuel a media feeding frenzy can be devastating.

Had Fr. Ritter — knowing full well he was guilty as charged — made the survival of Covenant House his first priority, he would have immediately stepped aside until the various investigations were complete and he was exonerated (if the evidence was circumstantial and inconclusive).

Instead, since he not only controlled the organization, but also the mailing apparatus, no one was able to stop him from communicating directly with his donors to protest his innocence. Obviously, his original board of directors was in his pocket and too powerless (or scared) to take action. Only after months of investigation — and irrefutable evidence of the priest's guilt — did Ritter cave in and leave. But the damage to Covenant House was far greater than if he had stepped aside immediately.

Once this destructive and reckless priest was gone, the actions of Covenant House were completely correct in every way.

Compare the Covenant House approach to making a quick, clean breast of it to how Richard Nixon handled Watergate or how Bill Clinton and his lawyers dragged out and obfuscated the various investigations into his alleged misdeeds. Had any of White House occupants — or the utterly incompetent sycophants on their personal staffs — been in charge of the Bruce Ritter debacle, Covenant House would have gone out of business in a New York second.

Instead, once Ritter was out, his successors operated under the basic rule of sound public relations, as articulated by Evelyn Lawson:

> Good public relations means letting people in on what you are doing.

8.

This then raises questions about your organization: Do you have any plan in place for your own reputation management? Is your board empowered to ask for the temporary stepping aside of a manager or employee while an investigation runs its course? What exactly is covered in your by-laws on these subjects?

4

Predictions:

The Most Diverting Sales Letter
Ever Written

It's axiomatic: Some of the most compelling prose being written today arrives in your mailbox — or office in-box — FOR FREE.

Direct mail copy must be powerful; it has to interrupt and keep on interrupting until some action is taken.

If something comes along to interrupt the interruption — a telephone ringing, a baby crying, someone knocking on the front door — chances are the sale is lost.

The letter that follows was written for *Predictions,* a newsletter published out of Boca Raton, Florida. I'm a bit hazy on who the publisher was — either Lee Euler or Joel Nadel.

I only noted having received this mailing a couple of times, so it could not have been a huge success. But, in the words of Arizona direct marketer and Harley-Davidson aficionado "Rocket Ray" Jutkins:

There are no failures; only lessons.

Besides, for sheer delight, this effort ranks with the best short fiction being written today.

The letter starts on the front of the six-by-nine envelope:

In the upper left-hand corner of the envelope in roman type.

The 100% Guarantee
a short story by
John B. Palmer

Chapter One

The letter that started it all arrived in Joel Adler's mailbox on a cold Saturday morning a few weeks before Christmas. It was an ordinary-looking blue envelope, no return address, sandwiched between a copy of Time and a handwritten letter from Joel's son Tim, a college senior, undoubtedly asking for money.

Joel sorted quickly through the mail, found nothing that riveted his attention, and turned back to the morning paper. "QB Hurt: 49ers Super Bowl Hopes Plunge," screamed the banner headline on the sports page. "I'll have to remember that for the football pool," Joel thought.

Perhaps it was the Super Bowl reminder that caused Joel's glance to shift to the little blue envelope . . . for it was then that he noticed the line printed discretely on the envelope just to the left of his name:
"SUPER BOWL WINNER: 100% GUARANTEED. $1."

Now intrigued, Joel ripped open the envelope. Inside he found only a very short letter, which, in its entirety, read as follows:

Dear Sir:
 The winner of next month's Super Bowl game is
known to me. For the sum of one American dollar in cash,
I will reveal the name to you. If the team I name does not
win, your dollar will be returned within 72 hours and you
will never hear from me again.
                                    — Balthazar Balash

Well, as you can imagine, Joel was hooked. "What's this guy's gimmick," he wondered. "He can't be making any money at a dollar a clip." Joel extracted his wallet, removed a wrinkled one-dollar bill, inserted it in the reply envelope and tossed it in the outgoing mail basket.

Shortly after New Year's, another little blue envelope arrived at the Adler household. The letter inside read, as follows:

(continued inside)

Inside the envelope was a 12-page letter with no letterhead. The copy was set in Courier (typewriter) type. Here is that letter.

(continued from the envelope)

Dear Sir:

The winner of the Super Bowl game will be the San Francisco 49ers.
                    — Balthazar Balash

Of course Joel didn't believe a word of it. But the office betting pool was a small one. And even when he pocketed his winnings, following San Francisco's dramatic upset victory, he hardly thought about the little blue envelope.

A few weeks later, the next blue envelope arrived.

Dear Sir:
The winner of next month's election for Prime Minister of France is known to me. For the sum of five American dollars in cash, I will reveal the name to you. If the candidate I name does not win, your five dollars will be returned within 72 hours and you will never hear from me again.
                    — Balthazar Balash

Joel had little interest in French politics, but he was sufficiently intrigued to risk five dollars to see what would happen.

What happened was what the newspapers called "Stunning Upset in French Vote." "Boy," thought Joel to himself, "I could have made a bundle betting on that one. Wonder what's next."

Next came a blue envelope guaranteeing the winner of a basketball playoff game — for $10.

Joel made a few side bets at the office, and then made a pleasant profit when the prediction came true.

After the fourth prediction — for $25 — the surprise winner of a big mayor's election — Joel was baffled, confused, and even more intrigued. He felt the need to talk things over with his old friend Jay Sampson.

"Jay, as a commodity broker, you're in the prediction business yourself. What do you make of all this?"

The broker puffed on his pipe thoughtfully. "Look, Joel, you know as well as I that no one can see into the future. It's just a gimmick of some kind."

"Maybe so," Joel replied, "But you've got to admit that four upsets in a row is pretty darn good."

"Or pretty lucky. I'd like to see this Balash character try to predict something in *my* racket."

"Then take a look at this," said Joel, tossing a blue envelope onto the broker's desk.

"Fascinating," said Jay. "For a mere fifty bucks, he will tell you whether the price of gold will be higher or lower on June first than on May first. Are you inclined to take the risk?"

"Well, uh, I already have. Here's his answer." The familiar blue sheet had only one word on it: "Higher." Joel smiled sheepishly. "I, uh, thought I might sell that mutual fund on May first and, well, buy some gold."

The June 1 closing fix on gold in London was $22.50 higher than the May 1 close.

And the next four predictions, which cost the new partnership of Adler and Sampson $100, $250, $500, and $1,000 respectively, were equally surprising and equally correct. The two men, who had made quite a bit of money in investments and side bets, were utterly mystified.

"Look," said Jay at one of their weekly lunches that fall, "I know I said I didn't believe in magic. "But, well look — this Balash has made nine correct predictions in a row, and at least seven of them were big surprises. The odds against that are astronomical."

Joel readily agreed. "Unexplainable things do happen all the time. I don't know if it's what they call a miracle or what. I just know that I'm darn well convinced."

"I've got to admit that I am too," said the broker. "In fact, I can hardly wait for prediction number ten."

"Then have a look at this," said Joel. "It came in the morning mail." The blue sheet read as follows:

Dear Sir:

On September 27, there is a fight for the WBC heavyweight championship of the world. The winner is known to me. I will sell you that name for the sum of one million American dollars in cash. If the fighter I name does not win, I will refund your one million dollars within 72 hours.

— Balthazar Balash

The two men looked at each other long and hard. Then, as one, they whipped out their pens and started calculating. "If I re-mortgage the house . . . " "I've had an offer on that land in Hawaii." "I can put together a syndicate — I know Gustafson and Whitman would go for it . . . "

And so it went. Within a week, the syndicate had been formed. One million dollars to buy the

name of the winner, and four million more to
place the bets discreetly at Las Vegas and
London bookmaking parlors.

The huge sum of cash was transmitted, and
two weeks before the fight, the blue envelope
came. The syndicate gathered in Jay's office to
open it. Joel was the first to speak. "It's
Walker," he shouted. "Walker — - the four-to-
one underdog. That means sixteen million dollars, gentlemen. Sixteen million dollars!"

Chapter Two

Walker lost.

Chapter Three

The money was never returned.

Chapter Four

Final Report: The Balthazar Balash Case

Investigative Unit, Los Angeles Police
Department

Based on records found in the apartment abandoned by Balash the day after two parcels containing $1 million cash each were sent to his
Post Office box, the method used was as follows:

Initially, Balash sent out enough sales letters
to produce at least 1,024 responses. Half of
these customers (512) got a letter predicting
that San Francisco would win the Super bowl.
The other 512 got a letter predicting that
Cincinnati would win. When San Francisco won,
he used the money sent in by the 512 winners to
make refunds to the 512 losers.

Next, for the French election, he sent one candidate's name to 256 of his remaining customers

and the other name to the other 256. Again, he paid off the losers with the money sent by the winners.

Now he had only 256 customers left. 128 got the name of one basketball team, 128, the other. For the mayor's election, 64 people were sent each name. For the gold prediction, 32 people were told "higher" and 32 were told "lower."

And so it went, right down the very last prediction, when he had only two customers left. Each of these customers had been given, by the luck of the draw, nine correct predictions. They were well and truly hooked. Of course they didn't know that there had originally been 1,022 other clients.

One customer (an Arab oil sheikh) was given one fighter's name for a million dollars, and the Adler syndicate was given the other fighter's name for another million. The Arab presumably is quite happy now, and so, we may assume, is Balthazar Balash, who disappeared with two million dollars in cash, and can almost certainly never be traced.

Conclusion: In the business of predicting the future, some people may be quite good indeed — but there's no such thing as a 100% guarantee.

Anyone investing in the advice of predictors is hereby advised to act cautiously.

Dear Fellow Investor

Now that I have your attention, I would like to recommend that you very cautiously make a mod-

```
est investment in the services of some of the
best investment predictors in the world today.

There is a new, inexpensive but extremely pow-
erful investment advisory service called, sim-
ply, PREDICTIONS: SPECIFIC INVESTMENT FORECASTS
AND RECOMMENDATIONS FROM THE WORLD'S TOP FINAN-
CIAL EXPERTS. . . .
```

The letter then goes on to pitch the newsletter, *Predictions.*

Points for Marketers to Consider

1.

When I first received this letter, I read it with relish — up to the point where the story ended and the pitch for the newsletter began. I remember being simply delighted at finding such a nifty piece of prose in my mailbox. I put the letter down to think, for a moment, about the two guys who had bet the ranch and wondered whether I would have fallen for the same ruse. (I wouldn't have.)

The point is, *I put the letter down..*

Freelancer Malcolm Decker likens a sales letter to trout fishing with barbless hooks when he was a boy in Maine. In order to land a fish with a barbless hook, Decker explains, you have to keep a constant tension on the line all the way to the net. If you allow the line to slacken at all, you've lost the fish.

Same thing with a sales letter. If the prose suddenly goes slack and you lay the thing aside, chances are good you won't pick it up and start reading it again. And, even if you do, you will come back into the middle of the argument.

A letter is an interruption to the normal thought process. An interruption of that interruption is usually fatal to the sale. Chances are the mailing will be left on the table unread and then gathered up with the sports pages and tossed in the recycling bin.

2.

The Balthazar Balash letter is wonderfully written. But, clearly, the overpowering message left with the reader is that you are going to get screwed by anyone who claims to be able to predict the future. So, while it's a spectacular piece of prose, it negates the entire concept of the product being sold. In that sense, it is cute; it is clever. But it is, ultimately, destructive. Compare this letter to Bruce Ritter's fund raiser for Covenant House telling of the three kids who showed up at his front door. Ritter was able to make an easy, logical segue into the product he was selling.

3.

Not a single benefit to the reader is expressed anywhere in this long opening. No mention of what the reader is supposed to do or look for.

4.

In the words of freelancer Jack Maxson — whose elegant prose put Brookstone's *Hard-to-Find Tools* catalog on the map:

Your job is to sell, not to entertain.

5

Boardroom I

Martin Edelston: How a Bookish Ex-Ad Salesman Created the Most Efficient Company in the World

GOD.

So proclaims a giant orange-and-black glass sign over the door of the sanctum sanctorum of Martin Edelston, founder and proprietor of Boardroom Reports and its series of spin-off newsletters, books and seminars. On entering, the tiny and crammed outer office with its two desks and mélange of files, papers, books, computers, in-baskets and bizarre decorations, you are greeted warmly by Edelston's wonderfully upbeat and accommodating secretary-factotum-den mother, Helen Brennan, who then opens the door to Edelston's office and calls in, "Marty, your visitors are here!"

It turns out that "God" is called Marty by everyone from office boys, secretaries and copy editors to vice presidents. Even his three children who are in the business call him Marty. When Brennan answers the phone, she chirps, "Marty's office!"

After a moment's wait, God-cum-Marty shuffles through the door. The first impression: a hulking, owlish, ex-hippie of medium height with quizzical eyes behind horn-rimmed glasses and an Adlai Stevenson forehead topped with a full mane of overly long and untidy dark hair — gray at the temples — combed straight back. This day "God" was clad in a navy blue sports jacket over a startling American flag rugby shirt, dark trousers and black earth shoes.

However, within four seconds it is apparent that the "God" thing is an elaborate put-on; Edelston is a big kid who is idolized by his employees, an incredibly low-key paterfamilias whose business day is spent playing host to a parade of colleagues and visitors, all of whom enjoy access and who are looking for advice, affirmation or a decision on everything from a headline to offer copy on a direct mail order card.

When I first interviewed Edelston, his small corner office on the fourteenth floor of the old McGraw-Hill building overlooking Manhattan's 42nd Street was a topsy-turvy jumble of furniture, shelving, books, statues, prints and crazy electrified contraptions which, when switched on, shake, rattle and roll. The company has since moved to modern, antiseptic offices next to the Greenwich, Connecticut, railroad station. The old place was more fun.

As you thread your way through the clutter, Marty points to the corner where two deliciously tacky fake palm trees — their trunks fashioned of tin cans — reach to the ceiling.

"I never travel," Edelston announces. "I vacation right here. If I ever have the urge to sit under swaying palm trees . . . " he flips a wall switch on the far side of his desk and you hear the soft whir of an electric motor, whereupon the trees immediately begin to move back and forth ever so slightly, their tin-can barks clanking.

Edelston isn't kidding about not traveling. According to creative director Evie Randegger, he has not taken a vacation in 23 years and has never missed a day of work because of illness.

Edelston attributes his work ethic to his need to excel in athletics. He went from being the worst runner in high school to the best. At age 45, he took up karate, becoming a black belt 12 years later.

The Unlikely Mogul

This lumbering, gentle, ex-greeting card purveyor and former ad salesman has built a publishing empire that generates $125 million a year in revenue, and he does it with a magnificent team of just 80 employees, which tallies out to a sublime $1.5 million per employee. Not one of the Fortune 500 companies can touch Boardroom's efficiency, employee loyalty (call it adulation) or minuscule turnover.

Edelston's secret of success: the confluence of events and ideas that included a serendipitous journey through life, and insatiable curiosity about everything and everybody he ever came in contact with and a business philosophy adapted from Peter Drucker and W. Edwards Deming that has come to be known as I-Power (more about that later). Plus the genius of an untrained, intuitive copywriter named Mel Martin (more about him later, too).

A Dozen Jobs Later

Born and raised in Newark, N.J., Edelston went to the University of Newark, where he majored in business.

> I learned two things in college. If you take credit when business goes up, you had better take responsibility when business goes down. I also learned something else, but I forget what it was.

In the course of his life, Edelston held a dozen jobs before starting Boardroom. In his boyhood, he worked on a milk truck and behind a soda fountain. He sold greeting cards door-to-door and, later, behind a counter. He worked as a swimming instructor and life guard and sold advertising pencils, Yellow Pages advertising and billboard space.

At Hearst magazines, Edelston sold mail order advertising for *House Beautiful*; it was here he first met some of the men who would have a profound influence on his later success — copywriters Gene Schwartz and Henry Cowen and the brilliant Richard V. Benson. As he remembers it, instead of joining the *House Beautiful* advertising staff every day for long, liquid lunches at a Lexington Avenue gin mill, Edelston would be out hustling business. In those recessionary times, Edelston's sales were up even though everyone else's were down, a situation that so miffed his colleagues that whenever Marty came into the office, all heads would turn away from him. He was shunned. "I enjoyed it at the time; I couldn't handle it today."

The other great influence on his life was Frank Bettger's 1949 classic, *How I Raised Myself from Failure to Success Through Selling,* a book Edelston stocks in quantity today and hands out to anyone who'll agree to read it.

In a stunning burst of stupidity, Hearst took its top mail-order salesman and transferred him to liquor and travel sales for pre-Helen Gurley Brown *Cosmopolitan* — at a time when single women were perceived as neither travelers nor drinkers. After he was fired from *Cosmo,* Edelston did a quick turn selling for *Interiors,* when he was offered a selling job at *The Reporter.*

It was at *The Reporter* that Edelston met Mel Martin, whose later editorial and direct mail copy for Boardroom Inc., was almost entirely responsible for the company's exponential growth in the '80s and '90s.

Even though Marty could claim credit for 90 percent of *The Reporter*'s advertising sales, owner Max Ascoli refused to make him ad

Martin Edelston, proprietor of what may be the most efficient company in the world.

director. Not getting the job grated on Edelston. But in his gut he knew why; he was a feisty know-it-all.

> Every day I had an argument with somebody. Editorial . . . circulation . . . none of them like an ad man telling them what to do. They were doing dumb things and I told them so.

Early on at *The Reporter* — with its intellectual roots in book publishing — Edelston became a gluttonous reader.

> I tried to read everything — every book published — and at the time there were 50,000 new titles a year. How could I keep up?

Someone suggested he read only those areas he was interested in. "That was easy," Edelston says, "Jewishness and business. I read everything in those two areas."

So when Norman Podhoretz, publisher of the Jewish intellectual magazine *Commentary* offered Edelston the job of business manager, it was the opportunity to put together everything he had learned and believed in thus far in his life. "I had ten beautiful years there," Edelston exulted. "Everything was bootstrapped. I took circulation from 10,000 to 80,000."

A Fateful Lunch

From his reading, Edelston found he loved business books and disliked business magazines. The reason: books dealt with the how-to's of business: how to raise capital, how to manage people, how to close sales, how to market products and services, while the business magazines — *Fortune, Business Week, Forbes* — told readers what was happening at GM, AT&T and Goldman, Sachs. To Edelston, the how-to information was invaluable; reportage on business was useless.

One day in the early 1970s, freelancer Sol Blumenfeld called Marty and suggested they go into business together. Edelston and Blumenfeld had gone to grammar school, high school and college together. At lunch at the Vanderbilt, the two old friends poured out their dreams. Marty wanted to publish a magazine that did what business books did: tell how to run a business, not report on news of the business world.

Following lunch, the search was on for $1.25 million in venture capital. The search began in 1972 in the teeth of a recession; everyday the market shrank. Starting a magazine was out of the question.

It was then that someone suggested a newsletter, which could be done for a fraction of that amount. Edelston put up $30,000 and the Boardroom empire was born.

From Zero to $125 Million

When the concept of *Boardroom Reports* crystallized in Edelston's head — that of a how-to-do-it newsletter for business people — his initial investment of $30,000 was not a lot of money, even back in the 70s. But the ever-resourceful Edelston came up with what he thought was a brilliant idea.

> I made a deal with a number of publishers to run a space ad and give them a share of stock for every paying subscriber their publication brought in. It was a good deal for both of us.

Inventive, yes. Successful, no. It did not produce enough subs to get started. So Edelston hired copywriter Gene Schwartz to turn the ad into a direct mail piece. The headline:

**HOW TO READ
300 BUSINESS BOOKS
IN 30 MINUTES**

Generally speaking, the ideal size of a direct mail test is 5,000 pieces per test cell. The reason: The benchmark 2-percent response will bring in 100 orders, which become a statistically valid sample for tracking back-end performance. With groups smaller than 100 customers, analysis can be questionable.

For the initial mailing, Edelston broke the rules and made the following tests:

- Five lists.
- Two pieces of copy.
- Cheap paper vs. expensive paper.
- Individually typed envelopes vs. labels.
- First Class vs. Third Class

Total amount of all tests: 17,000 pieces.

Boardroom Reports was up and running. Edelston went looking for more money and found one lender: Maxwell Dane, the Dane between Doyle and Bernbach.

Edelston scheduled a mailing of 50,000, but found that with editorial and production expenses, he could not afford the drop. It was Milt Smolier of Names Unlimited who taught Marty to mail 10,000 a week for five weeks rather than do a single drop of 50,000; the initial nut isn't so huge and mailing in waves provided a steady cash flow for the young business.

At that time, Boardroom's offices were at the New York Public Library, where editor Stan Zarowin was clipping short bits from dozens of business magazines and business columns from newspapers and general interest publications. Finally, when it was determined that Zarowin needed a real office, Edelston rented space at 500 Fifth Avenue at 42nd Street and borrowed a desk from his old friend, Don Howard, of Don Howard Personnel.

Two Hiccups

Boardroom Reports expanded geometrically, getting to 200,000 subscribers in a faster growth pattern than *Business Week, Fortune* or *The Wall Street Journal.* It was at this juncture that Edelston experienced the first hiccup in his growth.

Since the Boardroom control mailing was a bill-me offer, the company was cash-starved. Edelston immediately switched to cash-with-order; up-front response took a nose dive, but the company was saved and became solvent. Although money was pouring in and Marty was mailing aggressively, he had no long-term plans. Edelston called this his "period of substantial delegation. Now I don't delegate; I coordinate."

Edelston rented office space from Doyle, Dane, Bernbach until 1980 when an offer he couldn't refuse came up: a floor in the old McGraw-Hill Building on West 42nd Street. He signed the lease and told his accountant to put aside the $600,000 needed to fix it up. "We don't have $600,000," the accountant said.

Hiccup number two. Edelston had a huge empty floor of the McGraw-Hill Building. Because of liberal concessions, no rent was due for many months, but the problem was nasty and nagged at him. He spent every weekend of the summer of 1980 sitting on the beach at the Jersey shore wrestling with what to do. The solution he came up with:

build half the floor, enough to move the marketing department into the new offices while editorial remained behind at DDB. Edelston split his days between the two offices.

Eventually cash flow allowed him to complete the move.

A New Product

It was M. Lincoln Schuster, co-founder of Simon and Schuster, who said: "One book is a product; two is a line." The secret of successful direct marketing is to have more than one product so that you can generate additional sales from your existing customers. One of the great elements of Edelston's success over the years: taking existing editorial material, repackaging it in a different format and offering it for sale to his customers and outsiders. At this time Edelston created *The Book of Business Knowledge,* which was a huge success; whatever was mailed in its behalf produced gigantic amounts of cash.

At this time, Edelston's ace copywriter, Mel Martin, began to hit his stride with the revolutionary copywriting technique he dubbed "fascinations." Where most direct mail copy creates needs, makes bold promises, offers benefits and more benefits, Mel Martin created pages and pages of teasers. For example, his mailing for Edelston's spin-off newsletter, *Bottom Line/Personal,* mailed in a white #10 envelope with the huge teaser:

WHAT NEVER TO EAT ON AN AIRPLANE

Created in 1987, it was mailed continuously through 1995. In 1994, Boardroom mailed a mind-blowing 16 million pieces of this venerable effort. The only change: new envelope copy:

BILLS IT'S OKAY TO PAY LATE

For Edelston, Mel Martin was a secret weapon whose work was bringing in millions of dollars of revenue. More about Mel Martin later.

More Than a Hiccup

In 1988, Edelston signed with a computer company to create a model that would forecast profitability, but no one in the place could make the numbers balance. Something was seriously wrong with the model.

So Edelston dispatched his circulation director, Harry Sailer, down to the Skidaway Island, Georgia, lair of consultant-guru Richard V. Benson.

Sailer's charge: to figure out where the model was off.

Sailer flew down on a Thursday night and met with Benson on Friday. Friday night Edelston called Benson and in a lighthearted way asked if he and Sailer had figured out the mistake with the model. "There's no mistake in the model. You got too fat. You have to cut your overhead tremendously."

Edelston took an inventory and realized both Benson and the model were correct. "I had six office boys," Edelston admitted. "I didn't need six office boys." Over the weekend, Edelston created a position paper and realized his very survival depended on cutting his staff by one-third — downsizing to 80 employees from 120. Plans were made; generous severance packages were put in place; the deed was done the following Friday.

When asked if it had been the worst day of his business life, Edelston said, "I never thought about it that way, but yes."

Although it was excruciatingly painful to Edelston, the company was saved. Today, Edelston presides over a publishing empire that includes six newsletters, a slew of spin-off books and a masterfile of 4.5 million buyers.

Marty Edelston learned his lesson. This sobering experience — combined with his editorial and business philosophy, enables Boardroom to mail 125 million pieces of mail a year — some 75 different mailing packages, each with six or seven test panels; these efforts generate $125 million in revenues.

And since Edelston reads and approves everything that goes into the mail — acquisition packages; billing and renewal efforts; inserts; book offers; you name it, Marty has nitpicked it to death — it is the same voice going out to prospects, subscribers and expires. This is why Martin Edelston is a true Method Marketer.

Marty Edelston and *I-Power*

When Martin Edelston founded his first newsletter, *Boardroom Reports,* he brought a lifetime of study to the table, an insatiable desire to know about everything and a set of internal antennae rivaling an AWACS radar plane.

In the words of Boardroom creative director Evelyn Randegger:

> Marty is endlessly curious. Life experiences are very impor-
> tant to him. He seeks knowledge in everything he does. When he
> sees something, he immediately wants to know how it works.
> Nothing escapes him. When he arrives in the morning, if any-
> thing is amiss — from a co-worker's smile to a vase of flowers —
> he picks up on it. He is an expert on type styles, on headlines, on
> design. He continually challenges you intellectually. And we all
> work under a fair amount of pressure.

Yet, everyone at Boardroom not only likes Marty, they worship
him. T'was not ever thus. Edelston:

> I started with an editor and a secretary. We worked together
> for four years. During that time I hired people and fired people.
> And hired and fired. And hired and fired. I reached the conclu-
> sion that something was wrong with me.

Edelston went back over all the resumes of people he had interviewed and phoned a psychiatrist in Raleigh-Durham he had once talked
to. "I think I can help," the psychiatrist told him. Once a month for a year
and a half, Edelston commuted to North Carolina "to learn how to run a
business. We would talk about problems and how to solve them."

Now, Edelston has consultants for everything: postal consultants,
strategic planning consultants, circulation consultants. In addition,
since "I am probably the last major mailer who pays full rate for all
brokerage services," he has no compunction about calling on the top
people in the industry for counsel. "If you are insisting on discounted
services," Edelston says, "it's hard to ask for free information." As a result, Michael Fishman of The SpeciaLists and the legendary Dave
Florence of Direct Media are a phone call away. "I never start a new
project without checking things out with at least one outside consultant," he says.

Disenchantment

For 20 years Edelston and his editors talked to hundreds of important
and successful management consultants, business school professors,
Wall Street analysts and business executives in a search for specific ad-

vice on how a company could improve productivity, creativity and profitability.

> Then about eight years ago, I began to feel uneasy. It was becoming very evident that there were major flaws in the ways American managers were handling their businesses. And as a major advice giver to America's managers, that meant there were flaws in the advice we were seeking and publishing.

Edelston's doubts were not only directed at American business, but inwardly — to his own business as well. Once after a grueling day of consulting with Peter Drucker, the great guru suddenly asked him, "How are the meetings in your company?"

"Pretty bad," Edelston admitted. "But aren't they bad at all companies?" Drucker's reply: "Have everyone who comes to a meeting be prepared to give two ideas for making his or her own department's work more productive . . . ideas that will enhance the company as a whole."

Drucker's suggestion — tossed off almost casually — changed Edelston's life and his business; Edelston began calling meetings; instead of asking for two ideas, he asked for three.

> I wasn't prepared for such a flow of ideas. I took detailed notes, lost some right away, and couldn't remember others. As a result, I wound up awed by the power of ideas but felt guilty, chagrined and embarrassed that I couldn't make them happen.
>
> Ultimately, almost all these initial ideas were lost because we didn't have a structure and process in place to make sure these things got done.

Drucker's scheme fell by the wayside. Boardroom was doing extremely well without the ideas.

And then disaster struck in the form of the computer model hiccup and massive downsizing, Edelston was chastened. "I wanted to bind up the wounds. When somebody makes a suggestion, you write down the ideas and you implement them."

Over the next two years, Boardroom became an idea factory. The system was institutionalized. The original name, the Continuous Improvement Program — or CIP — was a mouthful. What Edelston had stumbled on was a power program, one of Ideas, Ingenuity, Invention and Innovation, Intelligence, Imagination and

Improvement. It became I-Power — based on the Japanese system of "kaizen," or continuous improvement.

I-Power was an adaptation of the philosophy of W. Edwards Deming, the Bell Labs management genius brought to Japan by Douglas MacArthur following World War II and who was, in large part, responsible for Japan's massive resurgence as an economic superpower. Each year, Edelston awards over $100,000 to employees for their ideas. A former Boardroom employee said that when she was there, I-Power was something of a nuisance; she took it for granted. But in her new company, she has just as many ideas, but no mechanism in place to give them a fair hearing or implement them. She is currently very frustrated. Edelston's explanation:

> I cannot stress this enough. In order to foster a flow of ideas, the atmosphere must be totally free of negativity. People must feel comfortable about saying things right off the top of their heads, since that's where some of the best ideas come from.

I-Power has spawned a book of that title (*I-Power*, by Martin Edelston and Marion Buhagiar), as well as a series of nationwide seminars to spread the gospel. Edelston so passionately believes in I-Power that he has, for the first time in his career, ceased to be a recluse. His photograph is featured in newspaper ads, and he actually makes an occasional speech.

From Tiger to Pussycat

Edelston himself is a changed man.

> I used to be a big arguer. Very confrontational. And then my son, Sam, came to work for me. I could not be confrontational with Sam. I couldn't fire Sam any more than I can fire my foot. He's part of me.

Realizing he couldn't treat other employees different from Sam, Edelston changed his style. He became very aware of his employees and his effect on them. "I don't take positions any more Edelston says. "I search for the truth." Now, in addition to Sam, Edelston's daughters Sarah and Marjory also work at Boardroom. As Boardroom Vice President Brian Kurtz says:

It's hard to work for Marty and not be a cheerleader. Everything in the company is done in a spirit of fairness. If everything is fair, you won't regret anything.

Edelston's words:

Tapping into the skills and knowledge of workers who, day in and day out, handle the actual work in offices and factories is the most powerful — and underutilized — engine of growth, ideas, strength and opportunity available to every American company.

At the same time, he does not delegate authority nor empower his people easily. Basically he makes every major decision — and a slew of minor ones — in every aspect of his empire: editorial, production, promotion, strategic planning. If it is determined that an outside copywriter won't get along with Marty, the copywriter doesn't have Marty for a client.

Further, writers and art directors complain that Marty nitpicks their work to death, to the point where so many changes are made, they can actually lose money unless the contract allows them to bill for extra time.

One of Edelston's consultants, Gordon Grossman, sums up the Boardroom experience this way:

Marty's a fascinating guy. Stubborn as hell — as all entrepreneurs are. But also very gentle. His employees are his extended family.

Edelston's concern for his employees caused him to pick up and move the company to Connecticut — a move triggered by the World Trade Center bombing. Edelston was living in New Jersey and the terrorists had announced they had plans to blow up the Hudson River tunnels. Suddenly Marty realized that his family members and all his other employees were at risk coming to New York via bridges and tunnels. He asked six top consultants their opinion about the future of Manhattan. All six said its future was behind it. So in 1994 — at age 65 — after a lifetime in the city, Edelston took their advice and moved to a modern building next to the Greenwich, Connecticut, railroad station — a quick reverse commute for any of his people who wished to remain in the city. Amazingly, only two or three employees opted not to go with him.

When asked if he would cooperate for an interview as *Target Marketing*'s Direct Marketer of the Year, Edelston was totally self-effacing. "It's not me," he said. "I am part of a team. If you were ask which part of the car is the most important, the answer is everything is most important."

On the subject of American society, history and business, Edelston is a brilliant talker and analyst. His predictions for the future are gloomy. When asked what kind of a world his new granddaughter will be growling up in, Marty draws inward and his voice drops to a quiet monotone:

> Entitlements are now something like 50 percent of the budget. In 1991, the government wrote checks for $115 billion to people earning more than $50,000 a year and $30 billion to $100,000 earners. Then there's the debt. The third big problem is the bureaucracy. And worst and hardest to deal with is the China problem Or India. Or Korea. Those countries have hundreds of millions of workers who are as well trained as our best people and who are willing to work for $30 a week. By the year 2025, the major economic powers will be gigantically changed and the U.S. will not be among the top ten . . .

"So I-Power is your legacy to America and American business?" he was asked. Marty brightened perceptibly.

"No," he said, beaming. "It's just the beginning."

6

Boardroom II

Mel Martin, Master of Fascinations: Marty Edelston's Secret Weapon

> Mel was one of the world's greatest copywriters,
> and nobody has ever heard of him.
> — Brian Kurtz
> Vice President, Boardroom, Inc.

You can count the creative geniuses who revolutionized direct mail on slightly more than the fingers of two hands: Walter Weintz, who dreamed up the penny mailings for *Reader's Digest;* Fred Breismeister, who discovered that long copy works better than short copy and turned John Stevenson's Greystone Press into the direct mail power-house of the 1960s; Greystone's Paul Michael, who originated the lift letter ("Frankly, I'm puzzled . . ."); Frank Johnson, inventor of the Johnson Box (the boxy headline you see over the salutation of direct mail letters) and the 17″ × 22″ bedsheet circular he developed for *American Heritage;* Johnson's brilliant protégés, Bill Jayme and Heikki Ratalahti; Gary Bencivenga who pioneered 12- and 16-page letters which were transmogrified into the magalog format; sweepstakes wizard Henry Cowen; Eugene Schwartz, who could pile more cock-and-bull benefits into a mailing than there are lights on the Rockefeller Center Christmas tree; Ed McLean, whose blockbuster letter for *Newsweek* in the 1960s started, "If the list upon which I found your name is any indication . . ." that wound up being mailed in the hundreds of millions; Linda Wells, whose invitational approach was (and is) not only perpetually successful, but has been lifted at least once by nearly every copywriter in the world; Donald Staley, the wordsmith behind J. Peterman, who turned catalog copy into some of the best short stories ever written; and Mel Martin, master of fascinations.

Mel who?

Martin.

Master of what?

Fascinations.

Teasers.

The taking of old-fashioned teaser copy — usually found on an envelope — and stuffing an entire mailing full of it, nakedly appealing to the emotions that drive people to action.

The Beginnings

The tortuous trek of Mel Martin, from laborer in the vineyards of advertising and publishing to rarefied heights in the pantheon of the greatest direct mail copywriters who ever lived, began modestly enough at the Sussman & Sugar agency and, thereafter, at the Friend-Reiss agency. It was at Friend-Reiss in the late 50s that he used to be called on by Martin Edelston, an aggressive young advertising salesman for Max Ascoli's now defunct *Reporter* magazine. Two decades later, that meeting would be to newsletter publishing what Ben & Jerry's is to ice cream.

In the early 70s, Mel Martin was hired as a copywriter by Herb Nagourney, the toothy publisher of *The New York Times* book division, whose business was built on running coupon ads in unsold space in the *Times*. While there, Martin created what Edelston considered to be some of the greatest book advertising ever written. "I would love to go through the *Times* on microfiche and find those ads," Edelston says. "Each was masterpiece."

After Nagourney and Mel Martin parted company in 1974, Marty Edelston hired Mel to write editorial material on a per-diem basis for his fledgling newsletter, *Boardroom Reports*. Quite simply, Mel Martin detested the work. So Edelston went along with Martin's idea to create a contents page. From 8:00 a.m. to 10:00 p.m. one day every two weeks, Mel Martin would boil down the contents of the newsletter into a one-page table of contents which ran on the cover. In Edelston's words: "Each contents page was a glittering jewel — far and away better than the rest of the publication." These contents pages were the birthplace of "fascinations." A sampling:

Mel Martin, Boardroom's secret weapon and inventor of "Fascinations."

Attire for women managers.
Traps in issuing checks.
Trend to watch: Retort pouch.
CORPORATE STRATEGY 14
How to stay out of court: Part 2 of Fred J. Halsey, Jr.'s series on
   avoiding litigation. The mistake that is the biggest single cause
   of business lawsuits; how to soften a potentially damaging
   statement made on the phone; ways to defuse an angry
   customer.

The front page of a single issue of *Boardroom Reports* might contain 60 to 80 of these teasers. You *had to* take a look!

Moving Into Direct Mail

Edelston proposed that Martin try a direct mail package to get subscribers for *Boardroom Reports*. The writer did not have a clue where or how to begin; he had only written ads — never a package. So Martin created an ad, and the two of them converted it into a direct mail package.

Here's Martin's #10 envelope for Boardroom's *Bottom Line:*
<u>Bills it's okay to pay late</u>
   ■ **<u>Supermarkets: Shocking new ripoffs</u>**
   ■ **<u>How to buy a house with no down payment</u>**
   ■ **<u>How to slash your property taxes</u>**
   ■ **<u>What never to eat on an airplane</u>**

Sometimes Martin's envelopes used a single fascination in jumbo type, covering most of the envelope face:

WHAT <u>NEVER</u> TO EAT ON AN AIRPLANE
or
WHAT CREDIT CARD COMPANIES DON'T TELL YOU

Here is his seven-year control for *Bottom Line/Personal:*

What never . . . <u>ever</u> to eat on an airplane

The dirtiest, deadliest airline in the whole world

• How to get VIP treatment in hospitals. (All patients are <u>not</u> treated equally.)

• Cruise ship rapes: The uncensored facts which even the news media won't touch.

• How to find out if someone has a "past" — criminal record . . . bankruptcy . . . or whatever they're hiding.

• The little-known casinos in Atlantic City and Nevada that offer the best odds.

• Deduct the cost of your hobby as a business expense, even if you never show a profit.

• How to get an Oval Office tour of the White House.

• Get a hotel suite . . . while paying for a room.

• How competent/incompetent are your lawyer and accountant? Check 'em out . . . secretly.

(And other surprising secrets you're not supposed to know.)

Dear Fellow American,

This letter is about information that's "none of your business."

Did you know that certain specific foods they serve you on a plane will lower your blood sugar count at high altitudes — leaving you tired . . . cramped . . . headachy?

Now, perhaps you're thinking, "Why would airlines want to make me tired and grouchy?" Well, they don't want to, of course. But they <u>do</u> want to slice the cost of each meal — so if it's cheaper, and (artificially) tastier . . . then — why not?!!

Let's talk about <u>survival</u>. You think, perhaps, that air safety is minutely scrutinized by the FAA . . . that all airlines regard careful maintenance as <u>sacred</u>? Well, some do . . . but <u>some don't</u>. And if an airline is losing hundreds of millions of dollars a year (as some are) . . . and Wall Street is whispering "Bankruptcy" . . . then there's a strong temptation to cut corners — a LOT of corners.

Talk to flight crews on some airlines, and you'll hear some real horror stories. Talk to the FAA, off the record, and they'll tell you that budget cuts have left them stretched to the breaking point. Maintenance records <u>are</u> being falsified . . . much too much of the time.

I'm telling you all this to illustrate a point: They tell us we're living in the Age of Information . . . and we <u>are</u> drowning in information. Unfortunately, most of it's <u>useless</u>. On the other hand, you're not getting the information that <u>really counts</u> because it's "none of your business."

Would you like to know which airlines are filthy, over-aged, under-maintained flying <u>cattle cars</u>? Sorry, it's "none of your business."

Which airline foods could ruin your day (at the very least)? How do you recognize an <u>Air Safety Alert</u>? (Signifies an extra element of risk . . . but not so great as to cancel the flight.) Which airports and airlines have the best security? The worst?

It's "none of your business," and you know why? Because it's <u>bad</u> for business . . . <u>bad</u> for a company's stock price . . . <u>bad</u> (i.e., embarrassing) for the executive bureaucrats who run a company. Nor will you ever learn about these things in magazines or on TV. Media executives are terrified of losing their airline advertising.

Well, <u>too bad</u>! Now you can discover what's <u>really</u> going on.

<u>TRY THREE FREE ISSUES OF 'BOTTOM LINE'</u>

Twelve years ago, I started an unusual 16-page, <u>biweekly</u> periodical that was unlike anything then (or now) being published in the U.S.

Unusual? Well, consider this: <u>BOTTOM LINE</u> accepts no advertising . . . has no glossy photographs . . . doesn't even run any editorials or letters to the editor.

So why are there now well over a million fanatically loyal <u>subscribers</u> (larger than Business Week, Forbes, or Fortune)? It's simple. We

give you what you can't find anywhere else —
covering all aspects of living . . . working . .
. playing.

Let me show you what I mean — with getting
your money's worth . . .

• Where to find the best buys in a supermarket
. . . positions where you're least likely to
look!

• Conventional wisdom: You can't push an insurance company when it comes to collecting money.
Wrong! Here are two proven ways to get your
check within days.

• Thinking of suing your lawyer for malpractice
. . . or incompetence? There's the hard way
(favored by most people) and the easier way.
Here's how to prevail. Quickly.

• Canceled check for fire insurance proves
you're covered. Right? Wrong.

• How stockbrokers unload securities from their
own inventory at a higher than market price . .
. and the evidence is buried in fine print on
the confirmation slip.

• Collect interest from two money market funds
at the same time, on your same spare cash.

• Want to sell your house in a bad market?
Here's an unconventional, off-the-wall approach
that gets results . . . and fast.

• The richest, lowest-priced hunting grounds in
America for antiques.

Where does BOTTOM LINE get this kind of information? Apart from our own staff of editors,
writers and researchers, we have an Advisory
Board of 165 leading experts and professionals
— all of them nationally renowned in their

fields. That means, when we're working on a story, we've got <u>authentic insiders</u> to help us out.

In a moment I'll tell you how to receive <u>three free issues</u> — but first let me tell you more about the unusual information we manage to uncover.

<u>LIVING BETTER — AND SAFER — FOR LESS</u>

Most people think you <u>must</u> have more money to live better. Not true. Money helps, of course, but inside knowledge also works. For example . . .

• Best ways to get "bumped" from your reserved airline seat — and pick up a free travel voucher for taking the next flight . . . sometimes a <u>free round trip</u>.

• How and where to get the best deals when joining a health club — you can save <u>plenty</u>. And how can you spot a club or sports center that's best avoided?

• Outwitting hotel thieves: The best places to hide valuables in your room.

• How to outwit a mugger in a self-service elevator. (One of the <u>worst</u> big-city traps.) And what do you do if you're a woman, and you're attacked in the hallway of a big-city hotel or apartment building? Scream "Help!"? NO . . . there's something <u>else</u> far better.

• Where to obtain a 100% legal second passport — recognized by the U.S. Government — giving you huge advantages at home <u>and</u> abroad.

• Book a vacation cruise at 50% - 60% below the regular price. (And the cruise lines to <u>avoid</u>.)

• The gruesome story about duty-free shops. (Not talked about in the travel industry!)

• A simple way to prevent Montezuma's Revenge.

• What airlines avoid telling you, because they're key ways to squeeze more money from you. (Nasty . . . nasty!)

• Many home safes costing hundreds of dollars are semi-useless. Why . . . and what <u>should</u> you buy?

• Looking around for a small home tractor? Two things you should do: Check your Consumer Reports . . . <u>and</u> something else.

• Ever been abused by an uncivil servant . . . humiliated by some self-important official . . . or given the runaround by a large corporation? Here's how to write a simple letter that creates instant havoc . . . gets financial satisfaction . . . <u>and</u> gives you sweet revenge.

<u>LIVING LONGER . . . LIVING HEALTHIER</u>

<u>BOTTOM LINE</u> has a big advantage over other consumer periodicals: We own an independent medical publishing division. This gives us access to the latest in medical breakthroughs . . . and we know what's really going on in the health-care industry. For example . . .

• Why some patients are given favored status in hospitals . . . almost <u>preferred treatment</u>. This little-known information could save your life.

• How to learn about medical discoveries <u>before</u> your doctor.

• Use sleeping pills <u>without</u> becoming addicted . . . and relieve a headache <u>without</u> drugs.

• Doc-talk: How to translate medical jargon on a patient's hospital chart.

• How to evaluate a nursing home — and the tip-offs that will indicate a rip-off (or worse).

• Alternative medicine: An Asian cure for the common cold that's amazing the U.S. medical profession.

• How and when blood pressure can fool you . . . and drinking alcohol without hangovers.

• Facts and fallacies about dental care . . . and the newest technologies already available.

• The two famous cold remedies that, taken together, can give you ulcers.

PLANNING FOR THE COMING YEARS

Tens of millions of Americans are living in a dream world.

Complacently preparing for retirement — thinking that everything is under control . . . planning for a certain income . . . assuming that they'll have a decent standard of living through their active years.

Sure . . . and do they also think they'll be getting their Social Security checks 10 or 15 years from now — undiminished in value? Well, DON'T COUNT ON IT.

BOTTOM LINE is an invaluable source of information that will help you live better no matter what happens. For example . . .

• The 20 safest banks in the U.S. — and the lemons, which spend their time lending to third-world deadbeats . . . and real estate hucksters.

• The 10 best places to retire in the U.S. —
everything is almost perfect: Climate . . .
health-care . . . recreational and cultural facilities . . . etc. Best of all, they haven't
yet been "discovered," which means property
values are still reasonable.

• The best . . . absolutely the greatest retirement discount deals in the country. Save
thousands and thousands of dollars on hotels
. . . insurance . . . all kinds of shopping
. . . airline and cruise tickets . . . and so
on. A discounter's paradise!

• The 10 best part- and full-time retirement
businesses — working right from your home, with
a low overhead.

DEALING WITH THE IRS — AND OTHER FACTS OF LIFE

Every issue of BOTTOM LINE is written in
easy-to-understand English — covering all kinds
of topics . . . including that institution
Americans love to hate. And here again, we can
help you . . .

• Why the most dangerous tax audit comes right
after you die. Yet . . . honestly . . . you can
actually fight back from the grave. (And your
chances are better dead than alive!)

• How a wife can deed assets over to a dying
husband — estate planning at its shrewdest.

• What you don't have to tell an IRS auditor —
and how to prevent a "fishing" expedition
through your records.

• A legal way to deduct your gambling losses.

• How to deduct a family vacation as a business expense. (Ingenious possibilities your accountant never showed you.)

• <u>Avoiding</u> a tax audit: What IRS computers are looking for on your return — and how to put them off the scent.

• Add up what you spend on your daughter's wedding and use it to reduce your income tax.

• When the bank can't bounce a check . . . and how to deposit an <u>unsigned</u> check.

• Safeguards for safe-deposit boxes . . . and the little-known vulnerability that makes you a sitting duck.

And so on . . . and so on. Do you see? <u>BOTTOM LINE</u> shows you how to do everything <u>right</u>: Taxes. Investments. Budgeting. Travel. Health. Fitness. Insurance. Banking. Estate planning. Managing your finances . . . your household . . . your career.

We show you how to make your money grow — <u>and</u> get the best value when you spend it. And everything you read is easy to understand . . . easy to put into action.

Best of all, we challenge misconceptions. Yes . . . this gets some people pretty agitated. Yes . . . they write us threatening letters sometimes. But <u>no</u> . . . it doesn't bother us because we have the editorial freedom that comes with <u>not</u> taking any advertising.

See for yourself why well over a million people read this unique periodical — in fact, we'll make you a special <u>12th Anniversary Offer</u> . . .

> <u>Act now and we'll send you three issues of</u>
> <u>BOTTOM LINE — absolutely free — as part</u>
> <u>of a one-year trial subscription</u>
> <u>at a substantial discount</u>.

If I'm wrong, and <u>BOTTOM LINE</u> is not for you, just return the bill marked "canceled." You can't lose — not even the cost of a 29-cent stamp!

Mail the free trial form today. And many thanks for reading this letter.

> Yours truly
>
> /s/ Martin Edelston
>
> Martin Edelston
> Publisher

ME:rgr

P.S. If you decide to stay as a regular subscriber, I'll send you a book that answers those items mentioned in this letter — along with <u>more</u> information, besides.

The Order Card

Here's Martin's order card copy:

> **DON'T SEND MONEY**
> *FREE. Yes, please send free three issues of BOTTOM LINE/PERSONAL. If I like the free issues, I may subscribe at a big saving off the regular subscription rate. If I don't like BOTTOM LINE for any reason, I'll simply return the bill, owe nothing and keep my three free issues.*

In fact, the copy is so strong for this newsletter that the price of the product is not mentioned anywhere on the order form. Nor is the price given anywhere in the mailing, thereby breaking an unbreakable rule that has been drummed into the head of every direct marketer since apprenticeship. (The exception, lead generation efforts — which this becomes.)

Mel Martin: Up Close and Personal

He was a very gentle man who did not like interacting with people. Rodale wanted him, and they just couldn't come to terms. He worked in his apartment at 81st Street and First Avenue. We talked a lot — mostly on the phone on weekends. He had a huge terrace and several thousand plants; he was an accomplished gardener and an aficionado of classical music.

— Marty Edelston

Mel Martin was also a very sick man — for years. "By my count, he had over a dozen doctors aside from his internist," Edelston said. "one specialist for each thing that was wrong with him."

Brian Kurtz, Edelston's brilliant young vice president, added: "He was an incessant smoker. In fact, if he ran out of cigarettes, he had to quit writing and run out for cigarettes."

The image that Kurtz and Edelston painted was reminiscent of Marcel Proust, who suffered terribly from tuberculosis and resided in an cork-lined room in Paris, venturing out occasionally in the cool of the evening when the lower humidity did not aggravate his delicate lungs. The difference between Mel Martin and Marcel Proust: Proust produced torrents of prose.

"Mel Martin was the world's slowest copywriter," Edelston says. "It would take him three or four months to write a direct mail package. He could get stuck for a month on a letter opening."

In the beginning, Martin used to do pencil sketches of how he wanted the packages to look. Eventually he taught himself to use the computer and, in Edelston's words, "became a first-rate, second-rate computer artist." He would design each mailing with tiers of fascinations, the most powerful ones appearing in the largest type. When he wasn't writing copy, Martin would read all of Edelston's newsletters — *Boardroom Reports, Bottom Line/Personal* and *Tax Hotline* — and turn the various stories into fascinations. He maintained a massive database of fascinations, including full annotations of which article appeared in which newsletter on which page and where on the page and on what date. When it came time to create a book from past newsletters, the

Master would go into his database of fascinations and cook up a mailing; Edelston's editors would then create a book based on Mel Martin's mailing package, not vice versa, as is the usual case in publishing.

Because he was so slow, Mel Martin could not support himself as a freelancer. Early on he asked Edelston for more money. The answer was no; cash flow wouldn't permit it. Finally, Edelston agreed to buy 25 percent of Mel Martin's time. Edelston increased the percentage as Martin's other clients died off, and he kept writing winning packages.

"He loved what he did. He used to deliver the finished copy to our offices himself — always perfect. The writing invigorated him. It gave him energy." Kurtz said. "I remember once right after a serious operation, he started writing a package and positively exuded energy. It was his best package. Think of it! He wrote his best package within days of being operated on!"

In 1990, guru Axel Andersson suggested that awards be given to long-term control direct mail packages — those efforts that have continued to work year after year, beating back all tests against them. Edelston's organization has won a staggering 10 Axel Andersson Awards. An amazing 16 million of the seven-year-old Mel Martin package, "Bills it's OK to pay late" (née "What never to eat on an airplane") mailed in 1994. Because Edelston was so protective of Mel Martin — paranoid that some direct marketer might discover his name and phone number and offer him a writing job — he would never reveal his name. As a result, Martin received no Axel Andersson Certificates of Excellence. Every time I did my Axel Awards slide show, I was forced to talk about "Marty Edelston's mystery copywriter."

Mel Martin died in 1994. His legacy: a powerful copywriting technique that made it possible for Martin Edelston to build a $100-million-a-year business and an extraordinary oeuvre of direct mail that will continue to generate profits well into the next century.

Points for Marketers to Consider

1.

Personally, I have always found Mel Martin's copy far more interesting and compelling than Martin Edelston's products, just as his Contents for the early *Boardroom Reports* were the best things it contained in terms of interest and readability.

Mel Martin was a classic Method Marketer. He had that unique ability to become the person to whom he was writing and figure out what was worrying the person lying awake at four in the morning and hitting those hot buttons.

Mel Martin took it one step further. He *created* all kinds of fearful scenarios (What never to eat on an airplane; supermarkets: shocking new ripoffs; What credit card companies don't tell you.) that you probably never would have thought of.

Study Mel Martin's copy. Short, interruptive paragraphs — often with each paragraph only a sentence long. No paragraphs longer than seven lines. In it, you will find at least five of Bob Hacker's six key copy drivers: Fear, Greed, Anger, Guilt, Exclusivity, Salvation.

You can't get bored with the copy; if one thing doesn't interest you, your eye flicks down to something **compelling.**

Knotty concerns — many of them hibernating in our subconscious — suddenly bubble to the surface.

What's more, Mel Martin's copy gives nothing away — with the possible exception of heartburn and angst.

If you want the answers, buy the product.

The copy is like eating peanuts; once you start, you can't stop. Unless, of course, it's to order the product — which, in the case of *Bottom Line/Personal*, more than a million people have done. Nothing subtle. Nothing cute. Nothing tough to figure out. Just pages and pages of brickbats.

Freelancer Pat Freisen has said:

> Normally, the best lead paragraph for your letter is buried somewhere in the middle of your first draft copy.

Take a close look at the direct mail you receive at home and in the office. You'd be amazed at the percentage of letters you receive in which the writer clears his throat, rolls up his sleeves, rubs his hands together, whereupon you are on page 2 and nothing has been said — no benefits, no promises; rather, it's a bunch of preachy crap that a good copy editor should have deleted.

Now take a close look at your current promotional material with a critical eye. I can think of two good reasons to do so — NOW.

(a) When Hemingway wrote a novel, he would put the first draft in a drawer and go off for six months fishing, or hunting in Africa or traveling the bullfighting circuit in Spain. When he came back to the novel six months later, he was able to read it with absolutely fresh eyes, immediately deleting the boring parts, shoring up the weak parts and enhancing the excitement. Chances are when reading your current control after a long time, you'll find words, phrases, paragraphs that can be tightened and made more exciting, more readable.

(b) The copy may need updating. A two- or three-year control may refer to world situations or prices that are out-of-date. You'll find this particularly true in Bill Bonner's masterful letter for *International Living* in Chapter 11 where he talks about huge profits to be made in the financial markets of Japan and Taiwan. Had this gone out in the midst of the Asian economic crisis, a disconnect would occur between the reader and what the letter was promising. As Bob Hacker has said, "This is a business of trying to get just one more order per hundred."

It's probably been six months since you read your promotional material. Do a Hemingway with all your current copy; you probably haven't given it a look for months. Do it now. And do it at least every six months.

2.

Mel Martin's copy — and instincts for what would excite a reader — were so strong, that when it came time for Edelston to create a book based on material from back issues, he had Mel Martin write the copy and the book contained what Martin had promised in his letter.

When the copywriter Bill Jayme was contracted to create an acquisition mailing for the launch of a new magazine, the editor and publisher would give him an outline of the contents, a marketing plan and a list of the lists his solicitation would be mailed to. When asked if he wanted to see some tables of contents for future issues — the various articles and features that would be published (if the mailing brought in enough subscribers), Jayme told them not to bother. "I'll decide what articles will be in the magazine," Jayme would tell them. In effect, the publication became as much Jayme's at the publisher's. "Why not?" Jayme once said to me. "When I write a letter, I'm writing to *my* people. They respond to *my* work."

Do you have such strong-selling promotional copy that your product should reflect what the copywriter has written rather than what the editor or product manager has come up with? After all, isn't it the copywriter who got inside the head and under the skin of people — thought how they thought, felt what they felt — and persuaded them to respond? In that sense, isn't successful promotional copy and design more important than the product itself?

3.

A corollary here. In direct marketing, a direct mail package or television commercial will begin to lose its punch. With rare exceptions, when consumers see a mailing come into their home or office repeatedly, more and more of them will say, "I've seen this before," and chuck it out unopened.

Whenever a mailing goes out, a certain percentage of the pieces should be reserved for tests of some kind — from a new envelope to a whole new mailing package to a new offer in an old mailing package.

A new mailing package, however, can create unplanned problems. For example, a copywriter and designer — with a new voice and a new look — can hype the up-front response. But, if what the new customer receives is the same old product and the same old fulfillment material — that in no way reflects the tone and look of the new offer — a disconnect will occur in the customer's head. "I don't remember ordering this!" will be the reaction. And back it may come or, in the case of a magazine, no payment will be sent.

When a dramatic new approach is taken in selling an old product, all the fulfillment material must be examined to make sure it reflects the new offer and the new voice to which the customer responded. Again, Method Marketing: getting inside the head and under the skin of your customer, thinking how he thinks, feeling what he feels and making sure that everything tracks.

> The sale begins when the customer says yes.
> — Bill Christensen

4.

Edelston creates books out of back issues of his newsletters. This means taking existing material, perhaps enhancing or changing or updating it slightly, and then repackaging it and selling it in a different format, disguised as brand new material for both an old and new audience.

What do you have in your shop that you could pull off the shelf, rework slightly and market to a brand new audience?

Isn't this a lot cheaper (and quicker) than coming up with a brand new product?

5.

How good is your internal reporting system? In two instances on the road to zillionairehood, Marty Edelston was taken totally by surprise.

> He signed the lease and told his accountant to put aside the $600,000 needed to fix it up. "We don't have $600,000," the accountant said.

And again:

> Friday night Edelston called Benson and in a lighthearted way asked if he and Sailer had figured out the mistake with the model. "There's no mistake on the model. You got too fat. You have to cut your overhead tremendously."

When Peggy and I started a newsletter in the family room of our Stamford, Connecticut, home, we never had more than three part-timers. All our other work was contracted out: design, printing, etc. Finances were not complicated. We had four checkbooks: one for the newsletter, one for my freelance copywriting business, a third one for *The Directory of Major Mailers* (we had a partner in that venture) and our personal checkbook. We knew what was coming in and what was going out. We would go down to the post office box every day and retrieve the Business Reply mail. If we found ourselves with a lot of cash, we'd go to Europe or Africa; if the bank accounts were down, we stayed home.

In a way, I'm glad our business did not take off like Edelston's; we might have run into the same trouble. I am an expert in the arithmetic of direct mail; running a sprawling company with a lot of overhead is another matter. If I had tried to leverage the business in the go-go 80s, I would, no doubt, have ended up in bankruptcy.

Do you have an expert in charge of your corporate finances? Are checkpoints and trip wires in place?

The one thing no businessperson likes is a surprise.

At the same time, remember what cataloger John Peterman said to an interviewer:

> Successful businesses are driven forward with different kinds of minds. Accountants can't make any revenue. They can

account for revenue and do a lot of good things. But the creative mind creates revenue.

6.

This, of course, leads to the question of cash flow. At one point, Edelston had tons of receivables — the result of offering a "bill-me" option. In the direct marketing of magazines and newsletters, a very standard offer is:

> Take one [or two . . . or three] issues FREE. If you like the product, pay the bill; if not, return the invoice marked "cancel," and that ends the matter. You owe nothing; you are under no further obligation; you keep the free issues.

As a result of this offer, you find yourself with a great many lookers and real collection problems. This is especially true if the first couple of issues are not terribly strong. Subscribers will hold the bill in one hand (in the case of a newsletter, an invoice for quite a lot of money) and the publication in the other hand and weigh the value.

Edelston, in a cash crunch, changed the offer from bill-me to cash with order only. His up-front response nose dived, but he (1) got paid; (2) wasn't sending out issues to people who would never pay; (3) wasn't sending out bills to people who owed him money. Now, as you can see from Mel Martin's *Bottom Line/Personal* letter, Edelston not only doesn't ask for money, but doesn't even tell you the price.

Should you examine the way you are generating money? How are your receivables? When was the last time you looked at your billing and collection series? Should you call in a consultant to run an analysis and compare how you are doing with others in the industry?

7.

Get Marty Edelston's book, *I-Power.* This is a blueprint for tapping into the creativity of your people — and rewarding them for it. Edelston goes into meetings with a fistful of $10- and $20-dollar bills and hands them out for good ideas. Remember, your people are on the firing line, talking to customers, seeing weaknesses in your operation. Make them want to participate. And make it worth their while. The money you hand out will pay for itself many, many times over.

7

Memorial Sloan-Kettering

The Astounding Carol Farkas Letter:
Fundraising at Its Most Elegant

Peggy and I received the following letter from our friend Jon Saunders, creative director at Bozell Worldwide, Inc., on Bozell letterhead.

Mr. & Mrs. Dennison Hatch
310 Gaskill Street
Philadelphia, PA 19147

Dear Peggy & Denny,

I have been asked to help raise at least $500,000 to assist the Home Care Program/Memorial Sloan-Kettering Center in completing its endowment.

The Home Care Program cares for homebound people living with catastrophic illness. It offers psychological symptom control, without charge to them and their families/significant others. Care is available 24 hours a day, 365 days a year. The interest from this endowment will enable the Program to secure the services of a home care nurse. The more money raised, the greater the number of people whose needs will be met in a compassionate and professional manner.

In order to help reach this goal, we ask that you kindly do the following:

1. Please forward a check for $10 (no more) made payable to "The Home Care Program, MSKC," c/o (Physician in Charge), MD, 1275 York Avenue, New York, NY 10021.

2. Please, retype this letter on your letterhead and send it to ten friends or individuals in your company or organization whom you know personally and know will be able to help. With your letter, please send the names of those who received it along with the enclosed list of recipients to date.

All contributions are fully tax deductible. No goods or services have been offered or received by you in consideration of your gift. Thanks for joining me in supporting this worthwhile endeavor.

Best regards,

/s/ Jon

Enc.

It started small. Carol Farkas, a volunteer at Memorial Sloan-Kettering in New York, sent this simple one-page letter to 10 of her friends on Manhattan's Upper East Side.

According to an April 3, 1997, story in *The New York Times,* the letters crisscrossed the top echelons of business, law and entertainment nationwide; contributions came in from the likes of Elizabeth Taylor, Carrie Fisher, Gregory Peck and Lauren Bacall. Not only did Lauren Bacall send in $10, but she sent the letter off to the Sidney Lumets, the Arthur Schlesingers, the Tony Waltons (he's a top set designer who was formerly married to Julie Andrews), Betty Comden and Adolph Green and the Mike Nichols (she's Diane Sawyer).

Mike Nichols, in turn, sent the letter to Elaine May, Steve Martin, Whoopi Goldberg and Frank Langella, Pete Peterson and Joan Ganz Cooney, and Nora Ephron and Nick Pileggi.

And so it went.

Never mind that the mailing brought in over 14,000 checks for a total of $251,000 for Sloan-Kettering. According to the *Times,* the folks at Memorial Sloan-Kettering treated Mrs. Farkas (wife of the former chairman of Alexander's department stores) like a pariah. In the words of the *Times:*

> The hospital has asked her not to speak to the press and has
> distanced itself from a chain letter that officials said privately they

considered tasteless and unbecoming to Sloan-Kettering's reputation.

While neither Sloan-Kettering's president nor director of fund raising, Alexander H. Chute, would comment to the *Times* on the promotion, a hospital spokeswoman said: "I think chain letters in general raise questions on the part of the U.S. Postal Service."

I spoke by phone to Alexander Chute, who reported that this letter "has been investigated by everybody and has been found to be totally clean. We have done nothing to encourage a thing; at the same time we couldn't stop it."

It is emphatically not a chain letter, because it doesn't promise the sender a jackpot, nor does it require a fee.

Yet, Cheryl Bell of the Metropolitan New York Better Business Bureau pompously proclaimed:

> This could damage the reputation of the charity because most chain letters are scams.

What poppycock!

Look at what has happened:

(1) A well-meaning amateur — with no fund-raising experience — sent a letter out to to 10 of her friends asking for a small donation to be sent directly to a cause she believed in. Clearly, she was an intuitive Method Marketer, having gotten into the heads and under the skin of her friends with absolute honesty. What's more she only asked for ten dollars; it's probably safe to assume not one of these stars and nabobs have been asked for so paltry a sum since they were in college.

(2) The ten friends were obviously in the upper education and income strata, because they had the wherewithal to get ten personal letters out along with photocopies of the list.

3) These ten, in turn, sent it to ten others in this upper league of power, money and influence.

(4) The United States Postal Service should be thrilled. Instead of going out at the brutally low Non-Profit Rate, all these letters were mailed with highly profitable First Class postage.

(5) The mailings cost Memorial Sloan-Kettering nothing. Zip. Nada. No creative. No production. No postage. No postage for reply mail. All revenue was pure profit!

(6) No fund raising agencies got their hooks into this promotion to claim their pound of flesh. Again, all revenue was pure profit!

In short, this is fund raising perfection.

As of July 1997, according to Chute, the promotion had brought in 24,000 new donors whose average gift of $17 made for a total of $408,000.

Imagine! Twenty-four thousand brand new donors whose combined net worth was in the tens of billions — people Sloan-Kettering would *never* have been able to reach under ordinary circumstances with ordinary pleas for money!

What's more, the scheme is self-perpetuating.

"Checks will probably be coming in long after I'm dead," Chute confided.

At the same time, be advised that this entire caper is an aberration; any fund raiser who tried to build a marketing plan and a business using this technique by itself would be positively nuts.

8

The J. Peterman Company

John Peterman:
Maverick Merchant Prince

We didn't know whether people would read long copy. We knew they wouldn't read short, boring copy, so we made the copy interesting. We hoped they would read it—and would buy.
—John Peterman

Summer surprised us, coming over the Starnbergeresee
*   With a shower of rain; we stopped in the Colonnade,*
And went on in sunlight, into the Hofgarten,
*   And drank coffee, and talked for an hour.*
                    —T.S. Eliot
                    The Waste Land

Everything is bathed in extraordinary sunshine.
*   The waiter brings me a Swiss omelette.*
Everyone I see is wearing a tie for breakfast.
*   When he enters, he's removing his glasses,*
and there's an apple color in his cheeks.
*   Lucky man's wearing a buffalo-plaid coat.*
"Bow-koo cold," he announces to the crowd.
*   Everybody laughs.*
                    —Donald Staley
                    Owner's Manual No. 44
                    The J. Peterman Catalog

To walk into the J. Peterman Company Store in Lexington, Kentucky, is like Proust taking a bite of that Madeleine cake. For inside, past a black BMW motorcycle and sidecar, past the rack of light tan, ankle-length cowboy dusters — Peterman's signature merchandise — is a large room chockablock with soft and hard goods of every sort from floor to ceiling — accessories and clothes circa 1920, but redesigned so as to be classically stylish for any decade.

The merchandise is reminiscent of the *fin-de-siècle* costumes from the steamer trunk in your Great Aunt Teeny's attic at the shore, where as a child you used to play dress-up on rainy days to recapture a gentler, innocent era — your grandfather's tweed jacket with leather elbow patches and his windowpane wool trousers. Here, too, is your Great Aunt Hallie's rust-colored, tea-length skirt that swirled with a romantic flounce, and her deep black jacket, its shapely, nipped-in waist and dozen small buttons — as stylish in the late 1990s as it might have been amidst the elegance and splendor, the bands and confetti streamers, the riotous good-byes and the basso profoundo honks of the great liner *Titanic* as she departed Southampton that fateful April day in 1912.

On the floor of Peterman's store you glimpse glossy yellow rubber snow boots, racks with umbrellas and walking sticks, hats for him and for her; before you is a glass case with shelves of antique brass miniature gewgaws — compasses, sextants, telescopes, along with tiny brass oil cans, cufflinks and necktie clips.

A massive red, gold and black Moroccan Child's Pavilion is used as a display case for sweaters, and couches and chairs have merchandise stacked on them. With few exceptions, everything in the place is for sale; those exceptions, such as a set of library chairs, are discreetly marked with little green tags on which is hand-written "FA" for Fixed Asset.

In the next room: a claw-foot 1920s bathtub with bright brass knobs, brass towel rings from the Grand Hotel and an overpowering canopy bed made in Kentucky from huge, hewn cedar logs (only $1,295, including a mallet for knocking it together); covering it is an authentic "power blanket" and a mountain of inviting pillows. And, ooooohmigosh! — hanging by the door — a pair of extraordinary gossamer silk pajamas which the catalog describes as:

> Dreams. Made possible by sweet evenings. Followed by sweet, irresponsibly late mornings. These will encourage that. And things undreamed. Hollywood Pajamas (No.45A3897). Very sexy Very comfortable. Goes nicely with a little Perrier-Jouet. The top goes very nicely without the bottoms (not if you plan to actually watch TV). Charmeuse silk. Noted for its effect on the wearer

and admirer. Charming. Lombardish stripes. Price, $165. Imported. Color: Cream with Black and Ivory Stripes.

And, astonishingly, sitting on a table out in the open for anybody to examine, fondle (and steal?), a magnificent 1875 Elkington Sheffield sterling silver tea service with a price tag of $12,500; if you want the silver tray that goes with it, add another $1,750.

In Peterman's store it's easy to drop a grand in the blink of an eye.

The Real John Peterman

The J. Peterman Company — behind Taco Bell just off Route 60 on Russell Cave Road — is housed in a former blue jeans manufacturing plant with a small flower-bedecked main entrance dwarfed by truck bays running along two sides of the building.

Covering the waiting room walls are 8" x 10" photographs of Peterman's celebrity customers — a veritable Who's Who of actors, actresses, rock and country musicians, including Paul Newman, Oprah Winfrey, Angela Lansbury and Jimmy Buffet.

A side door opened and in walked a tall, very trim man of indeterminate middle age; he was wearing a watermelon pink shirt, jeans and pointed boots. His dark mustache drooping ever-so-slightly around the corners of his mouth, and thin wire spectacles perched on the end of his nose were reminiscent, perhaps, of a young Rudyard Kipling. He ambled over with the easy, rolling gait of a cowboy, stuck out his hand, looked me squarely in the eye and said, "Hi, I'm John Peterman."

In Peterman's book-lined, tchotchke-filled office I told him I had been to the store and suggested, "Your pricing is strange."

"Strange how?"

"Some stuff is woefully underpriced and other things are unbelievably expensive."

"What's underpriced?" Peterman asked, a tad defensively. "I'll charge you more if that's what you want."

'Those great yellow rubber boots. Only 40 dollars."

"Less than that," Peterman purred. "Actually 32."

"But then I found an umbrella for $235. I mean, really! A $235 umbrella!"

When Peterman talks, he gesticulates — often wildly. Suddenly his hands went akimbo. "Hey, that's the Queen's umbrella. You want

The real John Peterman (not the Seinfeld character), maverick merchant prince and master merchandiser.

the Queen's umbrella, you pay for it!" He added, "I have a belief: if you produce first-rate quality, people want quality and will pay for it."

"And the silver tea service for $12,500. Anybody could slip one of those piece under a coat and make off with it.

"Try to steal that tea set, and you get burned," Peterman said. "A giant cage comes down on top of you. What's more, I keep a pet rattlesnake in the coffee pot."

"Seriously, aren't you taking one hell of a chance leaving that thing out like that?"

Peterman grew suddenly contemplative." I don't lock my car door in Lexington," he said. "I have an attitude; I trust you until you screw up. You can't go through life starting out by not trusting people."

He looked off into the middle distance. "Unfortunately, this will not work when we get into the big cities."

Peterman's office is what you'd expect of a world traveler whose eclectic tastes spawned the remarkable *Owner's Manuals.* Bookshelves lined with new and old books on subjects ranging from flying and fly-tying to a biography of George Patton. On the top shelves next to the ceiling: rows of old boots, suitcases, three ratty stuffed pheasants and a ten-gallon hat. His desk and side table are cluttered with memorabilia of every shape and description from model airplanes to autographed base-balls. Next to the door is his pantry — neat rows of sodas and bottles of Evian and a set of heavy glass goblets described in the catalog as follows:

Life on a Spanish Galleon.

You left Cuba 7 days ago for Spain.

You are becalmed. You are in the horse latitudes.

The shipowner's daughter is very beautiful. You are mysteri-ously ill. She is nursing you back to health.. In other words, things couldn't be better.

You are feeling "some improvement."

(You are in bed, in a cabin at the stern of the ship, the one with dozens of little windows.)

She brings you wine in a goblet. For "strength."

(Perhaps you would like me to stop here and explain exactly what kind of goblet. OK. An Irish goblet. Graceful, but not overly delicate. Early 15th-century in look; brilliant handblown lead crystal, tiny bubbles here and there.)

Two sizes: Large Goblet: Approx.. 7-1/3" tall, 4" mouth. Price: $40. Four or more, $35 ea. Wine: Approx. 6-1/2" tall, 3-1/2" mouth. Price: $38. Four or more, $33 ea.

Now where was I?

On the wall: a very splendid poster with a peacock next to a bot-tle of Cognac Jacquet and a faded photo of Babe Ruth in the Yankee dugout.

In one corner is a rack on which hangs every man's coat ever of-fered in the catalog — all in Peterman's size — including (of course) the horseman's duster and a replica of FDR's navy blue cape with scar-let lining, which Peterman wears on formal occasions.

Most intriguing of all was the drafting table in the corner covered with hundreds of snapshots of Peterman — the characters in his life and his trips around the world. Truly startling: candids of the office Halloween party with Peterman half out of a Roman toga and crowned with a laurel wreath while next to him stands his VP of Operations, John Rice, decked out in drag as television's dippy Dame Edna. No, Peterman said, we could emphatically not run any of those photos in the story!

The Early Days

The son of a Nyack, N.Y., banker, John Peterman wrote about the years he spent with the Pittsburgh Pirates farm organization in his 1993 catalog, *Booty, Spoils & Plunder:*

> When I was 7 my plan was to become Marco Polo.
> I would have gone ahead with it except I had a change of heart when I was 8. I decided to go into professional baseball.
> My dream actually came true. I played professional baseball when I was 20, 21 and 22. Then it ended.
> I started looking for work. When asked why I left my last job, I said it was because I couldn't hit a curve ball.
> I still had 307 other dreams left, but I decided to go back to the first. I still wanted to be Marco Polo.

What was it like playing in the minors? "It was just like the movie *Bull Durham*," he said, "but without all those candles."

Peterman spent the next 20 years "bouncing around midlevel sales jobs at General Foods and Castle & Cooke, "working as a kind of corporate circuit rider, covering the Southeast and calling on accounts in such towns as Knoxville, Tuscaloosa and Lexington."

In the course of his early career, he moved his family from Chicago to Atlanta to Lexington. Why did he settle in Lexington? "I was fired in Lexington," he said. That was 1981. The Petermans liked the city and decided to stay. He was unemployed, had a wife and four children, and owed American Express $10,000 on his credit card.

Enter Donald Staley

"When you don't have a job, you become a consultant," Peterman said. "I had a client looking for an advertising agency, and so I was interviewing agencies in New York on his behalf."

One of the agencies was Staley, Fox, whose proprietor was Donald Staley, a bespectacled, bearded word wizard whose background included stints with McCann-Erickson Worldwide, Wells-Rich-Greene and Ted Chin and Company. Peterman:

> My liking and admiration for him was instantaneous. Donald was the only person I had met in my life who was truly talented creatively. The way he would speak about things was not the way other people spoke about them And he was not off the wall. He is one of the five most creative people in the world (and I'm not sure who the other four are). I have not quite identified what creative is, but I think it is the ability to cut through all the rubble and get to the core of situations.
>
> Donald liked me because I had never spent any time in the advertising business and didn't know any of the buzzwords. To Donald, I was refreshingly naive.

In *Ad Age,* Staley recalled an early conversation with Peterman:

> We made a deal. I said, "As I start spilling out ideas in the course of our friendship, if we . . . want to go forward with (an idea for a business) and actually work on it, let's do it, and we'll split the pain and the misery and the fame and the money — if there is any — fifty-fifty," and he said fine.

Staley began writing the ads — and the extraordinarily literate and inventive catalog copy that is the J. Peterman Company hallmark.

The Early Deals

A restless dreamer and schemer all his life, Peterman forever had little side deals going. For example, in Lexington, Peterman and Staley started the National Houseplant Diagnostic Laboratory — a mail-order business devoted to healing sick houseplants. He ran a full-page ad in *The New York Times* (at the special "standby" rate of $10,000) asking readers to fill out a detailed questionnaire about their sick houseplant and send in a leaf. He got 300 requests plus coverage in *The Wall Street Journal,* the "Today Show," "Good Morning America" and radio stations nationwide — a publicity blitz he figured to be worth $500,000. The business didn't make it. In another business venture in the 1980s, Peterman was part-owner of a company that specialized in a local delicacy called beer cheese. And you should hear Peterman regale anyone who'll listen with the tale of how he and Staley had the Kentucky tourism account for a total of 18 hours. "I like the power, money and prestige," Peterman said in an interview. "But that's not the deal. The deal is the chase and the company remains successful. If I die, get killed or retire, I have built something that perpetuates itself, on and on."

The Signature Duster

On a trip to Jackson Hole, Wyoming, Peterman bought himself an ankle-length horseman's coat — standard gear in the West but unusual and distinctive back East. He writes in his catalog:

> People want things that are hard to find. Things that have romance, but a factual romance about them.
>
> I had this proven all over again when people actually stopped me in the street (in New York, in Tokyo, in London) to ask me where I got the coat I was wearing.
>
> So many people tried to buy my coat off my back that I've started a small company to make them available. It seems like everybody (well, not *everybody*) has always wanted a classic horseman's duster but never knew exactly where to get one.
>
> I ran a little ad in The New York Times and The Wall Street Journal and in a few months sold this wonderful coat in cities all over the country and to celebrities and to a mysterious gentleman in Japan who ordered *two thousand* of them.

That was 1987. Peterman sold 2,500 dusters and added three more items to his line — the New York Fireman's Coat, the Baker Street Coat with Cape and the Alternative Coat, a hip-length version of the duster. That year, revenues climbed to $560,000, and the company broke even. The following year, Peterman and Staley launched the first catalog.

But for Peterman, the late 1980s represented a perpetual struggle for money. At one point he owed a half million bucks to about 20 vendors and cut a deal whereby he would pay each of them $1,000 a week. To get money, he maxed out on plastic, tapped friends and began prowling the shadowy world of venture capitalists.

Eventually the search for money ended with two large investors

kicking in $3.9 million and leaving Peterman with 50-percent owner-
ship in his company. One of the agreements was written on a napkin.
"My philosophy of life on catalogs and business is that it must be simple," Peterman says. "Simple is elegant and sophisticated. And that goes
for deals, too."

The J. Peterman Company's first big hiccup occurred when
Wyoming-based Schaeffer Outfitters went out of business, cutting off
his supply of dusters. He had a clear choice: start over or start making
dusters himself. He chose the latter course.

"How in the world do you go about making such an unusual
thing as a duster from scratch?" I asked.

The question triggered something deep inside Peterman, for he
threw his hands high over his head and exploded with laughter:

> I have no fucking idea! We analyzed the thing and identified
> 22 elements: corduroy-lined collars, snaps, pockets on a slant,
> canvas material. Then I got on the phone and started tracking
> people down — where to buy fabric . . . snaps . . . I never did any-
> thing like this in my life!

The First Buying Trip

Several years later, when the catalog was beginning to catch on,
Peterman and Staley went on their first overseas buying trip — to
London. At Blake's Hotel, they bunked together to save money and
spent their days exploring the city and its environs, not so much looking for merchandise as for ideas and individual items from which merchandise could be designed.

"Sometimes we buy something just for one feature," Peterman explained. It could be a sleeve or lapel or a kind of button. That feature is
then incorporated into an original, proprietary design whose manufacture is jobbed out — preferably to a factory in the U.S. where it's
easier to maintain control.

"What I want to do is go back 50 years — no, a little more than
that, now. Back to the 1920s."

In London, Peterman and Staley not only prowled the shops on
Portobello Road and Camden Place, but did all the museums — especially the war museums.

On a mischievous whim, Staley and Peterman got it into their
heads to put the Blake's Hotel concierge to the test. "Actually, Blake's

did not have a concierge," Peterman said with a twinkle. "Just a couple of gals behind the desk."

Peterman asked if he could rent a Morgan for the weekend — a recherché little two-seater sports car favored by connoisseurs for its road-handling ability. Architect Frank Lloyd Wright reportedly thought it the ultimate automobile.

Word came back to Peterman from the Morgan people that he should have made the reservation three months prior to coming to London. However, the hotel manager had a brother who owned a Morgan and might be willing to rent it to a couple of Americans for the weekend. Blake's Hotel worked on the deal, but it never happened.

> We didn't get the Morgan. But the point is they went to huge lengths to get this. Yes, we were paying guests; but no one knew who we were to give us such special service. This is the way they did business.
>
> Donald and I looked at each other and said what wonderful, wonderful customer service.
>
> It made a deep, long-lasting impression on me about customer service.

Customer Service

The J. Peterman Company is run on the principle that merchandising and customer service are two equal pillars. His philosophy of quality merchandise is simple:

> Nothing begins to get good until it's been worn 300 times.

In charge of customer service is Peterman's elegant wife of 30 years, Audrey, tiny, trim and always dressed in J. Peterman clothes. Her telemarketing operation — which can handle up to 400 incoming calls an hour — is in a large, well-lighted room with chin-high cubicles. Along one entire wall are racks of hanging clothes and shelves of hard goods from the most recent catalogs; if a caller starts asking questions about a specific item, it is instantly available to any telephone sales representative who can immediately give informed answers. Overhead is a blue light that starts flashing when too many calls come in, whereupon everyone in the place drops everything and hits the phones.

"I know a lot of companies go outside for customer service," Peterman said. "But basically, if the people don't have an ownership of the product, they won't take as good care of the customers. We want to make sure we have control. If we screw up, we can control it."

No outbound sales calls are ever made, and the Customer Service Reps don't sell hard, up-sell or cross-sell. "If you want it, you can have it," is Peterman's telemarketing philosophy.

Peterman on the Road

In recalling his days of scrambling for capital to keep his fledgling business afloat, Peterman says, "I never needed money. I just need the things money could get. Money, to me, is mobility.

Peterman has fulfilled his dream of mobility, spending approximately 30 percent of his time traveling. For example, between June and November of 1996 he went on three major buying trips — to Italy, the Far East and Ecuador.

While he does enjoy traveling with some people, Peterman prefers to travel alone; he can go when and where he pleases and — especially in the Third World — he has only one person to worry about.

His motto might be taken from Kipling:

> *Down to Gehenna or*
> *up to the Throne,*
> *He travels fastest*
> *who travels alone.*

In countries where he doesn't speak the language — and that's most places — he always has at his side someone whom he knows well and is fluent in the language.

One time he was in northern Ecuador with a friend who had a shop in Quito. In the local market, the Indians were wearing a shirt that caught Peterman's fancy, so he bought a couple for a buck, took them back to Quito. His friend found a local factory that could make them and they went into the catalog as the Otavalo Mountain Shirt.

The $525,000 Refund

In the entrance way of the J. Peterman Company Store — and in his headquarters waiting room — is an extraordinary vintage motorcycle with sidecar. Originally built by BMW for Hitler's Wehrmacht in 1938, it was replaced by an improved model. The factory was dismantled; the tools and dies were stored in a mountain until the end of the war when Stalin, who had liberated the mountain, presented them to Chairman Mao. On a trip to the Far East, Peterman came across 70 of these bikes with sidecars still in the original crates — built by the Chinese in the late 1950s — and he bought them on the spot.

Taking delivery on 14 of them, Peterman had them painted a spiffy black with white trim and offered them for $7,500 in the *Plunder, Spoils & Booty* catalog, where they sold out immediately.

Enter the lawyers who told Peterman that since he was the last person to touch them, he was responsible for any liability claims that might arise from faulty manufacture or an accident. What's more, it turned out the bikes would never have passed EPA emissions standards; that 14 of them made it to the Lexington warehouse was a minor miracle. Peterman had the unhappy task of calling all 70 customers — including CEOs of top corporations and the King of Jordan — to say, alas, he could not ship them. The money was returned, and the order for the remaining 56 motorcycles was canceled. The other bikes sit under a heavy canopy of plastic in Peterman's warehouse waiting to become decorations for Peterman's future retail outlets. Only one is ridden with any regularity. The owner, John Peterman.

Corporate Culture

Early on, Peterman began surrounding himself with professionals. "I am not the highest-paid person in the company," he told an interviewer for *The Lane Report*. "Some people say that is stupid. Sometimes I question it, too. The point: In order to create a great organization, you need great people." Peterman:

> I don't want to play God. God doesn't want me to play God. And people don't want me to play God. If everybody waits for me to make a decision, decisions won't get made.

It's difficult in a growing company teaching managers how to manage. Managing in its simplest form is common sense. Trouble is, most people in the world don't have common sense.

There's more to running a company than training managers; it's creating a culture.

Nobody's ever been fired for making a mistake. In fact, if you haven't made a mistake I cast a jaundiced eye, because you're probably not doing anything.

It's a constant challenge.

I want people to develop themselves to a point where they can get a job somewhere else, but they want to stay because they like the culture here.

I have people who left and came back — not so much for the money, but because they liked the culture.

To keep new merchandise flowing into the catalogs, in addition to Peterman, eight or nine buyers roam the world. Twice a year they convene in London for a preliminary meeting and then descend on Lexington along with Donald Staley and freelance artist Bob Hagel, whose distinctive paintings have given the catalog its visual character over the years. There, in a large meeting room filled with newly-acquired merchandise, next season's catalog is hammered out, page by page.

Shipments arriving from across the country and around the world are taken into the spotlessly clean and well-lighted 115,000-square-foot warehouse and shipping center that makes up the largest single space in the building. Every item — whether hanging on racks or neatly stacked in carefully labeled cardboard boxes with large holes cut in the front for easy access — is encased in a heavy plastic protective cover.

"The merchandise comes in to our quality control center," Peterman says on a tour of the vast facility. "If we have quality control problems here, it's too late. That's why you don't see any of our Q.C people; they're all out in the factories."

Peterman ships within 24 hours of receipt of the order and has the capability of getting 5,000 packages a day out the door.

Explosive Growth

The J. Peterman Company revenues grew exponentially — from $560,000 in 1987 to $5 million in 1992. In the three years, 1990-1992, revenues grew at the rate of $15 million a year. By 1996, revenues topped around $70 million. In the works, plans for 50 to 75 retail stores (along with his two outlet stores in Vermont and Tennessee and the store in Lexington), giving him the advantage of a second distribution channel. In addition to his regular catalog, he introduced *Peterman's Eye* catalog early in 1996 and also launched successfully in Japan.

Peterman sees his main task as continuing to develop and protect the brand. "I do not have to control every aspect of the company," Peterman told *The Lane Report.*

> The only aspect that I must control is that the pubic image of the J. Peterman Company remains true to what it originally was, because that is what people still want today. If it changes to Gap or WalMart, then we've got a problem and I have not done a good job.

He added:

> Whatever we do — whatever direction we take — one-half the constituency of experts will say this is what I should do and the other half will say I shouldn't do it. I pay no attention to any of them; these guys are not in the fray.

The Seinfeld Connection

John Peterman became a household name in America as the result of becoming a character on the megahit weekly situation comedy, *Seinfeld.* The Peterman character was a bit of a nitwit who spoke in the florid hyperbole of Donald Staley's prose. The reference was over the heads of the majority of the audience; only a small portion of sitcom viewers matched the upscale demographics who received the Peterman catalog; most did not realize that John Peterman was a real person with a real catalog. I had heard that one reason Peterman did not give interviews was his irritation at *always* being asked about *Seinfeld.*

Because of his reputed annoyance with interviewers asking him about the television character, I vowed not to mention it; Peterman would have to bring it up, which he eventually did. As a result of this quirky exposure, the brand was far stronger than it otherwise would be for a mail order company of its size. Peterman:

I mean 37 million people hear the name on Seinfeld. When a Peterman episode runs on Seinfeld, do sales go up the next day? No. Does it raise name recognition? Yes. Will it make a difference later on? Yes.

Reporters constantly asked him what it was like suddenly being a celebrity.

I'm reminded of someone interviewing Willie Nelson and asking him how it felt to be an overnight success. "I like overnight success fine," Nelson said, "considering that I've spent the past 40 years playing in honkytonks behind chicken wire."

When not on the road, Peterman puts in 12- to 14-hour days in the office. Weekends are spent relaxing on the 500-acre organic farm in northern Kentucky where he raises corn, tobacco and cattle. No chemicals are used on the farm because Peterman is a passionate environmentalist. One reason may be his incessant travels throughout the Third World. "The U.S. is not one of the physical locations that's ruining the environment," Peterman maintains. "We're not perfect, but it's the Third World countries that are ruining the environment. Every time I come home from Africa or South America, Kentucky looks better and better."

What would he do to improve things in the Third World?

I have had significant experience in Third World Countries and I like them The worst thing that happens to them is the do-gooders. I don't agree with the missionaries and the Peace Corps. People go in, screw everything up and then they leave. The people are no better off. Oh, maybe they have 27 more latrines, but so what. We should not be imposing our values on these people. I've seen more harm done by do-gooders than good.

What about child labor?

Should children be working in factories? I don't know. Certainly not in this country. Do we use child labor? No. I was just in a factory we use in China and saw a lot of young people but not kids. They were 20 or 21.

From his vantage point as a world traveler and American businessman, Peterman is concerned about this country's drift toward more people being taken care of by the government. At the same time, it may be good for his business. "The more we move toward socialism, the more people want products that evoke individualism."

He added:" In our society you can dream . . . and with enough people dreaming, some will go out and do things."

At 60, John Peterman is an American original — in the prime of his life, at the top of his game. Another great world traveler said it this way:

> *I'd not give way for an Emperor,*
> *I'd hold my road for a King —*
> *To the Triple Crown*
> *I would not bow down —*
> *But this is a different thing.*
>
> *I'll not fight for the Powers of Air,*
> *Sentry, pass him through!*
> *Drawbridge let fall,*
> *'tis the Lord of us all,*
> *The Dreamer whose dreams come true!*
> — Rudyard Kipling

9

The J. Peterman Company II

A Donald Staley Sampler

River Kwai.

The bridge is there, still. It connects the gorges of Kwai Noi with Kwai Yai.

The bridge is sad and strangely excellent and stirring, as you would want it to be. Even if you never saw the movie, you can see with your own eyes that this bridge was better constructed than strictly necessary.

Thousands of POWs died building it: British and Indian, Dutch and French, Australian, even American. They are buried here.

When you come all this way to see these things, all the way to Kanchanaburi, you won't be disappointed. The valleys and jungles and gorges and streams are themselves strangely beautiful to see. But the bridge is the most beautiful sight of all . . . a monument to defiance.

Being built slowly and painstakingly better than it had to be, it became a way of getting back. It became the POWs' own agenda, instead of their captors'.

Rebellion, especially in any new form, is always worth a trip.

Wear shorts and short sleeves when you go. Ours are as good as any.

Cotton Twill Short-Sleeve Shirt (No. 63A6191), cuffed sleeves, combination zip and button-through double pockets, removable epaulets, side-slit straight hem; exactly right for the jungles of Thailand, or your backyard. Price: $58. Imported. Men's sizes: S, M, L, XL, XXL. Color: Stone.

Cotton Twill Shorts (No. 63A6394), pleated front, side and rear pockets, belt loops; we subtracted the British-issue side straps (Wm Holden would approve, Guinness would not). Price $42. Imported. Men's even sizes: 32 through 46. Colors: Khaki, Stone, or Red. Pls. specify.

Russian Navy Shirt.

Wait a minute. Does Russia really have a navy?

They do. Of course they do.

Watch CNN tonight. If they're wearing striped shirts like this, it's the Russian Navy.

Unless you see a dark-eyed girl paddling a green boat and her boyfriend laughs and smokes and his cigarette is slightly less than one inch long and permanently attached and he is wearing a not-bad-looking striped navy shirt — then it's France.

Unless it's New York.

But if the girl and her boyfriend are both blond, and pale smoky-eyed and he you notice, is deeply tanned and wearing some kind of striped navy shirt without any sleeves, then it's Finland.

Or the island of Sylt.

Or Krk.

Or Sukhumi.

Under a suit jacket, it's L.A. Or maybe Munich.

But when they're both wearing striped navy shirts, it's Zihuatanejo.

Or Sochi.

If there are two girls and one boyfriend and all three are wearing striped navy shirts, then it's definitely Russia.

Unless it's Central Park.

Russian Navy Shirt (No. 63A2915). (The red tape could have taken a lifetime. Ours. This, therefore, is a copy; a faithful copy. Like the original, it's "unimproved." Pure cotton. The blue is wonderful: dark, deep, moody. Maybe it's the Russian soul, coming back.) Price: $34. Men's sizes: S, M, L, XL, XXL. Color: Blue and white striped.

The small island of Dominica.

The home, since 1907, of a very good West Indian Bay Rum; it has a fairly quiet scent, less strong than anything called perfume, less strong than anything called aftershave, but not so quiet as to be boring. It is, in fact, quite sexy.

Sexy the way skin begins to smell from strong sun, saltwater, steel drums, breaking waves , moving palm branches, and giggling coming from somewhere.

Men have liked Bay Rum since Spanish Main days. They like it for the least complicated reason in the world: it smells good.

A decent gift which often turns into a lifetime habit.

10 oz. Shillingford Bay Rum (No. 63A1105). Price: $11.

"Pembs."

Saw something odd in the window of an horologist's shop in Amsterdam.

Had to have it.

"Proprietor out of town. A famous collector. Couldn't sell at any price." Et cetera.

Quite maddening.

Nine years later. A shop in Bath filled with rare birds (including the owners). Dried ferns. Love letters. Photographs of boys gone to war. Riding boots. Crocodile picture frames. Thousands of books. Wooden cameras. Wedding rings. And under some ivory capeskin opera gloves, partially hidden, this watch.

This replica identical, almost, to the original: a delicate leather strap enclosing a smallish pocket watch. Worn on the wrist or suspended from the neck on a chain, for deft, ladylike time checks.

A lovely thing, resonant of another, earlier, more-thought-given-to-each-little-thing epoch.

It also held a secret. An inscription on the back read:

Gloucester Education Committee
Perfect Attendance
10 Years
Margaret "Pembs" Hayward
1911-1920

Tallulah Bankhead would have killed to be so innocent.

Pembs Watch (No. 09A5386). Replica of turn-of century lady's timepiece, worn on wrist or as pendant. Price: $95. Leather strap, brass case and chain. Japanese movement. Quartz. 1-1/2" diameter face. Chain 38" long. Engravable back. (Make it good.) Imported.

"My advice . . . never buy
untrained ponies in Bombay."

— Lieut. General Sir Beauvoir de Lisle

(You can't imagine the number of complaints received by the War Office from indignant parents. So many young officers exceeding their allowances . . .)

Herewith: original "European" polo shirt. The polo shirt you can play polo in. Three buttons, not six. Noticeably lighter in weight, and comes with a number.

The significance? Number 3: The Home team. Pisces in the 12th house. Professions: Actor, writer, gardener, club owner. Geography: Montego Bay, Aruba, Penang, San Antonio.

Number 4: The Visitors. Aquarius in the 11th houses. Aviator, gentleman farmer, hypnotist. Saratoga, Princeton, London, Newport.

Authentic European Polo Shirts (No. 63A6484). 100% cotton interlock. Knit collar. Short sleeves. Colors: Red with white trim, plus "4" or Black and white trim, plus "3". Pls. specify. Men's sizes: S, M, L, XL, XXL. Price $58, Imported.

Invite friends to tramp turf between chukkas.

<u>Who?</u>

They voted him most likely to do something weird.

That suited him fine.

"Not sufficiently outer-directed," one teacher remarked. He vanished from their world into another. Larger. His own.

Wool Tattersal Vest (No. 44B3660). 100% wool. Further insurance that no one will every quite be able to classify you completely. Windowpane checks infused with 19th-century French resonance. (Or is it 19th-century Scottish?) Prosperous 5-button front, welt pockets, back belt with buckle closure. Notched lapels. Fully lined.

Don't look for him at the 25th. Conflicts with his harvest in Napa.

Color: Spiced Tattersall.

Men's sizes: 38 through 48.

Price: $130. Made in late 20th century Cleveland. Tennessee, actually.

Points for Marketers to Consider

1.

When John Peterman brought his signature cowboy duster back East, he unwittingly tapped into a stream running deep in the psyches of many who saw it.

People want things that are hard to find. Things that have romance, but a factual romance about them.

I had this proven all over again when people actually stopped me in the street (in New York, in Tokyo, in London) to ask me where I got the coat I was wearing.

Of course, Peterman, long, lean and lanky, looks like a million bucks in the cowboy duster. I tried one on in his store; being short, rotund and balding, I looked ludicrous.

Peterman and Don Staley put themselves inside the heads of a segment of the population who perhaps want to be something they are not — part of a another lifestyle in another era.

The concept might best be illustrated by the wild success of James Cameron's *Titanic.* As a direct result of this film, the cruise industry experienced a boomlet. Peterman immediately saw what had happened and contracted with Cameron's company to reproduce and sell not only the blue pendant that was the centerpiece of the story, but also various props and items — some of which were used in the movie.

"The more we move toward socialism, the more people want products that evoke individualism," Peterman said to me.

His entire business is based on being inside the heads and under the skin of this segment of consumers, thinking how they think, feeling what they feel, and creating wants for them. This is Method Marketing at its most sophisticated.

2.

Donald Staley hit on a unique copy approach, one that breaks the traditional rules of direct marketing. Instead of talking about a product — or even the benefits and features of the product — Staley creates a fanciful story about the product, often setting it in another age or an exotic locale.

While Peterman's merchandise is perfectly okay, could he have built this huge business with the typical, run-of-the-mill descriptive copy found in catalogs by Lillian Vernon, L.L. Bean, Victoria's Secret?

Not bloody likely.

3.

Ultimately, shopping John Peterman's *Owner's Manual, Booty, Spoils & Plunder* or *Peterman's Eye* is, above all else, _fun_. You find yourself giggling with pleasure at Staley's prose. The whole experience is a bit of a put-on, but the prose is so witty that you play along — and often order.

The question here: Is it fun doing business with you? Can you make it more so?

4.

The emotional hot buttons — or key copy drivers — Staley uses are flattery, exclusivity and salvation. The reader is flattered that Peterman would send so literate and elegant a catalog.

Inveterate catalog shoppers will notice some of the same items in different catalogs, Peterman's stuff is unique — exclusive. And Staley's copy — with his literary allusions and vignettes — conveys that sense of exclusivity. Ultimately, you, the reader, can be like the world travelers and sophisticates Staley writes about; buy this item, Staley is saying, and you will find yourself living a better, more glamorous life. Your friends will admire your taste and assume you prowled the little shops in Portobello Road or the Grand Covered Bazaar in Istanbul. Salvation!

What are the emotional drivers you use to get prospect, customers and donors to respond?

5.

This is a classic example of brilliant copy creating wants (as opposed to filling needs).

6.

For all the casual, laid-back, nonsell that Staley does, Peterman has his finger on every facet of the business. He said to me:

> Products, people's attitudes, paper and postage costs, everything is in constant flux. This is the business of managing movement. You can never say you're done with one thing and can leave it and move on to the next.

7.

In our 1996 interview, Peterman alluded to starting up a series of retail stores. As I pointed out in the opening of the Peterman story, his store in Lexington was a sheer delight — right up there with Fauchon, Harrod's, and Virgin Records. My understanding is that by the time this book is published, Peterman will have a store in the grandly renovated Grand Central Terminal in New York City, as well as others. My sense is that like Rodgers & Hammerstein's song about Kansas City in *Oklahoma*, Peterman had "gone about as fer as he could go" in the catalog business. His list at the time was made up of 217,700 twelve-month buyers (customers who had bought at least once in the past year). While respectable, it's not the 4.7 million catalog buyers Victoria's Secret has in its computers or Lillian Vernon's 3.2 million. In fact, Peterman's clientele is just 10 percent of L.L. Bean's 2.1 million. He has probably found just about everybody in the country who can relate to Staley's wafty prose, imagine wearing the item he describes (or serving dinner on it). To be sure, many others must have the same dreams of being in far off lands and living in other eras, but the literacy rate in this country is on the decline. To continue to grow his business, he probably had to expand beyond his catalogs to reach those folks of a similar mindset, who need to see, feel and try on the actual merchandise before they buy.

Can you figure out additional distribution channels for your products? If so, it is imperative to get professionals who know how to do it *right*. Whether you are going retail . . . or adding a catalog as an adjunct to your marketing efforts . . . or testing Direct Response Television . . . spend the money on professionals to guide you.

The worst thing in marketing is to do something half-assed and amateurishly and bomb; you've spent money and you are back to square one.

10.

The Teaching Company

Tom Rollins:
The Teacher Could Learn Something

Don't assume people are happy if they don't complain.
— Judith Schalit

In the June 1991 issue of *Who's Mailing What!* I reported on The Teaching Company, an entrepreneurial catalog founded by Tom Rollins, former chief counsel to the U.S. Senate's Labor and Human Resources Committee. I wrote:

Rollins had a dream. So he sold his house, cashed in his retirement money, borrowed up to the hilt and told seven of his best friends which day of the week he expected to be invited for dinner.

The dream: Identify the greatest teachers in American colleges, universities and high schools, videotape their lectures and make them available on audio and video cassettes via direct marketing.

Working with Roger Craver of Craver Mathews Smith, Rollins formed The Teaching Company and created a simple one-color catalog; meanwhile, legendary copywriter Tom Collins (co-founder of Rapp & Collins) wrote and designed the space ads offering lectures by the "Superstar Teachers."

In order to write that original article, I decided to order a product. I went through the catalog and settled on an eight-video series titled, *A Modern Look at Ancient Greek Civilization* by Professor Andres Szegedy-Maszak of Wesleyan University. The cost: $149.95 plus shipping.

Someone once said that if you could count the truly great teachers in your life from kindergarten through college on more than the fingers of one hand, you were lucky. I was lucky. At the Lawrence School, I had Elsie Ringletaube and Ralph Clark. At Andover, I had Patrick Morgan and Dudley Fitts. At Columbia, I had Charles Van Doren, Mark Van Doren, Eric Bentley and James Shenton, whose American history course was a true theatrical event. For Shenton's end-of-term lectures (the Civil War in winter and the 1920s in the spring), it seemed the entire campus showed up and practically hung from the rafters to see a truly great teacher do his thing.

Yes, Virginia, I have been blessed with superstar teachers.

And in my opinion, Szegedy-Maszak was no superstar. Mannered and pompous, he had all the charisma of a Philadelphia carriage horse. I suffered through three of the eight videos and recently chucked them all out.

Back then I asked Rollins how he could possibly consider this guy a superstar; being a lawyer rather than a direct marketer, Rollins hotly defended the course by saying that a lot of people liked it.

He did not try to get inside my head; he wasn't the least bit interested in listening to one of his paying customers. (And the video courses all cost in the three figures, as I recall.)

In effect — and in actuality — Rollins was telling an unhappy customer that he (the customer) was wrong.

How would an old-school direct marketer have handled me?

> Oh, gee, Denny, by all means send them back and let me replace them with another course.

No such offer was forthcoming. As a result, I never ordered again.

At the time, I took Rollins to task for simply sending the merchandise. No welcome letter. No course outline. No list of reading materials. No biography of the professor. No catalog of other courses. No order form. Rollins blamed it on a fulfillment house screwup.

The company has survived, and today I find myself bombarded with Teaching Company catalogs at the rate of two and three a month. Since I was burned once, I never order. But I called Rollins for an update. He now has about 100 courses and never rents his lists. A new string to Rollins's bow is the founding of Mirus ("Latin for 'astonishing' or 'wonderful'") University, where he will be able to confer a "Master's degree at home using SuperStar Teacher tapes as the foundation of your classes."

I asked Rollins why he keeps sending me catalogs when I bought once six years ago and never again. I asked why nobody called me to find out if I was satisfied or dissatisfied and why I never bought again. His response: He had only brought his customer service in-house in 1994. He's apparently been doing some outbound telemarketing — but not to me.

In the course of our conversation — in which I only wanted to get the story for my newsletter — Rollins accused me of sounding like I was spying for the competition.

The upshot: I didn't like Rollins' products, and I didn't like Rollins. After talking a second time to Rollins, I not only did not like his product, but I liked Rollins even less.

Rollins ignored a basic tenet of direct marketing:

> Properly handled, disgruntled customers can be your best customers.
>
> — Judith Schalit

11

Agora Publishing

Bill Bonner: Renaissance Man

After three failures and $70,000 in debt, Bill Bonner went on to create a sprawling international newsletter and publishing empire — one that's closing in on $100 million in annual revenues — and part of the year he runs it from his chateau in France.

Three secrets to this hands-off entrepreneur's success? Brilliant copy, an unconventional corporate culture and a deliciously contrarian philosophy.

Bill Bonner is the quintessential nontraditional entrepreneur.

Contrarian.

Oddball.

He publishes newsletters, some of which are disguised as exclusive membership organizations. He has amassed some 900,000 subscribers in the United States, with another 100,000 scattered around 105 countries. He was asked how many newsletters his company, Agora, publishes.

Rail thin and six-foot three with an angular face, high forehead and piercing eyes, Bonner, 48, was seated across from me at an antique mahogany dining table that would easily seat 30. The setting was the wood-paneled dining room of his magnificent Baltimore headquarters — an 1882 Stanford White mansion in downtown Baltimore restored to pristine Victorian perfection. He entwined his Paganini-like fingers while pondering the question in momentary silence. At length, he shrugged his shoulders. "I'm not sure what the total number of newsletters is," he said. "Maybe 40."

He explained that the business is completely decentralized. Separate entities exist in four of these exquisite turn-of-the-century

William Bonner, arguably one of the world's greatest copywriters. In the background: Agora's world headquarters, Chateau d'Ouzilly.

Baltimore mansions, plus sites in New Jersey, New Mexico, Florida, London and international headquarters at Le Chateau d'Ouzilly, three hours outside Paris; in addition, partnerships have been forged with companies in Canada and Germany. Any of them could be starting or folding newsletters at any given time, as well as publishing books (Agora has over 300 titles in print) and special reports, producing videos, putting on conferences or leading "Discovery Tours" to such financial havens as Ireland, Panama, Honduras, Belize, Nicaragua or Costa Rica, where his subscribers — flirting with becoming expatriates — are bombarded by local business leaders, government officials, lawyers and economists with facts about everything from the economy to starting or buying a business and real estate opportunities to tax advantages and acquiring dual passports. Bonner:

> There is this myth of the entrepreneur as a visionary who sees the way to a new reality and despite all the odds, makes it work.
> When I got out of college, I applied for a job at *U.S. News & World Report.* I was in the running until I was given psychological testing and they decided I wasn't fit. They knew something I didn't — that I was unemployable.
> This explains all my dismal failures.

Bonner refers to his attitude toward business as Zenlike; all business is a reflection of the people involved — not just the head person. He started with a group of eight people operating as a family. They worked hard and were productive.

> The next stage doesn't happen because you have a vision. Rather you acquire more people who figure out pieces of the puzzle. The result is we don't get where we intended to go but end up where we ought to be.
> Basically, you go along and you don't quite know where you're going when somebody comes along or something happens and gives you a bit of energy. Sometimes it's the kindness of strangers. You may not have the right idea, but the combination works. That's how things really happen. You go from one failure to the next. It's all hit or miss. And it evolves.
> You do nothing to stymie or top it. You put in energy. You let it happen.

The Epiphany

William Bonner grew up in Annapolis, Maryland, and following high school, his education included stops at the Universities of New Mexico and Maryland, the Sorbonne and Georgetown, where he stubbornly hung on to earn a law degree even though he knew he would never go into practice. Following the abortive job interview at *US News & World Report*, Bonner fetched up at the National Taxpayers Union in the early 1970s, where he had an epiphany; founder James Davidson — a high school buddy from Annapolis — introduced him to direct mail. "This is how we get our money," Davidson told him. "We write letters."

"You send letters and people send you money?" Bonner asked incredulously."

"That's it."

"I can do that."

What astonishes Bonner was that the National Taxpayers Union control effort was so bad, the Direct Marketing Association of Washington highlighted it as the worst letter ever seen. Twenty years later, Bonner can quote it verbatim; mystification is combined with obvious disdain:

Dear Dunce,

> We overheard some fat cat politicians talking about you.
> They said you were too dumb to know you were being ripped off . . .

Audacious, yes; nevertheless, it brought in money which goes to prove Hatch's rule that you can't judge good direct mail; rather, it judges you.

At the time, Bonner had no idea that direct mail was its own discipline and people all over the country were doing it. Instead, he was completely self-taught. Bonner:

> In this trade, you are well advised to start at the lowest level so you can see and feel and touch the mail coming in. You get an immediate sense that if it isn't a big stack, you're not doing something right.

In five years, Bonner's copy wizardry grew the National Taxpayers Union from a donor base of 5,000 to 120,000.

Bill Bonner's Chateau d'Ouzilly, down the road from David Ogilvy's Chateau de Toffou.

Calling it "the depth of stupidity," Bonner and a partner started a newspaper of political satire on the side; it was modeled after *Le Canard Enchainé* in Paris and London's *Private Eye*, both of which he visited on a European jaunt. Although "juvenile, amateurish and sophomoric," Bonner maintains it was very funny. They bartered services for advertising and printed enough until the money ran out. "D.C. didn't have a sense of humor," he discovered.

Flat-busted and living from paycheck to paycheck, Bonner persuaded friends and family to invest $70,000 in a magazine, *Frontiers of Science*, which wasn't as fast a disaster and so was a far bigger one. They went in the mail with good packages, and people sent in their money.

"The 40,000 subscribers we acquired suckered us into a level that kept us going for five years. Ultimately, the magazine lost $200,000."

My whole career has been marred and marked by a kind of arrogance. I never really understood that there were people out there who knew the answers to these questions and that I didn't need to find out from direct experience. I've gotten a little less arrogant.

Eventually, Bonner got fed up with Washington and its politics and politicians, lobbies, and lobbyists, the "chattering classes, the politics, politics, politics." In addition, he discovered that so much profit was being generated by nonprofits he became uncomfortable in the fund-raising arena. It was the start of the 1980s and two things happened simultaneously.

• Bonner read about Baltimore's Shopstead Program in which Mayor Schaeffer was offering derelict city buildings for $1 to anybody who would renovate them. Bonner took a drive around and gawked at all the beautiful buildings. He found a big, do-it-yourselfer dream house with elaborate details in a Baltimore slum for $27,000 and blew D.C. With years of handyman experience and having built two houses in his youth, Bonner was up to the challenge.

• In 1979, Bonner, Jim Davidson and Mark Hulbert — a former philosophy student at Oxford with Davidson who was currently working at the National Taxpayers Union — attended a New Orleans investment conference put on by hard-money promoter Jim Blanchard. In the hotel bar afterward, the three of them hatched an idea that would get them out of fund raising and into business — a service that would rate the performance of investment newsletters. Hulbert glommed onto the concept and created a discipline out of the incredibly complex morass of investment advice. His technique: subscribe to a slew of investment newsletters and, using a highly sophisticated computer program, set up an investment account on paper for each newsletter; buying what they said to buy, selling what they said to sell. With Bonner's powerful copy — coupled with the availability of the investment newsletter subscriber lists — the publication was launched and was immediately paying its way. *Hulbert's Financial Digest* became the Bible (and the bane) of the investment newsletter business.

At the same time, Bonner, who had done some traveling, got the idea for a lifestyle newsletter that fell somewhere between investments and travel. He launched *International Living*.

Where *Hulbert's* has always remained a relatively small circulation publication (currently between 20,000 and 30,000 depending on promotional activity), *International Living* got up to 50,000 subscribers very quickly and currently enjoys a worldwide circulation of 120,000.

Success Secret #1: Brilliant Copy

Bonner today is arguably the greatest direct mail copywriter in the world. His genius was probably inborn, springing forth almost like parthenogenesis. At the same time, he studied the work of the masters: the old rock-'em-sock-'em packages that brought in subscribers to newsletters whose lists National Taxpayers Union was renting with great success. Among his models: Pat Garrard, whose work for Howard Ruff's *Free Enterprise* got circulation up to 400,000, and *The International Harry Schultz Letter,* the work of a highly opinionated British gold bug and proponent of hard money investments who operated out of Switzerland. "Schultz was sometimes right and sometimes wrong," Bonner says, "but never in doubt."

Ultimately, it was the power of Bonner's inspired, benefit-laden copy that enabled Agora to go from zero to $80 million in 18 years.

Bonner's lead-in for the long-term control letter for *International Living* is basically the same today as it was when he wrote it in 1979. The letter has been tinkered with and updated, but the tone and much of the copy remains the same. He doesn't open with a lecture on the high cost of living in America nor the rooking you get from high taxes nor the incompetence of government nor the obscene crime rate. Instead, he immediately offers exclusivity and salvation, putting the reader into an idyllic lifestyle and promising that it can really and truly be had. Here's Bonner's classic letter, set in a roman type:

You look out your window, past your gardener, who is busily pruning the lemon, cherry, and fig trees . . . amidst the splendor of gardenias, hibiscus, and hollyhocks.

The sky is clear blue. The sea is a deeper blue, sparkling with sunlight.

A gentle breeze comes drifting in from the ocean, clean and refreshing, as your maid brings breakfast in bed.

For a moment, you think you have died and gone to heaven.

But this paradise is real. And affordable. In fact, it costs only half as much to live this dream lifestyle . . . as it would to stay in your own home!

Dear Reader,

I'd like to send you a FREE copy of a unique — and invaluable — report.

It's called *The 5 Best Retirement Destinations in the World.* And it tells you about the best places in the world for retirement living.

In one of the places detailed in this report, gentle sea breezes keep the climate nearly perfect, with mild temperatures year-round.

You'll find cliffs, hidden coves with secluded beaches, rolling hills, and high mountains nearby dotted with picturesque villages.

In this place, you can buy a beautiful villa, complete with lavish gardens, marble floors, and hand-painted tiles, for <u>less than half</u> what you would pay for an average house in your home town. (Or you can rent a waterfront apartment for as little as $340 a month, *including gas, electricity, a pool, a washer/dryer, a telephone, and a gardener)* . . .

. . . you'll pay up to 60% less for groceries than you are paying right now (farm-fresh eggs are 48 cents a dozen . . . and choice-cut T-bone steak is $1.75 a pound!) . . .

. . . you'll pay $240 <u>A YEAR</u> for complete and comprehensive health insurance, including medical, dental , and optical coverage . . . you can rent a car for $10 per day . . .

. . . you and a friend can enjoy a <u>four-course gourmet dinner</u> at a charming outdoor cafe for $12, including wine — for the two of you!

In short, paradise does exist . . . where $800 a month will buy you a comfortable home in a beautiful setting, pay for your food and utilities, a housekeeper, a gardener, country club dues . . . and even leave you with money left over for entertainment and travel!

Details on this and other retirement Edens around the world are included in a valuable report called ***The 5 Best Retirement Destinations in the World***. If you've ever thought of living overseas . . . or of owning a second home abroad . . . this report can turn your dreams into reality.

And this report is yours FREE simply for taking a look at an exciting publication called INTERNATIONAL LIVING.

. . . a publication that will help you discover and benefit from the many opportunities the world has to offer.

INTERNATIONAL LIVING will introduce you to . . .

. . . parasailing in Thailand . . . bungee-jumping in New Zealand . . . bicycling in the Highlands . . . bicycle tours in Britain and France.

. . . first-class travel opportunities for less than *half* the usual fare (it's all a matter of understanding the angles used by savvy travelers the world over).

. . . secluded hideaways in Bali . . . castles for sale in Ireland . . . villas on undiscovered islands in the South Pacific . . . affordable ways to travel in the world's most expensive cities, including London, Paris, Tokyo, and New York.

No other publication covers the world like INTERNATIONAL LIVING.

It brings the entire world, with all of its rich, rewarding, exciting opportunities, to your door every month.

And these are opportunities you can *use*. After reading an article in INTERNATIONAL LIVING, you can pick up the phone and arrange to . . .

. . . travel to exotic foreign lands . . . learn new languages . . . invest in booming overseas stocks . . . profit from foreign bank accounts

. . . start your own international business . . . get a job overseas . . . retire to a tropical paradise . . . buy a piece of prime real estate in the world's few remaining profitable property markets . . .

. . . these and many more exciting opportunities are available to you every month in the pages of INTERNATIONAL LIVING.

A different world

You read about one side of the world in your daily paper, you see it on TV newscasts. Murders. Wars. Airplane crashes. Politics.

But there is another side of the world . . . one you can't find out about by reading the paper, certainly not by watching TV.

It is a world of delightful opportunities . . . opportunities for fun . . . pleasure, financial security and profits . . . romantic discoveries . . . adventure . . .

It is a world full of things you can do to make your life more fun — and more profitable. You can . . .

• Sail away to the islands of the Caribbean . . . chartering a boat can be an affordable, as well as exciting and luxurious, family holiday.

• Spend a summer in the Lake District . . . or actually buy your own cottage in Ireland or a chalet in the Alps . . . do it right and the property will almost pay for itself. (I'll explain how in just a moment.)

• Make big profits on international stocks and bonds . . . overseas investments in fast-growing countries offer high returns as well as the safety of diversification.

I must emphasize that this world of international opportunities is available to anyone . . . not just the rich and famous. That's one of the major reasons we publish INTERNATIONAL LIVING . . . to show you how to benefit from the rich rewards of an international, jet-set lifestyle without spending a fortune.

Consider these items:

In February of 1985 we published an article explaining how to fly around the world for less than $1,000. At the time, that wasn't even half the regular fare.

In fact, it was so low that some subscribers didn't believe it was possible. One actually put us to the test. David Hendrickson and his wife followed our instructions and actually flew around the world — with stopovers in London, New York, Bangkok, Hong Kong, and Tokyo, for less than $1,000!

But that was back in 1985. What about today?

We told readers recently about an around-the-world airfare for $1,200. That's still *less than half* the regular fare.

Let me give you another example.

When we first started publishing INTERNATIONAL LIVING, we wrote that you could "buy an apartment on Spain's beautiful Costa del Sol for a little as $15,000." Here again, many people just didn't believe it could be done.

One of our readers decided to find out for himself. In 1985 he purchased a one-bedroom apartment in the Malaga area — with a view of the Mediterranean from one side of the terrace and the mountains from the other.

The price: $13,100. Not bad . . . especially when you consider that he can rent the apartment during the summer months for $500 a month . . . which means the place pays for itself just by renting it out in June, July, and August — months when he didn't plan to use it anyway.

INTERNATIONAL LIVING has been called the "ultimate travel newsletter."

It's that . . . and more. It's a newsletter for anyone who wants to broaden his or her horizons, visit foreign countries, make overseas investments, and save money.

Yes, save money. INTERNATIONAL LIVING will tell you:

• how you can pay for your travel expenses (and then some) to many places simply by shopping for bargains — electronics in

Taiwan, clothing in Hong Kong, leather goods in Morocco, gemstones in Brazil and Colombia, antique furniture and paintings in Great Britain, horses in Ireland, blankets in Mexico, wood carvings in Uruguay, watches in Switzerland, the list goes on and on. Some people not only pay their expenses this way . . . but they make a living at it as well!

• how to make use of international pension and insurance plans. You can *guarantee* your savings against inflation . . . and a number of other threats.

• about retirement havens where you can stretch your money beyond all recognition. Live like a king on a tradesman's pension. If you look beyond your own shores, you'll find that many countries around the world offer far greater benefits and advantages for retirees than does your own.

• about which overseas stock markets have been the best-performing over the last few years. The Japanese exchange nearly tripled from 1986 to 1990. The Taiwan market rose more than 1,000%. And because past performance is not always an indication of future performance, INTERNATIONAL LIVING makes sure its readers know which markets are the best investments *right now.*

• about one of the best — and still largely undiscovered — retirement havens in the world, where the cost of living is low and the standard of living is high. In this undiscovered, peaceful, charming country, you can hire a maid and a gardener for about $4 a day. Complete health care coverage, including everything from major surgery to house calls, costs $35 a year. And this is one of the few places in the world where real estate is still a good investment — and still cheap; you can buy a large house near the beach, with incredible views, for $60,000.

INTERNATIONAL LIVING will tell you how to locate the best accommodations anywhere in the world. Stay in a comfortable hotel in the heart of London for just £12 a night. Or stay in a quaint hotel on a Thai island for less than $6 a night. INTERNATIONAL LIVING will show you how to find the best place to suit your taste and your budget.

For the past two years, we've been researching the world's best accommodations. From cottages to castles, from monasteries turned hotels to public campgrounds, from pensions to *zimmer frei,* from bed and breakfasts to five-star luxury establishments. We've researched accommodations in 69 countries around the world. You'll get the full story in future issues of INTERNATIONAL LIVING.

In addition, you'll learn about real estate markets in foreign countries. Should you rent or buy? Every month, INTERNATIONAL LIVING tells you about real estate bargains in other countries, and then tells you how to take advantage of them.

Want to own your own apartment in London or Hong Kong? A thatched cottage on Ireland's wild West Coast? A bungalow on an island in the South Pacific? Or a hunting lodge in North America? INTERNATIONAL LIVING will give you the full details. Everything you need to know . . . and what you need to watch out for.

Our classified section alone is worth the price of the subscription. You'll read about special tours, available on a limited basis. About houses for rent or sale. About timeshares available for exchange. And you'll read about special situations, too — employment abroad, foreign investment opportunities, business openings, travelers looking for companions.

In a recent issue, for example, a widowed baroness offered to share her castle on the Rhine. In another issue, a reader offered bargain weekly and monthly rates for a Hawaiian estate with an elegant two-level A-frame overlooking a 200-foot waterfall with swimming pools, clear ocean views, lily ponds, an aviary, and other exclusive features. Another reader offered an entire island in the sunny Caribbean — for less than the cost of a stay at a modest hotel!

INTERNATIONAL LIVING will bring you a world of new opportunities. You'll read about ways to dramatically change the way you live — for the better. Romantic places to live. Luxurious places to travel. Inexpensive places to retire. Rewarding investments. Safe havens for rest, tranquility . . . places to let your imagination and your creativity soar.

No, you don't have to be rich and famous to enjoy an international lifestyle. INTERNATIONAL LIVING will help you understand that all you need is the special imagination to appreciate all the opportunities the world has to offer.

Real Estate

• The best property buys in one of the least discovered (and most beautiful spots in the Caribbean. The sand is just as white as anywhere else in this part of the world. The sea is just as emerald. But the real estate prices are unbelievably lower. We'll tell you where to look for beachfront acres for less than $10,000.

• How to purchase a home in the countryside of Britain for £10,000 . . . or a flat in downtown London for £11,700. You won't find prices like these on the open market . . . but, if you follow our advice, you'll realize how easy it is to own premier British real estate for a song.

• How to restore an ancient farmhouse in Perugia . . . for fun and profit.

• Why now is the best time in decades to invest in real estate in New Zealand. We'll tell you how to get in on the ground floor of this market — and what profits you can expect over the coming years as property prices here start to climb.

• How you can own your own Irish pub. What visitor to the Emerald Isle, after spending long evenings in local pubs drinking hot whiskeys and listening to ceilidh bands, hasn't dreamt of owning one? The good news is that it is easier — and less expensive — than you might imagine to turn this dream into reality.

• How to make a sure-fire investment in rental property in the Algarve . . . the South of France . . . Uruguay . . . or any one of a dozen other countries in the world with an active holiday rental market.

• How to arrange a trade — your house or apartment for a place in a foreign country . . . and get a home abroad for free. We'll detail who to contact . . . what to look out for . . . how to protect yourself . . . everything you need to know.

• Where to go for the best crayfish and clotted cream in the world. This tiny, completely unspoiled South Pacific island also happens to hide some tremendous property buys. A home with a magnificent sea view from the East Coast would cost you less than $25,000.

• With the long-awaited opening of the Channel Tunnel finally upon us, now is the time to take advantage of property buys in both England and northeastern France, where now-affordable properties will steadily skyrocket in price once Le Shuttle gets up and running. We'll tell you where to look, how to buy, and how much to spend.

• How to find an apartment you can afford in London, Hong Kong, New York, and all the world's most expensive cities.

Travel

• How to find a bed and breakfast for less than £12 a night in London . . . a hotel in Central Hong Kong, for $25 a night . . . or an affordable place to stay in any of the world's other major cities.

• How to make sure that you never — ever — pay full fare for an airline ticket again. (We'll show you how to save 50% and more every time you fly.)

• Where to find the most gorgeous (and inexpensive) white-sand beaches in the Caribbean . . . and the world's beautiful people who return here year after year.

• The best way to get the lowest hotel prices in Greece. (This simple little secret can be found in no guidebook.)

• When not to tell your travel agency where you're going. In some cases, this little travel trick can save you hundreds of dollars.

• How to take a world-class, luxury cruise for less than half the regular cost.

• South America's answer to the Riviera — without the crowds or the ridiculous prices.

• The top 10 adventure travel opportunities in the world.

• The greatest travel bargain of the decade . . . a delicate and unspoiled place.

• Europe's attic . . . where you can shop for the world's finest antiques at flea market prices.

• The advantages and disadvantages of using automatic teller machines abroad — and how to make sure your bank card will work in the country you're visiting.

• Travel clubs are mushrooming these days. Can they really save you money? Yes, but with some very important exceptions.

• Ritz-style luxury in Madrid for no more than the cost of a regular hotel room.

• Travel where tourists can't go. Obtain an independent visa for travel inside Myanmar. Make your way through the Central Asian Republics of the former Soviet Union without once contacting Intourist. Travel safely in Peru. Travel alone in China or Vietnam.

• How to gain entrance to the world's most exclusive, most private clubs and casinos . . . the kinds of places you thought only the rich were allowed to go.

• How to take your kids to Europe — and still enjoy the trip.

• A well-guarded industry secret: How to book yourself on a Mediterranean cruise at no charge.

• 8 easy ways to guarantee an upgrade.

• Why you should never refuse dessert in Finland . . . pat a Thai person on the head . . . or eat fish with your hands in Russia.

• Why (and how) every airline ticket is refundable.

• Not all discount travel agents are trustworthy or reliable. We review the nation's top discounters and steer you right.

• The 3 finest hotels in London . . . and the 5 best for your money.

• The best way to see Africa. You'll spend three months exploring the Dark Continent — for as much as most people spend on three-week package tours.

• The best place in the world to plan your honeymoon, your second honeymoon, or just a romantic tryst.

• The safest country in the world . . . the cheapest country in the world . . . the healthiest country in the world . . . and the sunniest country in the world.

• The best guest house along China's Silk Route. Plan to stay at least several days. (Warning: Avoid the garish new Tour Group Hotel up the road.)

• The cheapest tickets — to the world's hottest shows.

Taxes, Currencies, and Investments

• How to earn $70,000 overseas tax-free.

• Learn how tax havens work — and how they can be made to work for you.

• The world's up-and-coming tax haven. You've probably never even heard of this tiny, far-off paradise.

• The world's most user-friendly tax haven. Ensure the privacy of your financial affairs within an hour — and accomplish the entire thing by fax.

• Earn 300% and more on your next offshore investment. (We're not exaggerating. Our investment recommendations have earned our readers this much and more.)

• How to avoid double taxation on your foreign earnings.

• Cut your taxes 95% — by living in paradise.

• Learn how to live tax-free.

• Enjoy regular currency forecasts from a world-respected expert. They can help you best plan your travel — and make sure you get the most for every dollar you spend in a foreign country.

• Learn how to avoid "official" exchange rates and take advantage of more favorable rates on the open market.

• Why Switzerland is not the only — and perhaps no longer the best — place to have an anonymous bank account.

Retirement

• How to enjoy a million-dollar retirement — without touching your savings.

• Where you can enjoy free medical and dental care.

• Learn how to double your retirement resources — and live as though you had twice the income.

• Cut your grocery bills by 30%.

• 5 countries where you can retire in comfort and style on $1,200 per month, including a nice home, groceries, utilities, country club dues, even entertainment and travel.

• Where you can find dinner for two at an excellent restaurant for $10, including wine.

• Where health care is very inexpensive . . . an eye examination costs less than $4 and you can have a cavity filled for $7 to $10 . . . and in one of the places we have in mind membership in the national health care system is $35 a year.

• Where you can take a taxi across town for $1.50 . . . get a sandwich and a Coke for $2 . . . and catch a first-run movie for $3.

And Much, Much, More . . .

In this brief letter, we have only been able to skim the surface of the opportunities . . . adventures . . . money-making and money-saving strategies presented in each and every issue of INTERNATIONAL LIVING. And for every topic covered, INTERNATIONAL LIVING surveys the best information available . . . from government agencies, from private firms, from independent analysis.

On currencies, for example, INTERNATIONAL LIVING studies the predictions of world-renowned currency expert Robert Czeschin, editor of *World Money Analyst.* It would cost you hundreds of dollars to get this advice on your own. But this information comes to you in simple, concise form as part of your subscription to INTERNATIONAL LIVING.

The same is true for all the subjects INTERNATIONAL LIVING covers. You get information that would cost you hundreds of dollars annually, and take hours of your time to compile — if you had to arrange it all on your own. We put you in touch with a network of correspondents throughout the world. Writing from Great Britain, the Greek Islands, Hong Kong, North America, France, the South Pacific, and dozens of other areas around the world, these correspondents make sure you have the firsthand, unbiased information you need to benefit form your international travel or living experience.

SPECIAL INTRODUCTORY SUBSCRIPTION OFFER

And remember, when you take advantage of this special offer to subscribe to INTERNATIONAL LIVING for one year (that's 12 information-packed issues) for only $34, you'll also receive:

• A **FREE** copy of *The 5 Best Retirement Destinations in the World*, which will introduce you to the most attractive and exciting retirement options and opportunities in the world.

• Here's an even better deal. Try a two-year subscription to INTERNATIONAL LIVING for just $58. That's a savings of 50% off the regular price. And you'll receive a second **FREE BONUS —** *How to Get the Best Deal on Every Airfare You Buy.* Never again pay face value for an airline ticket . . . our report tells you dozens of ways to cut the cost of air travel in half.

INTERNATIONAL LIVING can change your life. By giving you more options, more alternatives in the way you live . . . and where you live.

And even if you never take advantage of any of the exciting ideas in each issue of INTERNATIONAL LIVING, you'll still find your subscription well worth the price. You see, INTERNATIONAL LIV-

ING is entertaining as well as informative. In can bring you the excitement and glamour of living and traveling in foreign countries even if you never leave your armchair.

INTERNATIONAL LIVING is your passport to a brighter, more exciting, more adventuresome future. Take advantage of this special opportunity to become a subscriber. This is the only way you will receive an invitation. INTERNATIONAL LIVING is not available on the newsstands.

So, please, send your subscription reservation immediately, using the enclosed envelope. We'll take care of the rest.

Sincerely,

/s/   WEB

William Bonner
Publisher

P.S. INTERNATIONAL LIVING will show you how to live the sort of life that used to be available only to the very wealthy. Try it yourself. If you're not completely satisfied, simply cancel your subscription. We'll promptly reimburse you for all the issues remaining in your subscription, no questions asked. And no matter what, all of the free INTERNATIONAL LIVING REPORTS are yours to keep.

Kathleen Peddicord, who oversees Agora's lifestyle group of publications, describes Bonner's approach as going after people's "points of maximum anxiety" — the things that they lie awake worrying about at four in the morning — and then hitting their hot buttons by turning them into benefits. "You can't save these people," Peddicord says, "but you can give 'em hope."

Out of the box, the launch package for *International Living* did 300 percent of breakeven and Agora was up and running. Bonner:

> When I was copywriting, I didn't understand the power of copy and the power of what I know how to do. I discovered that unlike a magazine, at the time, newsletters didn't require a lot of money. Subscribers paid you up front, and if the acquisition effort worked, you were cash positive from day one.

The secret of successful direct mail is (1) reaching the right person, (2) dramatizing an offer that is important and believable, and (3) making each customer feel good about doing business with you.

Believability is the key. Consumers and business people are becoming more wily, seeing through the hype and fakery that are disguised in elaborate personalization which can be accomplished with a computer.

Another kind of personalization is not achieved by technology, but found within the copy. An example is in the personalized thank-you letter Bonner writes to his new subscribers:

> . . . And please do not hesitate to call our TOLL FREE customer service line (800) 433-1528, if there is any problem. If the product you've purchased, or anyone in my organization fails to meet with your complete approval, I would like to know about it.
>
> Our company specializes in two areas — investment and travel. To a large extent, these areas reflect my personal interests. Perhaps you share these interests. If so, please allow me to take a moment more of your time to tell you about an organization I am involved with called The Passport Club. It's a very useful group that appeals both to my desire to travel and my interest in financial topics . . .
>
> . . . In short, I've found membership in the club to be a source of a lot of fun as well as a lot of profit.

Here Bonner is reselling his newsletter — and himself — as well as sowing seeds that should grow into a future sale. Freelancer Bill Christiansen has said: "The sale begins when the customer says yes."

What Bonner has done is inject himself personally into the correspondence with the new subscriber. It's obvious that Bonner (1) is a real person, (2) cares about excellence and customer satisfaction, (3) loves travel, (4) loves what he does, (5) is delighted to communicate that enthusiasm and share the benefits.

I call this "Reflexive Personalization," whereby the writer's personality comes through. Freelancer Richard Armstrong puts it this way:

> What makes a letter seem personal is not seeing your own name printed dozens of times across the page or even being battered to death with a never-ending attack of *you's*. It is, rather, the sense you get of being in the presence of the writer — that a real

person sat down and wrote you a real letter. A heavily computerized letter, by contrast, seems less personal.

Direct mail recipients, after all, don't need to be reminded that they are real human beings with real names. To the contrary, they need to be assured that the letter they are reading comes from a human being, not a computer and not a committee.

Ironically, it is sometimes more difficult for professional copywriters to write this kind of copy than it is for our clients (although Frank Johnson, Tom Collins, and Ed McLean were and are masters of it). Often it is the entrepreneurs and activists themselves — people like Joe Sugarman [*JS&A and BluBlocker marketing wizard*], Gary Halbert, Father Bruce Ritter, Howard Ruff [*newsletter publisher*], and many others — who have the gift for putting their persuasive personalities on the printed page.

The New Rules

For a newsletter publisher like Bonner, the game has changed and many of the old rules no longer hold. The business is now highly competitive and complex. Three other major players — KCI, Phillips and Boardroom — together with a slew of minor players are trolling for the same fish in the same ocean. Bonner still has the best lures.

But, unlike the old days, newsletter publishers must be prepared to wait three years to get their money back.

Bonner is quick to point out that, word-for-word, newsletters are among the most expensive products in the world, and when you are asking for $39 to $99 — cash with order — long copy is necessary.

"Copywriting is our business," Bonner says. And while he spends a great deal of time on copy as well as jobbing-out packages to such top freelancers as David Deutsch, Peter Betuel, Todd Weintz and Bob Bly, Agora's appetite for new packages is insatiable. As a result, Bonner started a school of copywriting.

A source of talent: St. John's College in his old home town of Annapolis, where the Great Books Program turns out smart, literate graduates who are open-minded, but without any career path. Agora pays them to learn, with about one of three making good. Agora writers spend most of their time on acquisition packages and the various divisions test any and all formats, with the exception of the double postcard (which has no room to sell).

Growing the Business

Following *Hulbert's* and *International Living,* Agora embarked on an aggressive expansion program, acquiring existing products and launching others. Among the acquisitions and partnership arrangements: the letters of investment gurus John Dessauer, Adrian Day, Doug Casey, John Pugsley and Dr. Gary North. Around this time, Florida publisher Joel Nadel launched an international investment newsletter under the fanciful title, *The Royal Society of Liechtenstein.* Nadel eventually ran into trouble with the local Better Business Bureau which decreed that *The Royal Society of Liechtenstein* was neither royal, nor a society, nor did it have anything to do with Liechtenstein. Nadel changed the name to *The Oxford Club* and sold it to Bonner. Today, *The Oxford Club* has chapters around the word where meetings are held and the names of the active members are held in strict confidence (i.e., the list is not for rent).

The Oxford Club is unique in that it is a membership organization with the main benefit being the newsletter, a technique Bonner used when he launched *The Highlander Club*, which goes to 73,000 opportunity seekers.

Sticky Wickets

When Bonner mailed *The Oxford Club* promotions overseas, his packages were promptly impounded by British authorities who informed him that publications offering investment advice had to register with the government. Bonner engineered an end-run by acquiring Fleet Street Publications in London and becoming the largest publisher of financial newsletters in the United Kingdom.

A student of history, Bonner had always been impressed with the Taipans made famous by James Clavell — a group of 18th century buccaneer Scottish traders and drug pushers who introduced opium into China and ignited the famous Opium War (which did not see closure until July 1, 1997, when Britain's great war prize, Hong Kong, was ceded back to the Chinese).

In 1987, Bonner launched *Taipan*, his first letter that did not have a guru figure writing it. Rather, it is positioned as a fast-moving opportunistic vehicle that investors can use to make money.

Other Agora investment newsletter properties: *Tax-Wise Money;*

World Investor, acquired from Hong Kong entrepreneur Mark Tier; and *World Money Analyst.*

After a sputtering start in the health newsletter business, Agora is now finally on track with *What Doctors Don't Tell You,* edited by investigative journalist Lynne McTaggart; *Health & Longevity* by cardiologist Dr. Robert Willix, Jr.; *Dr. Bob Arnot's Inside Health Letter;* and *Dr. Atkins* [of diet fame] *Health Revolutions.* According to Group Publisher Kathleen Peddicord, all are staff written and heavily edited by those whose names are in the titles.

Other acquisitions along the way: Pickering & Chatto, a London-based academic book publisher; Welt Publishing; and John Muir Publications, a New Mexico-based publisher of travel, automotive and children's books.

Success Secret #2: The Corporate Culture

When Beth Dent answered a classified ad for a list manager, she arrived to find the entire basement of the Agora mansion under water, the result of a burst pipe. The first person she saw was a janitor in overalls soaked to his knees and wielding a giant push broom. She sailed through the first interview and was told she would be meeting with the president and owner, Bill Bonner, who, to her astonishment turned out to be the guy she thought was the janitor. Bonner told her that 40 people had been interviewed for the job and had been turned down because they didn't know the answer to one question.

The question: What is a Cheshire label?

Dent knew and was hired.

A dozen years ago, the Baltimore office of Ziff-Davis downsized, leaving 22-year-old Kathleen Peddicord without a job. When she showed up at Agora for an interview as copy editor, she was so grossed out by the rundown house amidst the projects that she was tempted not even to apply. In the interview, Bonner asked her if she know what a style book was. She said yes, she was familiar with the University of Chicago version.

"Here we use the Associated Press," Bonner told her.

"I can live with that," Peddicord said and was hired.

Today, Peddicord heads up the Agora Lifestyles Group — another totally independent profit center made up of *International Living* and the health newsletters.

Sitting over a drink in a yuppified little bar near one of the Agora mansions, Peddicord suddenly went off into a rhapsodic monologue:

> All of us at Agora know how lucky we are. This is a completely atypical corporate environment. The only boss I've ever really had is Bill, and I really have no boss. I cannot imagine working in another environment.
>
> Some people like structure and like to be directed. They would be miserable at Agora with its freewheeling laissez-faire management. New people come in here and their eyes open wide. What to me is so appealing is that ideas are respected and thought to be important just because they are ideas. It's a very indulgent idea that ideas are important. If you like that, you'll be happy here. I get to lead Discovery Tours and spend time at the chateau in France. And I love coming here in the morning; there's nowhere else I would rather be on most days. It's filled with young, energetic, smart, thinking people. You walk into these beautifully restored Victorian mansions and see 24-year-olds in jeans and sneakers. It's a young place. I'm one of the oldest people in the company. I'm 33 — almost over the hill.

Sandy Franks, a 10-year veteran of Agora, came out of hospital public relations and started as a marketing assistant buying print for direct mail. Bonner taught her how to create mail plans and how to get packages through production. Eventually she took on more and more responsibility until now she is one of three in charge of Agora's Opportunity Publishing Group, which publishes business and entrepreneurial advice and information.

She and her colleagues are responsible for all aspects of the business: acquisition and renewal marketing, results analysis, copy, editorial, all mailings — even data entry, fulfillment and customer service. Since every issue of every newsletter goes out with an insert, on the side Franks also overseas the creation of add-on reports and products that can be piggybacked. She says:

> I love this job. Never in 10 years can I look back and say I hated one minute of it. Bill Bonner is a believer in letting people have their head. He'll give you direction, but always says, "Do what you think is best." He tolerates mistakes because he knows that's how you're going to learn.

The Chateau

In the typical corporate culture, if the CEO/owner bought a vast spread in the French countryside and spent six months a year there, it could have a devastating effect on morale. Not at Agora where the Chateau d'Ouzilly welcome mat is out for any Agora associate who can get there. On her most recent trip to Europe, list manager Beth Dent finessed a visit to the chateau. The reason: she'd heard some 22 other Agora colleagues were in residence. Bonner claims, "Never were 22 Agora people there. More like a dozen. But we may get more next year."

Success Secret #3: Contrarian Philosophy

Bonner passionately believes in his enterprise and "lives it." If *International Living* tells subscribers how to flourish overseas, Bonner sets the example with a French chateau. His personal money is invested in the funds operated by his newsletter gurus. Given the red-hot performance of the stock market, Bonner admits he could probably have done better with an index fund. *Hulbert's Financial Digest* found that the recommendations of Agora's *Strategic Investment* newsletter have lost an average of 7.3 percent annually for the past five years. "Our advice has been bad," Bonner admits. "Our advisors have been smart enough to dodge their way around this."

Bonner calls the last 15 years of the roaring Dow an "aberration" and says his gurus are "temporarily out of phase."

> You cannot have the economy growing at 2 percent a year while the market gains 10 percent and more. It's got to come to a crashing halt at some point..

So why would subscribers renew a newsletter of investment advice when it has consistently lost money for five years. Group publisher Ruth Lyons was quoted in *Worth* as saying, "People read it for the focus, rather than the investments." And, according to Lyons, conversions and renewals are "pretty good."

To Bonner, information is available anywhere. The *opinions* based on that information are what he is selling. His subscribers are buying opinions; they want to be led in health, in financial advice and in lifestyle enhancement.

When Bonner suggested that newsletters of the 21st century will take the form of "e-zines" delivered exclusively over the Internet, he was asked how he planned to protect his intellectual property from cyberthieves; they could download the copy and disseminate it worldwide in the blink of an eye. He shrugged off the suggestion with disinterest.

> Opinions have no real value after a lot of time. Once in the public domain, they aren't worth anything. And they aren't worth anything to someone who hasn't paid us.

The secret of his copy — and his publications — is that Bonner makes his prospect want to get into his loop. His sales letters tell people exactly what he's doing, but they have no value until the reader buys into the relationship — allows Bonner to tap into the prospect's credit card — so he can say, "O.K., pal, you're one of us now."

To meet Bill Bonner — with his "aw shucks" demeanor and disarmingly casual reference to his many failures — one wouldn't expect the steely undercurrent of self-confidence that was revealed in *Worth:*

> We live or die by our ideas. We believe that the way we see the world is essentially righter than the way most people see the world

Over a million people across the country and around the world have bought into that idea.

Bonjour from Ouzilly

Three years ago, after Bill Bonner had become the largest newsletter publisher in France and England, he decided he needed a base of operations in Europe. Fascinated with architecture and aware that they could buy real estate in the boonies for relatively little money, Bonner and his wife toured the French countryside and settled on an old chateau sited on an ancient Roman road near Poitiers. With no plumbing and poor electricity, the mini-castle will take five years to renovate. "I'm a builder and handyman," Bonner says matter-of-factly, "and [I've] built a couple of houses."

The result: Bonner and his wife, the former Elizabeth Philip, and their six children spend the summer in France. Weekdays, Bonner devotes 12 hours a day to his business; weekends are spent wielding saw, hammer and trowel. In addition, he holds creative seminars for the copywriters of his far-flung enterprise; associates from Baltimore and elsewhere are always welcome.

In the summer of 1996, Laura Johnson and Nina Camp of the Agora Health Publishing Division joined the Bonners at the chateau for five months of working on breakthrough direct mail. Here is an excerpt from Bonner's letter home, published in the corporate gossip sheet, *Agora News:*

> I know many of you in Baltimore think that we are goofing off here in France. Not so. Nina, Laura and I are diligently at work. We get to the office at 8 AM. We would like to start earlier but it takes a while for last night's wine to drain from our heads. We work until the postman comes at noon.
>
> He's amazing. He drives right up to the office door, hands us our mail with a smile, shakes hands, and takes our outgoing mail — even if we don't have stamps for it. Don't worry, he says, you can pay me tomorrow. What a system.
>
> Anyway, we take off for lunch and try to get back by 1:30 PM or 2 PM. We'd like to get back sooner, but it takes a while for the wine from lunch to settle. Then, we work until 8 in the evening.
>
> Not a bad schedule. We also have a productivity schedule. We're doing 8 packages in the next 8 weeks. Atkins. Arnot. Taipan. Willix. McTaggart. Oxford Club. International Living. And one package to be determined. In that order. Our target is to beat current controls by an average of 20%. (Laura and I are counting on Nina to blow away the controls on a couple of her efforts.)
>
> We're inspired by the realization that the greatest ad man of our time — David Ogilvy — lives right down the road from us. I see his name from time to time on the FedEx man's delivery roster. He has a giant chateau that is open to the public. What is it about copywriters that makes them want to buy a chateau?

Points for Marketers to Consider

1.

Bill Bonner is the quintessential Method Marketer who can get inside the heads and under the skin of the people he is writing to and *become* those people.

Or rather, become that person.

Method Marketing means thinking and talking to one person at a time. You may be reaching a group — indeed, a huge segment of the population — but, ultimately this is one-to-one communication.

Malcolm Decker put it this way:

> The letter itself is the pen-and-ink embodiment of a sales-person who is speaking personally and directly to the prospect.
>
> The letter is the most powerful and persuasive selling force in direct marketing once the product, price and offer are set. The writer creates the salesperson, usually from whole cloth, and you must be certain that his sales representative is truly representative of your product or service, as well as of your company. He is likely to be the only "person" your market will ever meet — at least on the front end of the sale — so don't make him highbrow if your market is lowbrow and vice versa. Make sure he speaks your prospect's language. If he's a Tiffany salesman, he writes in one style; if he's a grapefruit or pecan farmer or a beef grower, he writes differently. ('Cause he talks diffurnt.) I develop as clear a profile of my prospect as the available research offers and then try to match it up with someone I know and "put him in the chair" across from me. Then I write to him more or less conversationally.

2.

Bill Bonner's letter — eight pages worth — has hit on virtually every possible scenario the restless person might dream of: retiring in affordable splendor overseas, exotic travel, adventure travel, timeshare trades, investing overseas, saving money on taxes, making money in currency exchange. Some possibilities are mentioned two and three times in the letter (presumably, if you skipped around, you'll catch this same idea later).

Have you looked at your product or service and thought through (1) every possible benefit and (2) every possible prospect who might bite?

3.

The letter copy is entirely devoted to *results*. If Bonner talks about an island in the South Pacific, he transports you to the white beaches and the murmuring ocean. No mention is made of the miserable 14-hour flight to Tahiti, nor the connection — a nasty, noisy, dangerous little puddle-jumper that dumps you off in this alleged paradise so jet-lagged that you're a zombie until a couple of days before you come home.

MBA magazine said:

> Consumers want 1/4" holes, not 1/4" drills.

Is your sales and promotional material talking results (i.e., benefits) or features?

4.

In the fall of 1997 I attended two Direct Marketing Association (DMA) events — a telemarketing conference at Disney World (Ugh! I hate mice!) and a database conference in Chicago.

A neophyte attending the sessions would quickly be led to believe that all direct marketing hinges on database exotica and the telephone when, in fact, the workhorse of direct marketing is direct mail.

Both conferences were filled with enthusiastic specialists all talking to themselves in incomprehensible technobabble and not giving two hoots about understanding any direct marketing discipline beyond their own.

For example, at the telemarketing conferences, the breakout sessions and panels were highly technical; all the plenary sessions featured "inspirational" speakers — a marketing guy from Marriott and a futurist from the American Future Society. Most astonishing was the Canadian woman who regaled us at lunch with the two defining achievements of her life: climbing Mount Everest and learning to pee in a bottle without ever getting out of her sleeping bag.

Suffice it to say that none of these speakers enhanced anybody's further understanding of direct marketing and, as such, were a total waste of the several thousand dollars that DMA member companies spent to send each person to the conference.

Contrast these specialists with Bill Bonner of Agora, who has created a multifaceted international publishing empire that is completely decentralized. The group publishers are responsible for their own purchasing, editorial, and acquisition marketing (including list research and selection, copy and design, testing, receipt and recording of orders — even data entry and fulfillment). In addition, they are in charge of conversions, renewals, customer service, telemarketing and the creation and marketing of ancillary products to increase revenues.

What Bonner may be losing in decentralization, he is more than making up in morale, loyalty and a corporate culture to die for; above all, he is creating a cadre of direct marketing "general practitioners" who are becoming expert in every aspect of the business.

DM News columnist Martin Gross put it most succinctly:

> Whoever knows only one direct marketing skill, whether it's art direction, copywriting or list management, does not even know that properly.

Where the oh-so-full-of-themselves tunnel visionaries at the telemarketing and database conferences are forever consigned to being bit players on the direct marketing stage — or, at best, supporting actors — Bill Bonner is turning out superstars.

5.

Are you delegating responsibility? Should you be more hands-off?

6.

Are your people empowered to make decisions — and mistakes?

7.

Do you treat mistakes as part of the learning process that ultimately makes your people more knowledgeable and more valuable?

8.

Or can you honestly say, as John Peterman said:

> If something fails and it destroys you, you should have been a nine-to-fiver. To be an entrepreneur, you can't be afraid of failure.

9.

Ultimately, what is your corporate culture? Precisely at quitting time, are the halls filled with employees scurrying out the door? If so, why? Are you not paying them enough so they have to leave for second job? National Business Furniture owner George Mosher told me he makes a point of paying higher than industry average. "It may not bring me better people," he said, "but it enables me to keep better people." He added, "The more lower-paid people you have working for you, the more chances you have for error."

10.

It's fascinating to compare the management styles of the two great newsletter publishers — Martin Edelston and William Bonner. Edelston is obsessively hands-on, controlling everything from the strategy to the minutiae of his empire; Bonner is hands-off, giving his people free rein to succeed or fail on their own. Both styles — although 180 degrees apart — are responsible for the creation and success of multimillion dollar newsletter empires.

12

Absolut Vodka

Absolut B.S.

All of us have watched the Absolut advertising campaigns over the years — the vast sums of money spent on turning the Absolut bottle shape into everything from a swimming pool to a Christmas tree. The magazine insert — where an Absolut bottle literally lighted up in the sky — was remarkable.

But Absolut went over the top in terms of insensitivity when it delivered to me — and 249,999 other households — via the newspaper on Father's Day Sunday a blue envelope covered with little Absolut bottles with tails designed to look like sperm. "You're one in a million. Happy Father's Day," proclaimed a small message on the envelope flap. The headline: "ABSOLUT DAD." Inside, an Absolut sperm silk necktie.

(1) I am not — and never have been — a father.

(2) I wake up every morning thanking God that I am sterile.

(3) While my drink is vodka, I don't like Absolut. I find Absolut has a nasty little edge to it — a bite or aftertaste I cannot abide.

Did the smartypants creatives at TBWA/Chiat Day — perpetrators of this hugely expensive joke — get inside the heads of their readers and think through the deep hurt they would cause the guy with a low sperm count whose wife has been desperate for children for years and whose in-laws consider him less than a man for not producing fine, fat grandchildren? How would he — and his disappointed wife and sneering in-laws — feel when this blue-sperm Absolut necktie arrived with the Sunday paper on Father's Day into a lonely home that had never reverberated with the laughter of children?

With all the Absolut millions irresponsibly dumped down the sewer by TBWA/Chiat Day, wouldn't it make sense to (1) build a database of Absolut customers; (2) bump them up against a file of households where the presence of children was known; (3) say "thank you for being an Absolut drinker" by sending a sperm tie; (4) persuade them that a bottle of Absolut is a splendid gift to give on just about any occasion; (5) create ads that include a coupon for free or self-liquidating Absolut premiums to be awarded with proof-of-purchase (which would expand the database)?

In the words of Raymond Rubicam:

> The object of advertising is to sell goods. It has no other justification worth mentioning.

This spawns Hatch's Rule:

> Most general agencies — with their pathological terror of accountability and measurable results — aren't worth the powder to blow them to hell.

13

QUEST/77:
Robert Shnayerson

The Amazing Story
of the Editor Turned Copywriter

This is the story of remarkable sales letter that pulled in over 600,000 subscribers to a new magazine . . . continually beat the best efforts of the industry's top writers for more than four years . . . and, most astonishingly, was written by a man who never attempted a direct mail solicitation before or since.

In 1984, Robert Shnayerson agreed to an interview, and we met in a midtown Manhattan apartment-office. He came in nattily dressed, with a full head of silvering hair that made him look a decade younger than his 56 years. Right away he set the scene of the times.

Early in 1976, a bloody civil war was raging in Beirut; every night television news was parading a series of decapitated bodies through America's living rooms in full color. The country was just coming out of shock from Vietnam and Watergate. In a political aberration, the voters had rejected the Establishment candidate in favor of a Georgia peanut farmer.

Shnayerson's own life was a shambles. He had just resigned from *Harper's* magazine after new management had done violence to all he had achieved there. His beloved wife of 23 years had recently died. And he was realizing more and more that he had spent his entire career as an editor "contributing to the misery of the world." He was ripe for change.

By coincidence, as he was leaving *Harper's*, Shnayerson was approached by a magazine consultant — Arthur Murphy, formerly of Time Incorporated — who had a client interested in starting a new magazine. Shnayerson listened, and liked what he heard — the possibility of a magazine that was upbeat for a change, an elegantly produced publication that dealt with excellence, achievement and hope, but at the same time "would not be sappy." Best of all, he would have carte blanche in the running of it, and there was plenty of money to get the thing going.

Shnayerson went back to his apartment, and on his old Remington typewriter in the bedroom wrote out the prospectus for the new magazine. It was accepted. Agreements were signed promising Shnayerson and his staff a free hand. All systems were go. For a man who describes himself as "a congenital, deep-dyed Irish pessimist," these were heady times.

Magazine consultant Jack Ladd was hired to do the computer modeling and get the publication launched, and one of his early dictums sounded vaguely like the Claude Rains' line in the last scene in *Casablanca*: "round up the usual copywriters."

Several world-class freelancers were brought in to create the launch mailings for subscriber acquisition. In Shnayerson's eyes, the efforts did not capture what QUEST/77 was all about. And he was right; those initial test mailings did not work.

Shnayerson asked if it would be all right if he took a shot at writing at his own letter. The consultants, marketing professionals and circulation people winked and smirked — smug in the knowledge that editors never beat the professionals — and told him to go ahead.

Starting with his original prospectus, Shnayerson went back to his old Remington and began to spill his guts. Here is his six-page letter, printed on high-quality 6" × 9" tan stationery with the big QUEST/77 logo and address in the upper right corner of page 1.

> "I'm Robert Shnayerson, editor of
> QUEST/77 — a new magazine for closet
> optimists, people who suspect the
> world is NOT going to hell. You're
> invited to become a Charter Subscriber,
> receive the premier issue and save 25%
> while you're at it."

Dear Reader:

For 20 years I helped edit three of the
world's best magazines: Time, Life, and

Robert Shnayerson whose very first direct mail letter hauled in more than 600,000 subscribers to his magazine.

<u>Harper's</u>. Last summer, after five years as editor-in-chief of Harper's, I took a hard look at my profession.

Journalism had trained me to assume that every day in every way, things were getting worse and worse. I <u>enjoyed</u> that notion. Yet all around me was contrary evidence. New life-styles, inventions, works of art, world records. The quiet heroism of ordinary people coping, healing, teaching. The unknown best and brightest in a billion

corners of the earth — unknown because good
news isn't news.

I'm tired of journalistic myopia. Fed up
with publications that appeal to our worst
instincts. Let other editors drag readers
through cesspools of mediocrity. I'm
interested in people as they really are —
and could become.

So I'm starting a new magazine about the
pursuit of excellence — the search for the
fully lived life, yours as well as mine.

A Fresh Look at Ourselves

QUEST/77 offers a fresh look at the human
condition. It takes a sophisticated stand
against fashionable despair and
disengagement. With drama, humor and zest,
it argues that happiness lies in expending
ourselves for a good purpose. It brings us
back to life, back to our senses, the full
use of our minds, bodies and emotions. It
asks: Who among us is admirable and why?
What in our lives is still wonderful, worth
celebrating, still excellent?

QUEST/77 is the first magazine to focus
directly on mankind's possibilities with all
the wit, clarity and sensibility that this
great subject demands. A superb-looking
bimonthly — stitched at the spine like a
fine book, crisp, elegant, richly
illustrated in color — it combines the
literary quality of the New Yorker, the
exciting photographs of Life and the lush
graphics of Audubon. It appeals to every
person who wants to excel, every person in
quest of the larger self that lurks within.

QUEST/77 won't promise to make you healthy, wealthy or wise; beautiful, strong or sexy. It won't claim to do for you what only you can do for yourself. It <u>will</u> show you the best in everything from art to humor, science to sports, It will leave you <u>exhilarated</u> by your own possibilities, or at least <u>enchanted</u> by the performances of others:

• <u>Gifted people in demanding occupations</u>: athletes, scientists, novelists, actors, inventors, painters, surgeons, explorers — not excluding feisty eccentrics who create their own worlds.

• <u>Gallant people who personify life, spirit and substance</u>. Free people who value excellence for its own sake ahead of fame, money or safety. Honest people who refuse to cheat, sell out or betray themselves. Joyful people who seize life and never settle for second best.

• <u>All people, famous or obscure</u>, whose achievements bolster our courage, advance our knowledge, delight our minds and refresh the human spirit.

QUEST/77 relishes adventure. Epic rescues. Solo voyages. Treasure hunts. Business comebacks. Mystical experiences. It reveals the human stories behind great inventions like the transistor. It introduces a Japanese daredevil who plans to dog-sled alone across the Antarctic. Tells you about other quixotic characters who keep trying to fly the Atlantic in balloons. It explores the most remote frontiers of human potential, from genetic engineering to space colonization.

An Examination of Life

QUEST/77 celebrates grace under pressure.
The examined life is one of its constant
themes. Who among us is astoundingly immune
to fear, hate, envy, moral cowardice? What
accounts for the agelessness of some
beautiful women and great old men? In our
pages you'll read the moving words of a
dying painter who spurned easy money in
favor of artistic freedom. You'll meet all
sorts of people who survived life crises,
public ordeals, imprisonment, falls from
wealth or power. People who've hit bottom
and bounced back, setting examples of
resilience for all of us.

QUEST/77 asks the world's finest writers and
photographers to describe things they
honestly admire, preferably on the basis of
personal experience. All kinds of things:
ideas, places, crafts, rituals and customs;
examples of artistic integrity, moral
courage and intellectual elegance.

We'll print informed opinions about the
"best" wines, beaches and airlines — as well
as the "best" poets, philosophers and
presidents. We'll give you practical
information about sex, health, food and
children. At the same time, we'll demand the
highest standards of taste, writing and
performance.

We'll apply rigorous critical judgment not
only to books and films, but also to new
fads, laws, buildings, scientific
discoveries, political speeches, peace
treaties, athletic performances and Supreme
Court decisions. We'll "review" such things
in order to explain why they're excellent

or how they could have been. We will seize
every opportunity to draw distinctions and
puncture nonsense. We will unabashedly
separate the best from the worst in all
callings, trades and objects.

First Issue: A Collector's Item

The first issue of QUEST/77 will appear in
February 1977 and I'm determined to make it
so memorable that you'll be torn between
displaying it on your coffee table as a
collector's item — and cutting it to pieces
to send clippings to your friends. In the
pages of this premier issue and those to
follow you will find:

• Spectacular pictures and firsthand
reports by eleven young Americans who
climbed Mount Everest and wrote about it
exclusively for QUEST/77.

• A special 16-page section on Courage.

• World famous photographer W. Eugene
Smith analyzes his 10 best photographs
. . . six top American artists revealing
their favorite painting and how it influenced
them . . . Sam Keene: are humans inherently
evil or potentially good? . . . a salty
British adventurer's incredible sailboat trip
across South America . . . Loren Eisley: the
difference between holy and unholy science
. . . Green Liberation: how ex-city women are
faring on the land as self-subsistent farmers
. . . J. B. Rhine on his 50 year search for
ESP . . . the inside story of America's five
women airline pilots . . . Lox with Love: how
to run a great delicatessen . . . a photo
essay on Seattle, the nation's most livable
city

. . . profile of a master teacher: Robert
Penn Warren . . . the next Guinness Book of
World Records telling us the latest human
accomplishments.

    • Plus: Max Lerner on Thomas Jefferson,
America's only philosopher-king . . .
Frederick Busch: a day in the life of a
country pediatrician . . . George Plimpton on
the art of football coaching . . . the
adventures of two English girls who canoed
down the Congo River alone . . . Stan Lee on
why he invented Spider man . . . Paul
Goldberger: America's 10 best designed
buildings . . . Mark Vonnegut on megavitimin
therapy for mental illness . . . Richard L.
Rubenstein on what torture does to torturers
. . . Richard Ford: The world's best fly rod
maker . . . Sam Posey: Why I Quit Auto Racing
. . . James Cameron on living with a bad
heart . . . Harold Schoenberg: how to raise a
musical prodigy . . . John Cole on living in
a solar house . . . Edward Luttwak on the
pursuit of excellence in elite military units,
from British Commandos to the Israeli raiders
in Uganda.

    • Plus: Fiction by Cynthia Ozick, Tom
Boyle, Roberta Silman, Paul West, Gerald
Jonas, Martha Saxton . . . Poetry by John
Updike . . . Book Reviews by William
Saroyan, George V. Higgins, Margaret
Drabble, Richard Poirier, Leslie Fiedler,
Victor Navasky, Murray Kempton, Anthony
Sampson, Maxine Kumin, John Gardner, Joy
Williams, Gary Wills.

QUEST/77 may awe you — achievement does that
— but it will never bore you, never preach
windy sermons. It will be realistic,
specific, entertaining — full of lively

writing, great pictures, good thinking and a
sense of playfulness.

If you're ready for a new magazine that
talks up to its readers, not down to them
. . . embodies the excellence it pursues
. . . provides a relief from slackness and
slobbism . . . makes you feel larger, not
smaller . . . then you're ready for
QUEST/77.

Charter Subscriber Privileges

On newsstands, QUEST/77 will cost $2.00 a
copy or $12.00 for the six issues. But when
you reserve Charter Privileges in advance by
mailing back the enclosed card now, you gain
in these valuable ways:

Immediate Cash Savings. Instead of $12 —
your rate is just $9.00. Right away,
you're ahead $3.00 — a savings of 25%.

Perpetual Savings. You're guaranteed
preferential rates in perpetuity —
always the lowest possible price on
renewals and on any and all gift
subscriptions.

Volume I, Number One. Your subscription
starts with the premier edition — the
issue most prized by collectors, most
likely to increase in value.

Full Refund Guarantee. If ever QUEST/77
lets you down, just cancel and get all
your money back — a full refund of 100%
of your current subscription.

PLEASE DO NOT SEND MONEY NOW. We prefer
that you hold off payment until you've
had a chance to assess the premier

issue. To see for yourself whether it
delivers what it promises.

But don't hold off your reservation.
We'll be printing only so many copies of
our Volume I, Number One issue — no
more. To avoid disappointment or delay,
the enclosed reply form should bear the
earliest possible postmark — today's if
at all convenient. Many thanks!

                    Cordially Yours,

                    /s/ Robert Shnayerson

                    Robert Shnayerson
                    Editor

The letter broke every rule in the book. Start with the lead or Johnson Box (the section above the salutation, a visual device reportedly invented by a great freelance copywriter, Frank Johnson).

"I'm Robert Shnayerson, editor of *QUEST/77*, a new magazine for closet optimists . . . "

Having read some 600,000 mailings from 1984 through 1997, I cannot remember one long-term control that started with "I." According to Axel Andersson, who has analyzed the Johnson Box of more than 300 successful direct mail letters, the most common word is "you"; never "I."

Bob Hacker's operative rule here:

> The consumer doesn't give a damn about you, your company or your product. All that matters is, "What's in it for me?"

Yes, many exceptions exist to Hacker's, such as Martin Conroy's 25-year control for *The Wall Street Journal* which has (so far) brought in close to $1.5 billion in subscription revenues. Conroy's lead:

> Dear Reader,
>   On a beautiful late spring afternoon, twenty-five years ago, two young men graduated from the same college. They were very much alike, these two young men . . .

In analyzing this masterpiece, Hacker pointed out that where the typical magazine offer hits hard on product and price, Conroy had adapted a technique used by fund raisers who involve the reader in a powerful story. Fr. Bruce Ritter used this technique in his "dirty lady" letter.

Yet, Shnayerson plunges ahead, with prose buoyed by his enthusiasm and absolute belief in what he is doing. And clearly, the letter is coming from Shanyerson, so it does seem personalized and you suspend disbelief.

Other rules broken:

• Long paragraphs that create "gray walls" of type.

• Preachy copy (e.g., "I'm tired of journalistic myopia." "Fed up with publications that appeal to our worst instincts." "Let other editors drag readers through cesspools of mediocrity."). This is reminiscent of Jimmy Carter telling the country we were all suffering from a general "malaise."

• Much of the copy is more cerebral than emotional (e.g., "The examined life is one of its constant themes." "Who among us is astoundingly immune to fear, hate, envy, moral cowardice? ").

• The letter is full of "it" copy ("It introduces . . . " "It reveals . . . " "It will be realistic . . . "). Letters are supposed to be full of "you" copy, not "it" copy.

• The letter is emphatically not scannable or easy to read.

> The letter *must* be quickly scannable: that is a reader should get the gist of the proposition by reading the (1) eyebrow, (2) lead paragraph, (3) crossheads, (4) wrapup, (5) P.S. If not, send it back for surgery, because without a strongly integrated skeleton the body of the argument will slump.
> — Malcolm Decker

• He compares *QUEST/77* to other magazines — ("it combines the literary quality of the New Yorker, the exciting photographs of Life and the lush graphics of Audubon . . ."). Generally, you want to stay away from talking about the competition; it's imperative the prospect focuses on your benefits rather than those of others.

• A direct mail letter with no P.S. is inconceivable.

> Always include a P.S., say experts. It can restate the guarantee, premium offer, or major benefit or make a provocative point

that kicks the reader back into the letter. use a hanging indent —
the entire message is positioned to the right of the P. and S.

— Don Hauptman

The letter pulled 6%. By Shnayerson's own admission, the promotional copy was better than the first issues of the magazine itself;
where the magazine was slick and glossy, the letter had an earthiness
that gave voice to the feelings of those who received it.

Over the next four years, there was a string of tests against it, written and designed by the very best in the industry. Meanwhile,
Shnayerson's control went through many variations: a sweepstakes . . .
even a hokey computer version . . . as well as new copy tests.

But for all the tests and razzle dazzle against it — like the cat in
the old folk song — the original letter kept coming back, its raw emotion and bold honesty simply overpowering the competition. "Even
today it still mystifies me," Shnayerson said, "why those top guys
couldn't beat it."

In retrospect, it's obvious why the professionals kept losing. Quite
simply, Shnayerson was a good writer who had become totally involved
in his product and passionately believed in it. And when that kind of
involvement and passion burns through a piece of copy with such literate ferocity, you can chuck all the old rules right out the window. *No
one could beat Shnayerson!*

The Demise

By the summer of 1980, with the magazine now called *QUEST/80,* the
mailings had come full circle and were back to the original invitational
size "I'm Robert Shnayerson . . . " letter. The Rapp & Collins Agency
was hired to come up with some new marketing concepts. They began
talking about a Quest Award for people who did outstanding things
and trying to build it into something akin to the Academy Awards.
Instead, Shnayerson came up with the "Giraffe Society" to honor those
people who weren't afraid to stick their necks out. He created a special
issue devoted to 25 people who had stuck their necks out in the past
year. What's more, he invited readers to become members of the society for $2 each, and to nominate people they knew who had stuck out
their necks. From among 350,000 subscribers came an immediate
$30,000 cash, 15,000 applications for membership and an avalanche of
letters, every one of them as passionate and earthy and moving as

Shnayerson's original. He had found an extraordinary constituency of Americans yearning for excellence long before "In Search of Excellence" became a catch phrase.

But in November of 1980 the whole thing blew up. According to Shnayerson, the magazine's backers — The Worldwide Church of God, a Christian fundamentalist organization headquartered in Pasadena, California — who had originally promised complete hands-off treatment, now began to exert editorial pressure; Shnayerson and his staff quit. Advertising dried up, and the magazine died several months later.

Points for Marketers to Consider

1.

Bob Shnayerson had two problems with QUEST/77: He was probably ahead of his time and he obviously had the wrong backer.

Reread his 1977 letter and see if it doesn't resonate with just as much power some 22 years later.

> I'm tired of journalistic myopia. Fed up with publications that appeal to our worst instincts. Let other editors drag readers through cesspools of mediocrity. I'm interested in people as they really are — and could become.

Dissatisfaction with the media today is rampant. Everyone knew what Bill Clinton was and elected him anyway. Congress is a national joke.

Bob Shnayerson got it right; the politicians and talking heads today have it wrong.

Bob Shnayerson was able to get inside the heads of the people he was writing to and talk directly and conversationally with them.

And relate to them in a powerful way that resonated in the deep heart's core.

This is Method Marketing.

2.

Bob Shnayerson said it best to me that day:

> I believe if you're gong to be the editor of a new magazine, you — the editor — must try to write your own direct mail letter, even if you're a terrible writer.
>
> You have to think through what this magazine is . . . what the benefits are to the subscriber . . . and then write a 4- or 6-page letter with all the passion and intensity of your last will and testament, as though it were going to be carved in stone and signed with your blood. Even though this letter may never be mailed, you will have created a document that your circulation copywriters . . . . your advertising promotion people . . . and your editors can work from. It's an absolutely essential step in any magazine start-up.

So, why stop with magazines? Logic dictates this would be an invaluable exercise no matter what the product or service — consumer, business or fund raising. Whether you're a banker with a new mortgage offer . . . an insurance underwriter with a new policy . . . a product manager with a new piece of merchandise . . . a merchandise manager with a new catalog . . . . a fund raiser with a new cause . . . or a broker with a new investment opportunity . . . you should sit down — however painful it may be — and write your own deeply felt "I'm Robert Shnayerson . . . " letter to serve a credo, constitution, wiring diagram and marching orders for everyone involved in the project.

Who knows . . . you might find yourself with a winning mailing that beats all the so-called "experts" — just as Bob Shnayerson did!

14

First Bank of Troy, Idaho

Whatever Happened to Customer Delight?

Bob Hemmings is one of the great men of direct marketing. Now in his early 80s and proprietor of the Hemmings IV Direct agency in Pasadena, California, Hemmings is dapper, intense, powerfully built, immediately recognizable with his Adolph Menjou mustache and a bone crusher of a handshake. Look for Hemmings and chances are you'll find him on an airplane, either en route to taking care of a client or just returning from giving a seminar on direct marketing.

In his younger days, a friend of Hemmings was Frank O. Brock, president of the First Bank of Troy, Idaho. Troy's population in 1960 was 514; Brock's bank had 6,000 active accounts—12 times as many people as lived in the town. He had customers in 45 states and around the world as far away as Pago Pago.

What was Brock's secret?

Hemmings recalled that Brock knew precisely what business he was in.

> I am in the financial services business to help provide finances for my customers from the cradle to the grave.

Brock once made a loan to a man who had robbed the bank five years before. He was caught and served three years in prison. Brock said: "He had learned his lesson. I don't hold past mistakes against him. He is a much more stable individual now."

According to Hemmings, Frank Brock paid personal attention to all his customers. He cared. He understood his customers and knew practically all of the them by their first names; whenever a good loan customer ran into financial difficulty, the bank carried him—without dunning notices or piling up interest charges—until he was back on his feet. Brock's entire day was spent in his office going over his list of customers and clipping newspapers. Whenever someone would marry, die, move away, give birth, etc., he would send a remembrance. All of his customers received a personal note or a telephone call at least once a month from Frank Brock. The current buzz phrase for what Brock did: Continuous Event Marketing.

Brock's other main function was greeting new depositors. When the child of a customer reached a certain age — let's say six — the kid would receive an invitation to come to the bank with his parents. There he would be greeted at the door by none other than bank president Frank Brock and given a formal tour of the facilities (the vault was a favorite), then brought back for a welcoming chat in the president's office.

At the end of the conversation, Brock would take out a brand new crisp $1 bill and present it to the child and then lead the little tyke up to the teller's window where a passbook savings account would be opened in the kid's name. With great ceremony, the child would give the teller his new one-dollar bill and the teller would present the president with the passbook who, in turn, would present it with a flourish to the child.

Later, in high school, the kid would open a checking account. Later still, this young man would go away to college . . . go into the Army . . . get discharged and get a job in a distant town or another country . . . but always keep the accounts at that original bank. He knew the president. If he ever needed to borrow money, he could do so on his name alone. If he ever needed cash, it immediately would be wired to him, no questions asked. If he ever moved back to town and wanted a mortgage, it was a piece of cake. Wherever that kid was in the world, Frank Brock was HIS personal banker.

Hence 6,000 active accounts in a town of 514.

This is textbook database marketing — and with no regression analysis, no sophisticated modeling, no CHAID, thank you very much. Rather, it is the story of a brilliant personal banker, a marketer whose business was the continual delight of his customers for better or worse, in sickness and in health, for richer, for poorer, till death did they part.

Years later, Hemmings phoned the bank. Frank Brock had long since died, but Hemmings got the chief cashier alongside whom he had worked so many years before. The bank had been bought out by a larger bank. "Is the new president still going over the customer lists the way Frank used to?" Hemmings wanted to know.

"Aw, hell, we're so busy with paperwork and dealing with the computer, nobody has time for customers any more," he said and then added, "but, you know, maybe we should."

Today, bankers — and many marketers — have become so dependent upon the computer they have lost touch with the fact that a database is not about blips on a reel of tape but, rather, warm, living, breathing, *human people*. The computer could do some of what Frank Brock did; for example, with continual updates and overlays, it might keep track of which bank customers had moved to new homes and send a congratulatory note—but long after the fact. And, no doubt, that would be after it had smugly turned down the mortgage application, enabling another bank to write the business.

What's more, computers can't read the newspaper and make a note of births, engagements, weddings and deaths and act on them. To my knowledge, nowhere in the modern world is to be found a savvy, yet caring and forgiving computer-literate banker who has the knowledge, wit and decency to not only make money from customers but, at the same time on a highly personal level, make the bank's family of customers feel good about themselves and feel good about where they are stashing their hard-earned cash.

In the words of Peter Drucker:

> The computer is a moron.

So are today's bankers.

15

Western Monetary Consultants

William R. Kennedy:
Warren Buffett Wannabe

The strange saga of the Western Monetary War College and what happened when his entire faculty flunked basic mail order math.

When I started to receive mailings from Western Monetary Consultants offering an all-expenses-paid junket to San Diego, for myself and my spouse, warning bells went off in my head and the red lights of my built-in shit detector started flashing.

The first mailing arrived as a #10 First Class letter with my name and address typed on the front of the envelope and a live 22-cent stamp (then the cost of a First Class letter) in the upper right-hand corner. The only other piece in the mailing was a reply envelope, also with a 22-cent stamp affixed to it. That's 44 cents to start. The piece was known technically as a Letter-Lope, elegantly lasered on high quality buff-colored linen paper by the Kurt Volk Company in Connecticut. Cost of lasering and mailing this piece in quantities of 1 million was 14 cents. Since the mailing was not printed all at once, but rather sent in waves as names became available, the cost was more like 17.5 cents each.

Add to this the cost of lists — roughly 6 cents a name — and the total cost of this mailing was around 67.5 cents or a staggering $675.00/thousand.

I received several of these efforts, sent to different aliases that I used to track who was mailing what. One came to "Duckworth" Hatch, indicating the list was *The Duck Book* for opportunity seekers, published by a strange fringe character named Robert White, who, as I recall, had been murdered in Haiti.

Others of this mailing came to Sy F. Hatch, A. Hatch and Sy Hathaway, all code names from George F. Wein's Select Information Exchange, a clearing house for financial newsletters.

At that time in our professional lives, Peggy and I were emphatically *unqualified* to receive this offer or any of the subsequent follow-ups.

The initial mailing came in the form of a memo from Bill Kennedy:

C O N F I D E N T I A L   M E M O

DATE: August 25, 1987

TO: Sy Hathaway
          210 Red Fox Rd.
          Stamford, CT 06903

FROM: William R. Kennedy, Jr.

SUBJECT: Being my V.I.P. Guest (deluxe accommodations provided) at a high-level, 4-day Monetary Investment Conference (closed-door sessions) held in Colorado and elsewhere.

SOURCE: Edward Harrison (File 108.D201.BO/ HATHAWAY)

Maybe I ought to apologize now for unintentionally wasting your time (and my money). Despite careful prescreening, over half of those who are referred to me — and that may include you — are just not qualified to receive this memo. Let me explain . . .

My aim is to reach responsible, serious,
substantial investors who meet AT LEAST THREE of
the following seven financial prerequisites:

(1) A net worth in excess of $450,000; (2)
Investment liquidity of $80,000 or more; (3)
Annual passive income of at least $35,000; (4)
Total income of at least $100,000; (5)
Investment activity of $4,000 or more monthly;
(6) Personal line of credit no less than
$40,000; and (7) Commodities holdings of
$15,000 or more.

If you meet three or more of these criteria, I
want you to join me, at my expense, in an
unusual thinking/learning/earning "experience"
— four days of meeting (and getting to know
personally) leaders in the public and private
sectors. People like Maj. General George J.
Keegan (Ret.), a former head of Air Force
Intelligence. Here is your chance to learn from
world-renowned experts . . . and, also, to form
rewarding friendships with people of substance
and achievement.

You (and your spouse) will be treated like
"visiting royalty" while we explore a
potentially profitable investment field that's
under-priced, under-researched, under-exploited,
and really underrated.

If you qualify, detach and return the bottom of
this memo. (Or call me collect.) You'll get all
the details posthaste. No risk, no cost, no
obligation. And, even if you join me for those
four all-expense-paid days, you still won't be
obligated to invest in anything!

Which isn't to say that Sy Hathaway, like 928
previous guests, will not want to emulate my
unique "accumulation" methods which let you

acquire rapidly appreciable and immediately
marketable precious metals — for LESS THAN 35¢
on the dollar.
- -
                CONFIDENTIAL INFORMATION REQUEST

Referral 108.D201.BO2
                        Dear Mr. Kennedy:

Sy Hathaway   I meet THREE OR MORE of
210 Red Fox Road   your financial prerequi-
Stamford, CT 06903   sites. Therefore, send me
                             full   details (no cost or
                             obligation) on how I may
                             profit as YOUR PERSONAL
                             GUEST for four all-expense-
If name/address is   paid days of discovery.
wrong, please print
correction   Sign Here X_____

                             Date_____Phone (_)_____

What was going on? How could anyone possibly make money
sending the exorbitantly expensive efforts to people on the Select
Information Exchange and *The Duck Book* lists — low-end investors
who are one cut above opportunity seekers? Could a small potatoes investor and spouse really get a free junket to Colorado or San Diego?
What was the catch?

We sent away for more information, and the four-part follow-up
series — coupled with telephone efforts — was an eye-popper. Here
were 9″ × 12″ hand-addressed outer envelopes, embossed portfolios, a
slew of personalized pieces including 3-part airline vouchers, application forms, 4-color brochures singing the delights of San Diego's Del
Coronado Hotel and, in a Jiffy-bag effort, a slickly-produced audio
cassette. All five efforts were mailed First Class, with 22-cent stamps on
the reply envelopes. (With normal Business Reply Mail, return postage
is not paid until the envelope is actually in the mail; putting on 22-cent
stamps represents huge wastage.)

A typical follow-up effort arrived in a 9″ × 12″ First Class envelope with a 56-cent stamp affixed. The letter was on handsome linen stationery; the three-color letterhead proclaimed:

U.S. Monetary War College & Investor Clinic

December 17, 1987

Sy F. Hatch
Margaret Hatch
210 Red Fox Rd
Stamford, CT 06903

Once again, Mr. & Mrs. Hatch

. . . I want you and your spouse to know how very happy I'd be to fly both of you to San Diego (as my personal guests) for our four-day Monetary War College and Investor Clinic.

Naturally, we'll pick up your expenses: round trip airfare, deluxe meals, V.I.P. accommodations at the famed Del Coronado Resort or similar luxury hotel), and personal amenities.

Also . . . feel free to extend your visit an extra week or so. Unwind. Relax in sun-drenched San Diego, "Climate Capital" of the U.S. Enjoy gorgeous beaches, lush mountains, desert oases, scores of recreational/cultural activities.

Visit Balboa Park, San Diego Zoo, Sea World, Seaport Village, Old Town — and nearby Mexico, too.

As your airfare is already paid, the extra cost is minimal. So why not combine a little profitable business (at our War College) with the pleasure of staying a bit longer? Say the word,

and our Travel Dept. will arrange everything for
you.

Cordially,

/s/ Bill Kennedy

William R. Kennedy, Jr.
Founder and Director

WRK/slh

<u>P.S.</u> Two of the enclosures (your USMWC
Application and reissued Airfare Voucher)
should be returned promptly; the other
items are personal, aimed at arousing your
enthusiasm for a San Diego visit.

The Order Form

Included were a "Prepaid Airfare Voucher" and a "Confidential
Application for Free Attendance" — both personalized and fully filled
out, both printed on two- or three-part forms, plus a map of San
Diego and fliers for local attractions. All you needed to do was check
off your choice of six dates and mail it back in the pre-stamped reply
envelope.

The form asked for no personal or credit information. At the bottom of the form was the following:

Financial Prerequisites and Statement
of Qualification

In order to qualify, you must meet *at least three* of the following seven
financial prerequisites:

1. *Personal net worth in excess of $450,000.*
2. *Current investment liquidity of $80,000 or more.*
3. *Annual passive income of at least $35,000.*
4. *Annual total income in excess of $100,000.*
5. *Monthly investment activity of $4,000 or more.*

6. *Personal line of credit exceeding $40,000.*
7. *Current commodities holdings of at least $15,000.*

I hereby certify that I have carefully read the seven financial pre-requisites, and that having met three or more of same, I qualify for complimentary attendance — free accommodations, free meals, free ground transportation, etc. I am willing to provide such additional information (including personal and bank references) as you may require.

X_____   _____
   Your Signature   *Date*

X_____   _____
   Spouse's Signature   *Date*

Kennedy was up-front about the object: An example:

> The average cost of over $3,000 per guest is incurred by the War College. This expense, initially underwritten by Western Monetary Consultants, Inc., is more *than repaid* by later earnings on attendees' precious-metals transactions. That's why attendance is strictly limited to those applicants who have the means though not the obligation) to make substantial purchases.

The Beginnings

Western Monetary Consultants was an outgrowth of a newsletter, *Western Monetary Report,* started in the early 1980s by a 40-year-old Montana-born geologist, William J. Kennedy, and his partner, Larry Brokaw, an expert on the Austrian School of Economics. They began sponsoring seminars for investors who paid several hundred dollars to learn the advantages of buying silver; and, oh, by the way, if you're buying silver, what a good deal you can get from Western Monetary Consultants.

Those paid seminars attracted not only high rollers, but also conservative, lunatic fringe, vicious anti-Semites and crazies who believed in aliens from outer space. These loonies were poisoning the atmosphere of the seminars, and Kennedy was not selling much silver to the attendees — which was the purpose of the seminars.

Enter direct marketing consultant Shell Alpert of Alpert, O'Neil, Tigre & Co., out of eastern Pennsylvania. (The partner, Tigre, was

William Kennedy, silver-tongued silver salesman who never quite understood the rudiments of marketing arithmetic.

Alpert's Yorkshire terrier dog.) It was Alpert who dreamed up Direct Marketing War College seminars in 1980, predating the famous Trout-Reiss War Colleges. For client Bill Kennedy, Alpert came up with the U.S. Monetary War College idea — persuading well-to-do investors to attend a free seminar that essentially would be a sales pitch for buying silver. When Alpert finally persuaded Kennedy to pay the airfare for the potential investor *and spouse* — over screaming objections of Kennedy's staff — the business took off like a rocket. Alpert's argument for picking up the airfare:

Don't lead with a clenched fist; lead with an open hand. Do
something nice for people, and they'll do something nice for you.

Once the signed application form came in, a screening process
was instituted to make sure the investor met Kennedy's minimum criteria. Those who did not were turned down.

Let's look at the arithmetic of this offer. The initial $675/M
prospecting offer from Volk generated responses from a high of 2% to
a low of well under 1%, depending on the list. Over the course of 1978,
the Volk package generated 400 to 600 leads a week for a total inquiry
list of 24,000.

Adding up all the money spent on promotion, follow-ups and
credit-checking, the cost-per-attendee was about $1,700. This was *be-
fore* the plane tickets were sent or the four-day junket expenses in San
Diego were picked up — an estimated $3,000 for two persons. So the
total cost-per-potential-buyer could be as high as $4,700.

When a group of investors gathered for the first briefing in the
lush surroundings of the Del Coronado, they looked at each other in
disbelief — and at Kennedy as though he were crazy. But Kennedy —
rough-hewn and charming — was straightforward:

> Look at it from my point of view. The way to get you here
> was to promise you a junket — just like the Las Vegas casinos. But
> there is one great difference. For a casino to make money, you
> have to gamble and lose. For me to make money, you have to in-
> vest — AND WIN!

Of the 1,600 potential buyers, 60 percent bought and 40 percent
did not. There was pressure to buy, but those who chose not to invest
were not treated badly. An estimated five percent were impostors —
people who slipped through the screening process and came along just
for the ride. Average sale was about 10,000 ounces at somewhere between $7 and $8 per ounce — for a total of $70,000 to $80,000.
Kennedy would buy silver at close to spot and add about a 10 percent
commission. Some buyers took physical delivery; others opted for a
system of commercial bank collateral financing, depositing their silver
in a bank vault as collateral against which the bank advanced money to
buy more silver, paying the bank low interest on the collateralized loan.
If the price of silver went up, the investor would be a big winner; if the
price slipped badly, there could be the equivalent of a margin call. War

College attendees bought approximately $110 million in silver. But was the promotion profitable?

Let's go back to the arithmetic

If a War College session had 50 attendees, of which 60 percent — or 30 of them bought an average of $80,000 in silver, that represented gross sales of $2.4 million — with commissions to Kennedy of $240,000. The cost-per-buyer was fixed at $1,700 for a total of $85,000. (50 x $1,700 = $85,000.) Junket expenses for 87 people (50 potential buyers plus 37 spouses) at $1,500 a head = $130,000. Total cost of the seminar: $215,000. Gross margin: $24,500. This would be okay if Kennedy were a one- or two-person operation. But he had 120 people on the payroll back at headquarters in Fort Collins, Colorado. And the price of silver dropped, which meant his attendees were getting margin calls and not buying more silver. We talked to one investor who made 100 percent on his money the first year; instead of taking the money out, he rolled it over and wound up a big loser.

Shell Alpert took issue with our estimate of Kennedy's markup.

> I suspect that the commission percentage you reported — 10 percent — is somewhat low, not only because the average spot price of silver was probably less than $7.20, but also because it doesn't take into account the additional charge (I think it's three percent) assessed when a Western Monetary client sells at "spot."

According to several sources, Bill Kennedy was a terrific guy but an abysmal executive. When he bought *Conservative Digest* from legendary northern Virginia fundraiser Richard Viguerie, he paid $1 million for a 25,000-circulation publication with 6,000 paid subscribers. With the purchase of *Conservative Digest*, Kennedy became a presence in Washington; he engineered private investor briefings at the White House and on the Hill. As his business mushroomed, Kennedy left the day-to-day operations to amateurs. In the words of *Conservative Digest* editor Scott Stanley, "He was backed up by cavemen — troglodytes!"

Shell Alpert was more charitable, claiming that Bill Kennedy held only himself responsible for the mismanagement. He wrote:

> Many of us who know Bill best, and worked with him on a daily basis, understand (albeit belatedly) that Bill was often *inten-*

tionally misled by those whose high-salaried jobs would have been jeopardized. It's a testimony to Bill Kennedy's capacity for friendship, loyalty, appreciation, and his unshakable belief that all his managers shared these virtues. It was not until he'd hired (doubtless too late) a competent chief financial officer, and had actually reviewed the irrefutable evidence, would he allow himself to believe how damagingly he had been betrayed by his "friends."

DM News reported Kennedy's attorney Gary Handy said there were no effective cost controls or cost accounting by management. Alpert elaborated:

> At Western Monetary, all figures concerning the company's profitability — and, except for the "total number of ounces" (in silver) posted at the close of each Monetary War College, gross sales as well — were at all times a very closely held secret. Only Bill Kennedy and, on occasion, his most senior officers were privy to these. Though no hard numbers (other than those directly related to War College promotion and fulfillment) were ever revealed during marketing meetings, the Western Monetary people in attendance often alluded to the fact that so-called "inside" or direct sales were supposed to generate enough CTO (contribution to overhead) to cover most or all of the Ft. Collins Headquarters' expenses.
>
> Insofar as our work (as the company's direct marketing consultant) was concerned, we were given only the information necessary to make strategic, creative and implementive marketing recommendations. For the purposes of response analysis, Western Monetary's operations people at first provided us only with intermediate numbers and certain cost "goals" — and then well over 18 months after we'd been hired. After Arthur Maranjian's appointment as Marketing VP, and at Bill Kennedy's insistence, we finally were furnished with more or less complete Monetary War College numbers. But even these reports were often contradictory and/or confused, and *never* included inside-sales CTO. Nonetheless, despite the fact that our professional purview did not extend to strictly management matters, I began to importune Bill Kennedy (every chance I got) to hire a capable controller or CFO.

In desperation, Kennedy went out to worse and worse lists which meant lower responses and unqualified leads. Merging and de-duping were sloppy; when investors received several invitations in the same mail, it blew the mystique and sense of exclusivity.

Sandy Clark, in his splendid seminar on direct marketing numbers, says "You can't lose money when you have an 11-time markup. If you can pay $5 for your product and sell it for $55, you will not lose money." Kennedy's markup was 10 percent — not 11 times — with 90 percent of his margin going for sales expenses. That left one percent for Kennedy.

According to broker Robert Chapman of Mutual Securities, Westlake Village, California — many of whose clients were involved in the Kennedy deal — the market for precious metals had been "burned out" since 1985. The aggressive selling tactics of Robert White (of *The Duck Book*), James U. Blanchard and Howard Ruff creamed the metals market. For the most part, hard money people, Chapman said, are fundamentalist Christian conservatives. "Reagan turned out not to be a conservative, but a wild man. With Iranscam . . . the Market Crash . . . the Jim Bakker/Jimmy Swaggert/Oral Robert debacles — all the fundamental values of these people crashed. Silver went down, and the banks made margin calls." When it was pointed out that Kennedy had 120 people on staff, Chapman said, "That's crazy! I do tens of millions a year with a staff of 10!"

By May of 1988, Western Monetary Consultants filed for bankruptcy under Chapter 11. While 1987 sales amounted to $163 million, it listed assets of $4 million and debts of $10 million. An exodus of top executives took place; none would talk to the the press. Kennedy's houses, cars and everything else went on the auction block. In an effort to satisfy creditors, *Conservative Digest* was sold. According to *DM News*, an ugly squabble over rights to the lists broke out between Western Monetary Consultants and Carnegie Marketing Associates of Los Angeles, who were reportedly owed $50,000. Of the 20 creditors, Alpert, O'Neil, Tigre was owed $60,000. Kurt Volk — who mailed an estimated 3+ million pieces — was the largest creditor.

Amazingly, many people firmly believed in Kennedy Redux. Even under Chapter 11, there was another War College with several million in sales. In the words of *Conservative Digest*'s Scott Stanley:

> When other guys would take Chapter 7 and say, "too bad, folks," Kennedy went Chapter 11. I think he'll turn it around. *The seminars were good.*

When asked if he would call it a case of mismanagement, Stanley snapped: "Put it this way, the guy did $163 million in sales in 1987 and is now in Chapter 11. What would you call it?"

Scott Stanley's rhetorical question seemed to sum up what happened: for over a year, Kennedy's people thought they were taking in millions when, in reality, they were taking in 10 percent of that. And nobody had the smarts — or the guts — to tell the emperor he wasn't wearing any clothes.

Shell Alpert suggested that Kennedy might have survived.

> If Bill Kennedy was able to continue doing his Monetary War Colleges, which (with constant refinement) had become increasingly successful, the outlook would be much brighter. But, since his War Colleges could no longer be financed, Bill would have to say that "the operation was a success, but the patient died."

Kennedy Redux?

In 1989, Kennedy was back in the mail with offers to attend his War College at the Del Coronado. This time, the mailing — postmarked 8 February 1989 — was a demure, beautifully produced little 4-1/2" × 6-1/2" invitation. No letter was included; rather it was loaded with a group of small pieces, such as: "What You Should Know About the U.S. Monetary War College and Investor Clinic" and "What previous graduates have to say about the U.S. Monetary War College and Investor Clinic."

Included were a bunch of testimonials from presumably happy investors. The major difference in Kennedy's offer: An investor had to buy silver before expenses were picked up. Even though Kennedy had wised up about giving away freebies to total strangers, it was obvious he had gone a bit bonkers, as evidenced by this "manifesto" on the back of one of the elements in the mailing:

> *"War is an apt metaphor*
> *for the never-ending*
> *fierce struggle — buyers*
> *pitted against sellers,*
> *and vice versa — which*
> *occurs in that dangerous*
> *place we call the 'market.'*
> *Still, it must be remembered*
> *that more investors are injured*

> *by their own ignorance*
> *than by others' connivance.*
> *Thus most fatalities*
> *of the free market result*
> *from suicide, not homicide!"*
> — William R. Kennedy, Jr.
> Founder and Director
> U.S. Monetary War
> College and Investor Clinic

On March 3, 1989, W.W. "Chip" Wood of Soundview Publications wrote me:

> I received this letter last week from the bankrupt bullion bully, William R. Kennedy Jr. Read the first 2-1/2 paragraphs; remember he *misspent* millions of dollars of client funds (even sending some a margin call on bullion he never bought for them!); and then tell me if you don't agree. Now, here's a *real* sleaze-master at work.

Enclosed was the following:

Western Monetary Consultants Bulletin

Dear Western Monetary Client,

Since 1979 I have provided political and economic advice to such leaders as Ronald Reagan, George Bush, and South African and Middle East government officials. I have been instrumental in providing financial support to the Freedom Fighters of Central America to assist in the battle against Communism. My greatest impact, however, has been to the investors in precious metals. Western Monetary Consultants clients annually purchase 30-50% of all investment silver and approximately 50% of all investment platinum.

Let me get right to the point of this letter.

I am stating this information not to blow my own horn . . . THESE ARE THE FACTS! I believe you should be aware of the impact my advice carries. What does this mean to you, as an investor? It means that the advice you receive from William R. Kennedy and his advisory staff at Western Monetary Consultants does and will have a very significant impact on the precious metals marketplace.

This letter distinguishes you as one we have chosen to receive our investment advice on an extremely select basis. You have received this mailing because you are both a serious investor in precious metals and are also familiar with doing business with Western Monetary Consultants. I've never seen an investment potential like the one I'm able to reveal to you now.

The information we have for you will require your immediate response and immediate action. The strategy will only be provided by calling:

1-800-544-5204

Your response will be met by a brief questioning to determine that you are not a competitor, and that you are in a position to take advantage of our advice.

This is a very limited window of opportunity; I anticipate the demand to strip away this opportunity almost immediately.

We have become very protective of our advice and wish to benefit <u>our</u> <u>clients</u> <u>first</u> . . . we will let our competitors find out the hard way — by watching.

Sincerely,
/s/ [Unreadable scrawl]
William R. Kennedy, Jr.
President

According to Arthur Maranjian and Shell Alpert, Kennedy's original partner Larry Brokaw and two others worked with the FBI to nail Kennedy in return for reduced jail sentences. Kennedy himself was sentenced to 16 years before parole in Federal prison for securities fraud; he served time at Leavenworth and is now in Lompoc. The other 14 Western Monetary Consultants executives who were indicted got off scot-free.

With a wife and three children (one of whom is retarded), Kennedy's tale is terribly sad.

Points for Marketers to Consider

1.

Bill Kennedy got inside the heads of his prospects and played to two key copy drivers: greed and greed.

Greed for a free junket to San Diego.

Greed at the possibility of instant riches in silver.

But, he wasn't a true Method Marketer.

It's amazing that with an offer of this power that his highest response was 2 percent. Three possible reasons: (1) He went to low-end lists where the names could not begin to have three or more of his financial prerequisites; (2) Consumers are generally savvy enough to know that if a deal sounds too good to be true, it is; (3); Consumers are generally savvy enough to know that if someone is offering them a free trip worth several thousand dollars, that obscene pressures would be put on them to spend tens of thousands of dollars.

In other words, he did not become his prospects and think through the possible objections and then overcome them in his promotion.

2.

Direct marketing is the diamond-hard and precise offspring of marketing, general advertising, promotion, POP, sales, advertising and public relations. It is the only discipline that is entirely accountable and measurable to within tenths and hundredths of a percent. It is a business of arithmetic, and clearly, no one in the Kennedy organization knew direct marketing arithmetic. Consultant Shell Alpert has been in the business for years and knows his arithmetic; but his claim was that Kennedy and his people never told him the real numbers.

For Alpert to give decent advice and create a profitable marketing plan, he had to know the cost of goods sold. In other words, if Kennedy sold an ounce of silver to an investor, how much did the silver cost — delivered — and what was left over for Kennedy? You then create best-, probable- and worst-case scenarios for attendance and sales at a War College session and work the arithmetic backward through the entire sales process to the lead-generation piece. Only then, can you come up with an offer.

An Analogous Situation

Seattle agency head Bob Hacker once had a client selling million-dollar homes in the desert outside Las Vegas. The selling cycle required 23 separate steps, starting with the lead-generating piece that brought the initial inquiry. The 23rd step: closing on the home.

It has been said that the measure of a great chess player is how many moves ahead he can think. IBM's Deep Blue computer finally beat Gary Kasparov because it could think thousands of moves ahead to Kasparov's 10 or 12. Same thing with marketing. Every one of Hacker's 23 steps had to be thought through — both in terms of the cost of the mailing effort and the message itself. If the cost-per-thousand of the original lead generation piece was too high, it would kill the profitability of the entire program. Other questions to deal with: what was said at each communications point? what information was given out when? when would a telemarketing call first be used? when would price be introduced? when would an invitation be extended to visit the development? what would the sales representative on site say to close the deal?

Hacker's premise: The marketing department must spend a lot of quality time on site with the sales rep understanding the motivators, the objections, the emotional drivers that brought the person to that point. Then you work backwards through the various steps.

With direct marketing — where the object is to consummate a sale as a result of a mailing or telephone call — the more you tell, the more you sell. In lead generation, the *less you tell, the more you sell.* Your object is to tweak the person's interest, yet not blab so much that it gives a reason to say no. Book-of-the-Month Club founder Maxwell Sackheim said about offers:

> Make it easer to say yes than to say no.

At the same time, the marketer has to anticipate what the objections will be and at what point they will be raised so they can be overcome; otherwise, the process will be derailed.

Clearly, none of this was done by Western Monetary Consultants. The War Colleges were shoot-from-the-lip propositions by arrogant men operating in the unbridled tradition of the Colorado silver barons of old: Leadville Johnny Brown and Horace and Baby Doe Tabor.

3.

Kennedy's list selection process was simply appalling. When I first wrote about Bill Kennedy's mailing back in May, 1988, I received a hot note from Janie Thompson of Carnegie Marketing Associates:

> . . . I would like you to clarify something in your May issue. Carnegie Marketing did the majority of list brokering for Western Monetary Consultants. We never ordered THE DUCK BOOK or SELECT INFORMATION EXCHANGE.

Janie Thompson and I had two long phone conversations regarding the mailings to "Duckworth" Hatch and "Sy" Hatch which were my *Duck Book* and Select Information Exchange (SIE) code names. After looking up the keys, Thompson determined that the mailing to Duckworth was from a list called "Millionaire's Manual" which was out of Robert White's *Duck Book* organization. "Sy" Hatch was a subscriber" to a gold and silver newsletter. Only I was never a bona fide subscriber.

A couple of years earlier, I had signed up with the Select Information Exchange for a bunch of trial subscriptions to financial advisories — $50 for 80 newsletters, or something like that. My agenda: to get the newsletters and mailings for my archive of direct mail. Under the system, SIE kept the money and gave my name to each of the publishers who, in turn, put me on as a short-term trial subscriber; later, they would then try to convert me. I never bought any of the newsletters. But for list rental purposes, I was lumped in with the active subscribers — high-rolling gold and silver speculators who paid hundreds of dollars a year for a subscription; a renter paid the same for my name as for an active, paying subscriber.

This is one of the many ways list owners screw over list renters. It's the same amoral code that permits magazines — for advertising rate base and list rental purposes — to call active subscribers, those who came in on the cheap, Publishers Clearing House and American Family Publishers (Dick Clark and Ed McMahon) Sweepstakes, when, in fact, they are people who want to win the $10 million prize and subscribe because they think it will help their chances of winning.

Here is one more example of why it is imperative to spend time digging deep into *exactly* where the names on a list you rent come from.

In renting lists, the product or service being delivered is less important than exhaustive research to discover the original source of the name — the mailing or telephone call or TV commercial that the person responded to.

Before you test a list, demand to see the mailing package and offers the names on those data cards responded to. Are they anything like what you are sending? Next, ask your broker who else mailed that list and, more important, who went back to that list for a rollout after the test. *Ask to see those mailing packages* as well. Who mails to which list is the most important — and highly secret — information in all of direct marketing. List owners will quietly tell list brokers, who will relay the information to their clients. This is done through networking and is almost never made public. Occasionally, you'll see an ad or mailing that deals with this incredibly sensitive area; but the information is often blind. (e.g., "This list has been used successfully by computer magazines, software companies, high-tech catalogs.")

In other words, as PCS Mailing Lists & Technologies president Jim Healy decrees: "It is imperative to know the original source of the name." If your broker can't — or won't — get you list-usage information, find a list broker who will.

For example, John Dough, an unsophisticated marketer with a new sports product may think his prime universe of potential buyers is *Sports Illustrated* readers. He will go out and buy a copy of the magazine and get from a list broker the *Sports Illustrated* datacard, which reveals the number of active and lapsed subscribers, the unit of sale (how much they spent), perhaps some demographics and the fact that, say, 80 percent were "mail sold."

This is the key. Mail-responsive subscribers are generally better (and more expensive to rent) than compiled lists, because the people on those lists have demonstrated that they buy by mail — subscribe to a magazine, buy merchandise from a catalog or books from a book club, etc.

However, a huge percentage of the *Sports Illustrated* "mail sold" subscribers came in from a sweepstakes offer. Many of the subscribers who buy the magazine do so only because they believe (erroneously) that if they purchase something, they have a better chance of winning the $10 million prize.

Will these *Sports Illustrated* sweeps buyers be interested in the new sports product being offered by John Dough? Not bloody likely, unless his mailing package is a sweepstakes offer — or at least *looks like* a sweeps offer.

This isn't to say that John Dough shouldn't test the *Sports Illustrated* list. But on his list test order he should specify: "**NON-sweeps**; mail-sold subscribers and renewers only." At the same time he might want to test 5,000 sweeps-sold actives and another 5,000 that were TV sold. But the various test cells should be kept separate with the results recorded separately.

4.

What should Kennedy have done to qualify candidates? Of the 1,600 potential buyers, 60 percent bought silver and 40 percent did not. In addition, approximately five percent were "impostors" — people who flatly failed to meet Kennedy's financial prerequisites and were not caught in the screening process. Yes, presumably some screening was done; but when 40 percent of those invited failed to buy, screening was obviously inadequate.

Usually, where the offer is for several thousand dollars in services and no commitment, the response form would request at least *some* financial information, such as bank accounts, credit cards, etc. Although forcing a respondent to supply personal information of this nature would cut down up-front response, presumably, the respondents would be more highly qualified.

5.

How were Kennedy's people compensated? Shell Alpert suggested that "Bill was often *intentionally* misled by those whose high-salaried jobs would have been jeopardized." Isn't it an error to compensate people with straight salaries, thereby giving them no real incentive to do better and better or to tell the truth to management when things may be going south? It costs six times as much to acquire a new customer than it does to keep an existing customer happy; what's more, in direct marketing, a customer often doesn't become profitable until year two or three. Many companies give hefty commissions on new business and then smaller commissions on ongoing sales. Shouldn't this be reversed? Shouldn't higher commission be paid on profitable business? Doesn't this give those on commission the incentive to make sure the operation is healthy and good customers are happy? Otherwise, aren't they tempted to neglect the good, profitable ongoing business in the scramble for high commissions on new business?

How are your people compensated? Is it to their benefit to tell management when things are going haywire? Or does it make sense for them to try to cover up problems?

16

NBC

Listen to the Murmur

> We're not inventing direct response marketing here. But the
> networks have looked down their noses at it before . . . There is an
> untapped opportunity for networks in transactions. This is about
> the future.
>
> — Don Ohlmeyer
> President, West Coast Division, NBC

According to *The New York Times* of May 1, 1998, in a moment of in-
spiration — or was it madness? — NBC withheld two 30-second commercials from advertisers and ran a promotion offering for sale videocassettes of *Merlin*, the mini-series viewers had just seen.

The result: over 100,000 videocassettes were sold.

The *Times* reported that the networks have shied off from offering videos of programming, because transactional business was associated with low-priced items like Veg-o-matic and ginsu knives. "We've
been trying to get away from cluttering up the air with too much
junk," said one television executive.

Junk?

Making an offer and asking for an order is junk?

Would that unnamed executive welcome a debate on what is —
and what is not — junk television?

To paraphrase Dwight Eisenhower's farewell broadcast, January
17, 1961:

> We must guard against the acquisition of unwarranted influence,
> whether sought or unsought, by an inside-the-Beltway media-po-
> litical complex.

Look at Washington. For months, tight-lipped, squinty-eyed, self-righteous politicians and media doyens on television and in print flailed Bill and Hillary Clinton for an avalanche of misdeeds: Whitewater, Filegate, Travelgate, "lost" Rose law firm billing records, Web, the McDougals, Monica, Kathleen, Gennifer, etc.

At the same time, these same smug elected officials and talking heads regularly excoriated the American people for our lax morality, insensitivity and general malaise in giving Clinton high marks for job performance.

The point is, these media-political complex members are all talking to themselves; they don't have a clue what makes the average person tick.

Suddenly Don Ohlmeyer from outside the Beltway had a major epiphany; it seems he discovered truth in the words of my first mentor, Franklin Watts:

> People love to be sold.

Duh.

My advice to the media-political complex is to heed Axel Andersson's rule for everyone in marketing and direct marketing:

> Take the streetcar or bus to work.

In other words, get out of the limo and start mixing with the folks you are pledged to serve.

Axel Andersson is unique. Happiness to Andersson is being surrounded by direct mail. Over the past 10 years, I have given Axel all our leftover direct mail — duplicates, merges, stuff not cataloged in the *Who's Mailing What!* His collection is so huge that he bought the house next door in Palm Coast, Florida, specifically to harbor his vast archive. Happiness to Axel is to fly to Philadelphia and hole up in the Clarion Suites, where he will analyze some 15 or more big cardboard boxes of direct mail that will have been carted over to the Clarion the day before.

Why the Clarion Suites — emphatically non-deluxe lodgings in in the middle of Chinatown?

> "Certainly I could stay at three-star hotel," Andersson says.
> "But first of all, I get a suite with a living room where I work and

a bedroom where I sleep. Secondly, the price is very reasonable. And thirdly, I see real people! At the Marriott or the Four Seasons, I would be among people just like me. I see those people everywhere. You can't learn anything from them!"

When Axel was running his hugely successful home study school in Hamburg, Germany, he hired one of his students to come work for him. The young man had graduated from two courses given by the Axel Andersson Akademy and was satisfied and grateful for this knowledge. The young man sat in the office next door to the president; and every time Axel entered or left his office, he had to pass this young man.

"I wanted to actually see one of my customers every day," Andersson says. "I wanted to have him constantly in my mind when I wrote an ad or a letter or talked to students on the phone."

Andersson also hired a professor at the local university as a consultant. As he said puckishly:

> Before I would test a new ad, I would run it by my former student and also give it to the professor for her reaction.
> If the student liked it, I would go with it.
> If the professor liked it, I would change it.

Of course, neither the former student nor the professor knew about the other or the real reason why they were hired.

As Don Jackson wrote in *2,239 Tested Secrets for Direct Marketing Success:*

> Listen to the murmur of your market. Create feedback loops in your database environment so that you can record what your customers and prospects are saying about your products, your service, your company, and your competition. There is no more valuable source of information.

17

The Eastwood Company

Curt Strohacker:
He Turned a Hobby into a Business

At the Eastwood Company, work is play and the customer is the real boss.

By the time he was 18, Curt Strohacker had owned 46 automobiles. One at a time.

The exception was a brief period when he owned four Austin-Healeys. Of course, in Chicago in 1963 you could buy a nine-year-old Chevy for $50, so buying and selling cars was a teenage rite of passage. Spend $100 and you had the wheels of a maharajah. This was possible because nobody took insurance very seriously. If you got into trouble, the neighborhood cop would confiscate your ignition keys and drive you home. Strohacker admits, "I never had car insurance until I was in college." He adds wistfully, "Things were different then."

Today, Curt Strohacker is president of The Eastwood Company. He mails a million catalogs to shoppers whose passion is either restoring old cars or collecting limited edition miniatures — cars, trucks, fire engines, military vehicles, airplanes and outrageous roadside buildings. His domain: a cramped corner office overlooking Route 30 in the Philadelphia suburb of Malvern, where he presides over 50,000-square feet of modern offices, a spotless warehouse containing more than 2,000 items and a retail store guaranteed to send do-it-yourselfers and toy collectors into orbit.

The Beginnings

From 1970 to 1982, Strohacker was an industrial salesman for products ranging from steel to fire-fighting equipment. His last job was with 3M, where he called on every imaginable kind of industry in the Philadelphia environs, from potato chip factories to U.S. Steel.

In his travels he learned about machinery: how things were made and how to repair them. When one of his customers who sold buffing wheels and compounds decided to call it quits, Strohacker felt he could make a go of it. In 1978 he invested $500 to form The Eastwood Company, taking the maiden name of his wife's grandmother. He printed an eight-page, black-and-white catalog at a quick printer in West Chester and tested two markets: antiques (the brass candlesticks crowd) and antique cars. In addition, he ran a space ad in *Hemmings Motor News* which had 200,000 readers. He quickly found car restorers were his market. The first order was for $170, and he was on his way. Because Strohacker wanted to keep his sideline business separate from 3M, he signed the letter in his catalog — and all other Eastwood correspondence — as "Fred Bailey."

One fascinating aspect of Strohacker's approach to business: long-term loyalty that goes both ways. Framed in his office is the company's first ad, its first catalog and the first order. That first buyer — White Post Supply, now one of the leading restoration shops in America — is still a customer. Products from the first catalog are still carried, the company still uses its first vendor and an Eastwood ad has appeared in virtually every issue of *Hemmings* since 1978.

How did that first ad pull? Strohacker yanks a ring binder off the shelf and tells you the precise cost per order.

As the business grew, he rented an office vestibule and put up shelving. Merchandise was delivered and stored there. He would take items home, where he processed and packed orders in his basement; finished orders were then brought back to his little rented vestibule for next-day pickups by UPS.

While he worked at 3M, Strohacker's wife and father-in-law took phone orders from 9 a.m. to 1 p.m. In the afternoon, an answering service kicked in. His customer list was typed so it could be reproduced on 33-up Avery® labels. Eventually he went to a service bureau. In 1979 a toll-free number was introduced; the 800 service went out of business the day the catalog dropped.

By the early 1980s, revenues had reached $400,000. He was working 40 hours a week for 3M and more than that for Eastwood, plus he had a wife and small baby. His wife ordered him to fish or cut bait; in 1983 the 3M umbilical cord was cut and Strohacker went on his own. "3M couldn't understand it," he recalls. "I was making a lot of money for them."

The First Employees

About that time, a young college graduate named Jim Shulman came looking for a job. Rail thin, with black hair, horn-rimmed glasses and an owlish mien, Shulman sported a degree in history and a nascent career that ranged from selling toilet cleaning chemicals to sets of china on the phone. "I could fog a mirror, type and file," says Shulman. "I was alive, and I showed up."

Pennsylvania was the ideal venue for Strohacker's fledgling business. It has the highest number of registered antique car owners in the United States; the Antique Automobile Collectors Association (AACA) was founded there in 1935 with headquarters in Hershey. As a result, two major antique auto shows are held annually — in Hershey and Carlisle, both prime events at which to move merchandise. However, Strohacker and Shulman needed transportation. Enter Brett Snyder, who waited tables at a Chinese restaurant in nearby Devon. For his sideline business of peddling used books and magazines, Snyder had a van with bald tires and a rocky transmission. If Eastwood fixed the transmission and bought new tires, Strohacker wanted to know, would Snyder contribute his van to help at car shows? The first of many symbiotic relationships was formed; at that year's Carlisle show, the van opened for business with Strohacker and Shulman purveying auto restoration equipment and Snyder selling old copies of *Life*.

Today, Snyder is operations manager; Shulman advanced to become Eastwood's director of new business development before going off on his own as a consultant in 1997.

A Company of Car Nuts

When he joined the company, Shulman was not into cars. Instead, he was an avid collector of fountain pens, wind-up Victrolas and 78 rpm phonograph records. For years, his pride and joy was the tackiest

American automobile ever, one of just 1,500 1962 Chrysler Imperial LeBarrons designed by Virgil Exner. Shulman's was metallic baby blue with white leather interior, free-standing headlamps, giant fins, rocket tail lights, square steering wheel, a 413 cu. in. V-8 engine that develops 350 horsepower and more gewgaws and chrome per square inch than any American car ever built. Shulman's vanity plate proclaimed: THE MERM, a tribute to Stanley Kramer's 1963 comedy, *It's a Mad, Mad, Mad, Mad World.* In a race scene, Ethel Merman whacks Milton Berle, who is driving this very model, and shouts, "We're in the Imperial! Why are we last?"

Strohacker, who has a weakness for little English station wagons, owns a Morris, a 1967 Austin Mini-Countryman and an Austin-Healey sports car. Product Manager Henry Hauptfuhrer has spent the past 20 years (on and off) restoring the 1960 MGA of his boyhood. Ask Marketing Director Kaye Broom what she drives, and she'll tell you a Toyota Camry. "Now ask me what I own," she suggests.

"What so you own?"

"A 1950 Cadillac, a '78 Trans Am and a '64 Ford F-100 Pickup," she replies. "Since I was a little girl, I have always loved speed."

Manager of Resources Charlie Sonneborn owns 15 collector cars, including a 1941 Lincoln Continental Cabriolet, the same model driven by Bette Davis in *Whatever Happened to Baby Jane?* Sonneborn's vanity plate: BABYJANE, naturally.

About 80 percent of Eastwood associates — men and women alike — are car enthusiasts; Strohacker would like it to be 99 percent. "The inmates are in charge of the asylum," Shulman said.

Listening to the Customer

When he started Eastwood, the most popular item was a restoration kit Strohacker designed — three buffs, three compounds and an instruction sheet. But the product that put Eastwood on the map was a $32.95 spot welder that could attach to any AC arc welder, enabling the user to do factory quality work; professional machines at that time were selling for $300 to $400. It is still a top-seller, although the price tag is now $50.

With the exception of some paints, Eastwood's merchandise is not car- or model-specific; tools are generic and the merchandise is

Curt Strohacker proudly shows off one of his grand obsessions, a vintage British mini.

skewed toward metal fabrication, welding, sandblasting, glass repair, interior care, rust prevention, painting and detailing.

While the company is strictly a marketing operation that does no manufacturing, Strohacker and his team are constantly on the prowl for new products as well as wide open to suggestions on how existing products can be modified or new ones created.

An example: Based on input from serious car restorers, Eastwood's research and testing team came up with a design for a sandblast cabinet that can fit anywhere and will travel flat, thus saving the customer a small fortune in shipping charges. It is now being manufactured exclusively for Eastwood, which owns the patent.

The Call Center

Fully 75 percent of Eastwood's associates are required to spend a minimum of five hours a month in the inbound telemarketing facility on the ground floor. For the new hires, call-center certification is the first order of business — learning how to talk to customers and then upsell. "I can't make money selling a $4.95 can of paint," says Hauptfuhrer.

So what happens when a customer orders a $4.95 can of paint? The telephone sales representative (TSR) asks what the person is working on. Chances are Eastwood has the additional tools and supplies needed for that particular job and any related tasks. The upsell helps out the customer as well as turns an unprofitable sale into a money-maker. Of course, car restorers love to talk about what they are doing, and the TSRs have to resist the temptation to chat.

What happens if the question is too technical? In 1986, it was determined that too many people were calling the order desk with technical questions, so Eastwood set up a separate help line where highly trained technical people can talk a customer through a difficult restoration problem. Complicated questions are bounced over the the help line; while advice from the help line is free, TSRs are fully trained in selling — and upselling. No one is exempt from duty in the call center; Strohacker himself can frequently be found with a headset, looking intently at a computer screen.

Until 1998, if an inbound overload occurred — such as the result of a television commercial — the word was quickly spread and qualified associates tore down to the call center to help out. During the great blizzard of 1996, 10 associates camped out in the office for three days so phones would be attended. "Companies spend thousands of dollars on corporate bonding and team-building seminars," says Kaye Broom. "Here, all it takes is a good snowstorm."

Plus, as Broom suggests, call center duty blurs the difference between managers and workers that contributes to Strohacker's philosophy of team building.

Brooksmith Associates (later BSA, then Acxiom, then MorTech, which it is today) designed Eastwood's original telemarketing software in 1983 under the direction of Jim Shulman. "You have a college degree," Strohacker said to Shulman. "You're in charge of the computer."

In those days, Eastwood was getting an average of 30 orders a day; today, the daily tally can be in excess of 1,000.

In 1998, the MorTech system became operative throughout the

building; associates are now able to take orders right at their desks rather than going through what Broom called "stair aerobics" to rush to the call center during an overload situation.

The Ultimate Customer Contact: Auto Shows

The most important interaction with customers occurs at the annual convocations of auto enthusiasts. Just as hunters go hunting, some 50,000 autoholics converge on central Pennsylvania for their yearly fixes.

Returning to their roots, the Eastwood crew loads up a giant tractor trailer with at least one of every item in the catalog and sets up shop in a 40' x 60' tent that is completely electrified, enabling them to demonstrate everything from stitch welders to the new sandblast cabinet. Overhead, a giant helium-filled blimp proclaims Eastwood's presence. The associates work like dogs from seven to seven, go off for a good dinner and start all over again the next morning. They sell in 110-degree heat as well as ankle-deep in mud. In 1994, the tent at the Carlisle show collapsed under the weight of a spring snow. "The tent company came and fixed it," Strohacker recalls. "We were back in business in two hours."

"At shows, we reach different people than those who buy by mail," Shulman explained.

> Like Brigadoon — the mythical Scottish town that comes alive one day every century — these people come out of the muck every year, often clutching a tattered catalog they picked up at last year's show. Sure as hell somebody will come back with a half-used can of paint he bought last year complaining it wasn't right. We apologize profusely, give him a new can of paint and chuck the old one in the garbage.

The eight to 10 shows a year they attend represent a minuscule percentage of the overall business; Shulman called it "Kamikaze Retail." But the face-to-face contact with customers keeps the company vital and supplies it with the ideas needed to keep coming up with new products.

For example, an entire subculture of auto restoration is the 50,000 members of the National Street Rod Association (NSRA) —

fanatics who acquire pre-1948 vehicles and modify them with all kinds of garish accessories and paint schemes. These folks have their own special needs, and Eastwood means to serve them.

Shulman himself attended about 40 auto shows a year and scheduled his vacations around these events. As a result of his travels, he discovered a trend: an upsurge in interest in '70s cars. This trend has been mirrored in the kinds of products being ordered by Eastwood customers.

Eastwood Automobila

In 1989 Strohacker got it into his head to restore a 1951 GMC panel truck to mint condition and emblazon it with the Eastwood logo for use as corporate signage — much like Budweiser's Clydesdale team and wagon. Restoration took far more time and a lot more money than anticipated. Could they turn the disadvantage into an advantage?

Ertl, a manufacturer of collectibles, was selling a 1:43 unpainted scale model of the very same panel truck with a slot in the roof for use as a bank. Eastwood ordered 2,500 replicas of the truck painted with the Eastwood logo, which it then offered in the catalog for $15.95. It was an immediate sellout. A second edition of 5,000 sold out the following year. Suddenly Strohacker found himself in the limited edition collectibles business with a catalog he titled *Eastwood Automobila;* it catered to a completely different audience — with merchandise at a far lower price point — than Franklin Mint or Danbury Mint.

Recent developments in the model collectible business have not been kind to *Automobilia*. Ertl and others decided that since they manufactured the unpainted scale models for others to decorate and sell, it, too, could paint up its blanks and sell them. In effect — and in actuality — Ertl went into direct competition with its own customers. Not only that, Ertl is creating infinite numbers of these little models, thus blowing the whole concept of limited editions out of the water.

The Sears Connection

In 1994, Strohacker saw a photograph of Sears Direct Marketing President Vachel Pennebaker standing next to a vintage MG, and called him cold. The result: a symbiotic, highly profitable relationship in which the Eastwood catalog is given a Sears Shop-at-Home Service cover and mailed to Sears buyers. Yes, Sears makes a lot more money than if it simply rented its list to Strohacker (which it wouldn't); but results are higher when a Sears book goes to a Sears customer who can use a Sears charge card. From Strohacker's point of view, he is reaching a vast, virgin universe of car tinkerers outside the mainstream; not members of antique auto clubs or associations, not readers of *Hemmings Motor News,* but those who are restoring cars.

For Eastwood, the Sears Shop-at-Home connection was an eye-opener. Quality standards are high as Sears requires all suppliers and partners to adhere to the letter of the law because of its fluorescent profile. As a result, Sears worked with Eastwood to help improve everything from the accuracy of catalog descriptions to customer service. Many Sears suggestions have been incorporated into Eastwood's own catalog. Although the Eastwood catalog does not offer vises, its vise mount metal brake is shown gripped by a Craftsman vise — as a tip o' the hat to Sears.

The Egalitarian Corporate Culture

People who work at Eastwood are "associates" rather than employees. Instead of top-down management, teams have been created. On walls throughout the company, interspersed with giant prints of great old automobiles, are posters that proclaim: TEAM (Together-Everyone-Achieves-More). Only Strohacker and Shulman had private offices, and Shulman's was demolished. Freestanding partitions now separate the associates' work spaces; like call-center duty, this tends to blur the difference between managers and workers. "It's tough," admits Strohacker. "Some people don't want to be on teams. They want to be told what to do. I've got to change that."

Where is Eastwood headed? Does Strohacker have a master plan?

"I've more than fulfilled my personal needs," he says. "No, I have no master plan. Let's just see what evolves over the next few years."

He added: "It's hard to tell sometimes whether we're working or just having fun."

Points for Marketers to Consider

1.

Curt Strohacker is a textbook Method Marketer. He doesn't have to get inside the head and under the skin of his customer. *He is his own customer.* If Strohacker had not started the Eastwood Company, as a restorer of vintage automobiles he certainly would have been an avid buyer of its products (or the products of some other company that would have filled the niche Eastwood discovered).

2.

Because Strohacker is his own customer — and because the majority of his associates are car aficionados and, therefore, customers — the entire company is structured from the customer's point of view. Consider:

- The first exercise for any new employee is to become call-center certified. This means weeks of learning the various product lines, being able to communicate knowledgeably with technically oriented customers and — above all — learning the art of upselling. This means turning an unprofitable $4.95 order into a highly profitable $49.95 order.
- Strohacker has a customer service department — an elite cadre of phone representatives who can listen to a customer's concerns or problems on a free help line and offer assistance on the phone. These are not order takers; these are experts in automobile restoration.

3.

Eastwood engenders absolute trust in its customers. Remember Jim Shulman's description of kamikaze marketing at the car shows and how the company will replace a year-old, half-used can of paint gratis.

This is reminiscent of L.L. Bean, who once said:

> I never consider a sale complete until the merchandise has worn out and the customer is satisfied.

Or my first boss and mentor, publisher Franklin Watts:

Dealing with a customer is like making love to a widow; you can't overdo it.

4.

As well as call-center duty, Strohacker and his associates attend vintage automobile shows for three purposes: to generate a presence, to make sales and to have face-to-face contact with customers, which keeps the company vital and supplies it with the ideas needed to keep coming up with new products.

18

Honda Motor Company

Turning a Negative into a Positive

Always convert a disadvantage into an advantage.
—Elsworth Howell

To the Ralph Naders and yellow journalists of the world, the 1995 recall of 8.8 million cars of 11 manufacturers for defective seat belts was a glorious event — a victory for consumerism and fodder for the news industry. According to *The Wall Street Journal*:

> Spokesmen for the Honda Motor Company and Nissan, the two companies with the largest number of cars affected, denied that their subsidiaries in the United States would conduct recalls, in which all the cars must be repaired. Rather, they will conduct "voluntary service campaigns," in which letters about the problem will be sent to car owners and repairs will be made only if consumers request them.

Put an American direct marketer in charge, and you'd see the biggest quick spurt of new car sales since the end of World War II. Here was an absolutely gorgeous opportunity to get inside the head and under the skin of 8.8 million dispirited owners of grungy old rattletraps and give them the opportunity to smell the inside of a new car. The Message:

> This dumb thing has happened. Not serious. No deaths and no injuries. And we certainly want to replace your seat belt fasteners at no charge. Just make an appointment with our service department to have the job done.
> Meanwhile, in the short time it takes to do the job, you and your family are invited to enjoy a loaner — a stunning new

Honda XZ-123 with its sporty lines, power plant for driving pleasure you never dreamed possible and magnificent new surround-
sound CD player. What's more, you'll receive a Gloria Estefan CD
— our way of saying "thank you" for coming in.

And, by the way, if you love the new Honda XZ-123, here's a
cash-back certificate worth $1,000 towards its purchase. Make
your best deal with the representative — including the trade-in
— and, when it's finalized, pull out this certificate, and it's as
good as $1,000 cash in your pocket.

Why conduct a "voluntary service campaign?" Fire the PR people
and put a marketer in charge who knows how to turn a disadvantage
into an advantage!

19

The Oreck Corporation

David Oreck:
The Most Famous Voice in America

He surrounds the country with his message

Anyone who listens to the radio — just about any radio, any station, any time of day — is familiar with David Oreck's voice and his offer for you to take the "Oreck Challenge" for 15 days free. Since he got into broadcast direct response in 1993, he believes he has become the second largest advertiser on the CBS Radio Network. Whether you listen to Rush, Dr. Laura, Dr. Joy or any of hundreds of programs on thousands of stations, you've likely heard David Oreck's radio commercials.

"Shoes don't ruin carpets; dirt does . . . "

"Hi, I'm David Oreck. And I'm proud that over one million of my Oreck XL vacuum cleaners are . . . "

On background, Oreck revealed how many individual radio commercials he would be running in 1997; let's just say the number was well into the millions. Surely his is the second most famous voice in America. On Madison Avenue, casting directors are actively looking for voices like Oreck's.

Rewriting the Book on Direct Marketing

Attend any direct marketing conference, consult with any direct marketing consultant, read any book on the subject, and you'll be told:
• 15- and 30-second direct response radio spots don't work

• If a product is being offered at retail and you try to market it direct, you'll wreck your retail distribution network.

• "Self-mailers don't work and are not worth testing," avowed the late guru Dick Benson.

In the case of Oreck Corporation, wrong, wrong and wrong again. David Oreck is a revolutionary who is knocking conventional direct marketing wisdom — and know-how — into a cocked hat.

An Unlikely Radio Star

Headquarters of the Oreck Corporation is a 140,000-square-foot building in a New Orleans suburb on the east bank of the Mississippi River. Go in the main entrance on River Road and you get a sense of David Oreck, the guy. In a massive glass case is a stunning three-foot scale model of his favorite toy, a modern replica of a 1930s Waco YMF5 open-cockpit stunt plane that he flies in and out of air shows across the country. On either side are parked two mammoth Harley-Davidson motorcycles; one is brand new, the other a 1960s model that has been restored to pristine perfection.

To your right, just down the hall, is an imposing stand-up desk behind which is David Oreck himself — trim, very bald and nattily clad in a blue suit — presiding over a room full of nondescript, sand-colored cubicles; he is deeply engrossed in a telephone conversation. Behind him: signed photographs of the legendary General David Sarnoff, founder of RCA, and test pilot Chuck Yeager of *The Right Stuff* fame.

"Curious executive offices," I said to him later. "No waiting room."

"We run a business," Oreck snapped with a good-natured smile. "People shouldn't have to wait."

The stand-up desk is just outside Oreck's cluttered, dark-paneled office where the first thing that catches your eye is a two-foot long scale model of an antique Stearman biplane he used to fly; suspended in the corner by a single thread, the yellow and blue model is spotlighted for dramatic effect. Other objects that dominate the office: huge museum-quality, multi-colored quartz crystals — millions of years old — that gleam in the subdued light. Why the obsession with quartz? "I want some things in this office that are older than I am," said Oreck with a twinkle. He's 73.

David Oreck, the New Orleans-based entrepreneur of floor-care products whose mellifluous voice surrounds America with millions of radio commercials every year.

The Early Days

David Oreck was born in Duluth, Minnesota, where he spent his first 17 years. During World War II, he served as navigator and radar officer on B-29s, flying missions into Japan from Saipan and Tinian.

After the war, the young veteran fetched up in New York City where he got a job as a salesman with the RCA wholesale distributor owned by David Sarnoff's brother. (It was Sarnoff who became world-famous as a very young man in April, 1912, when, as a wireless operator working atop the Woolworth Building in New York City, he picked up the distress signals of the sinking *Titanic*.)

The products RCA offered: RCA television sets, Bendix and later Whirlpool appliances. In the course of working himself up to vice president of sales, Oreck became close to General Sarnoff and stayed around longer than he normally would so "I could sit at the feet of the master." At one point he accompanied Sarnoff to a congressional hearing in Washington where the General testified on standards for color television.

Oreck's stories about the General include one on his management style. According to Oreck, if it was time for RCA to get rid of an executive who was privy to current information, he would not be fired outright; instead, he would be put "in the deep freeze." The man could stay in his fine offices in solitary splendor, collecting his paycheck but never seeing a piece of paper, nor attending a meeting. After six months of isolation — when any information he had in his head was thoroughly stale — the man was handed his walking papers.

In 1963, one of the principals of the distributorship died and David Oreck left to start his own corporation with offices at One Rockefeller Plaza. "Did I say offices?" Oreck asked. "It was an office — one small room."

Unable to make a success of upright vacuum cleaners, Whirlpool gave Oreck exclusive rights to market them throughout the United States. Oreck believed the concept of the machine was great, but thought the design was flawed. "Tell us what you want," he was told, "and we'll make it for you with the RCA Whirlpool label on it. Oreck:

> On a cold, snowy day in Chicago I was carrying the vacuum cleaner under my arm, à la Willy Loman, calling on Marshall Field and the other big retailers when the call came. In New

Orleans, the RCA-Whirlpool distributor was fighting for last place and frequently winning. Would I be interested in taking it over? I flew down to New Orleans that day. The sun was out. It was beautiful. I was still in my heavy winter overcoat. I said to myself, "Wow, I'm missing something here." In 48 hours I bought the business from a fellow who was floundering, and it went from last to first in two years.

The year was 1966. Oreck became well-known in the area not only for his television commercials but for his pioneering work in direct mail. It was Oreck who developed the "XL" or Extended Life trademark which he licensed to most of the RCA distributors.

Why the Oreck Vacuum Cleaner is Unique

Of the three types of vacuum cleaners — canister, upright and electric broom — virtually all required powerful, heavy-duty (and therefore, heavy) electric motors. The reason: When today's dirt is sucked in, yesterday's dirt has to be pushed out of the way. With the Oreck, dirt and dust are brushed and sucked in and then blown up the handle with a high-speed impeller. The dirt falls down to the bottom of the bag from the top. Since it didn't have to lift yesterday's dirt, the job could be accomplished with a light, high-speed motor that used very little current. A great deal of weight was saved with no sacrifice in performance.

In those early years, Oreck sent the product to Germany for design and manufacture. At first he marketed his machine the traditional way — through retail stores. He used independent reps and house salesmen to cover the country. Oreck:

> Unfortunately, retailers don't sell. They point. Go to a retail store and ask the clerk what the difference is between the $150 machine and the $200 machine and he'll tell you that the difference is $50.
>
> I had a product that was light and durable; the competition called it a toy and implied that it was light in performance and durability.
>
> The big retailers muscled us; what with all the deductions and returns, we couldn't make out. So in 1967 I stopped selling retail and went into direct mail.

Oreck knew something about the mail order business because at one point he bought a defunct home-study business that taught radio and television repair in Spanish. As freelancer Bill Jayme has said:

> Of all practical advertising media, only direct mail offers a sufficiently large canvas for telling a complex story.

Distribution Channels

Eighteen years ago, Oreck began manufacturing his machines in the United States. The current model has a powerful, durable motor and brushes with over 11,000 bristles turning at a mind-boggling 6,500 rps. "Other brands' brushes look bald in comparison to ours," Oreck maintains. Over 1 million Oreck XLs are in use in homes and office and in 50,000 hotels around the world. His offer is as strong as his machinery. For the floor dirt, he sells the XL with its powerful little motor and extraordinarily light weight. For above the floor dirt — upholstery, table surfaces and light cleaning — he gives away free a little four-pound vacuum so powerful it can lift a 16-pound bowling ball.

Today Oreck Corporation markets its products in myriad ways:

• **Licensees.** In 1994, Oreck had 35 floor care-centers — retail establishments that exclusively sell Oreck Products. That number is now more than 200 — with 70 of them company owned — and growing.

"These are not franchises," Oreck explains.

> In franchising, you pay a fee to get the franchise plus you pay an override on sales and generally there is an assessment for advertising.
>
> We have no franchise fee, no advertising assessments, no overrides.
>
> A licensee can get into the business for $75,000. That's $55,000 to get set up and operate for six months and $20,000 for merchandise. We train them in Houston, get our local people to assist in site selection and provide them with architectural drawings (they need about 1,000 square feet). These are mom-'n'-pop operations. The average store can make a 60 percent gross profit. Of course, many do a lot more than that.
>
> And, to date, we have not had one single failure.
>
> Right now we're running ads for more licensees and they are working well.

• **2,000 Traditional Multiline Dealers.** These are small appliance stores that specialize in cleaning equipment and carry a number of different brands. Seeing how well they do with Oreck products, many owners are dropping their other brands and becoming exclusive Oreck licensees.

• **Syndication.** In addition, Oreck syndicates via direct marketers. American Express has sold more than 375,000 Oreck machines for revenues of over $100 million. For these accounts — from American Express, Spiegel, Sharper Image, Comtrad's and department stores like Marshall Field's — Oreck creates the mailing piece, prints and mails it, pays the postage, takes the orders, ships the merchandise, and takes back the occasional returns. The account never sees a vacuum cleaner.

• **Oreck's Own Efforts.** In addition, Oreck Corporation does its own merchandising of the products — by direct mail, space advertising, free-standing newspaper inserts, television and, of course, his ubiquitous radio commercials, many of which he writes himself. In fact, he wrote and performed a singing commercial. "Call this number if you want me to stop singing," Oreck said. "We were inundated."

On the floor above David Oreck's office is a state-of-the-art telemarketing site — complete with $1 million worth of predictive dialing hardware and software — and a total of more than 100 telephone sales representatives on duty from 7:00 a.m. to 11:00 p.m. As with Audrey Peterman's telemarketing operation at the J. Peterman Company (described in Chapter 8), a complete line of products sits in the center of the room; if a consumer has a question, the Telephone Sales Representative is just a few steps away from actual product.

Direct marketers who heavily use direct response broadcast can find themselves overwhelmed with incoming calls at odd times. For example, the entire response cycle to a direct response television commercial is approximately 15 minutes. If the line is busy — or there's no answer — the sale is lost. Oreck's overflow is funneled off to two outside telemarketing contractors — one in New England and one in the West — where dedicated TSRs take over.

Following the sale, Oreck's telemarketers call every customer to ask if everything is okay and to upsell other products. For example, generic bags do not fit Oreck equipment, so the after-market is considerable. Oreck:

> People welcome our calls. How often do people buy a $50,000 car and never hear from the dealer again?

• **Where Oreck DOESN'T Market**. He does not sell to mass retailers (e.g., WalMart, K-Mart, etc.).

Keeping Track

Orders that come in the mail all have individual keys, so tracking the source of the order is no problem. TV commercials all have their own 800 numbers. However, with some 7,000 different radio stations running millions of commercials, there simply are not enough 800 numbers, so precise tracking is not possible

Making It Easy to Order and Pay

When David Oreck urges you to take the "Oreck Challenge" — to try the XL for 15 days free and see if it doesn't pick up a lot of dirt your old vacuum misses — he means it. The challenge is really free for 15 days. Only when the customer decides to keep the machine is the credit card charged. For those who don't want to use credit cards, Oreck provides its own financing and currently has some 100,000 accounts.

Of machines shipped under the Oreck Challenge, only about 5 percent are returned.

Making It Right for the Customer

A few steps away from the telemarketing operation is another small room with his highest-powered teleprofessionals. Like Curt Strohacker's auto restoration experts, these are the Oreck representatives who know the products inside and out and who are there simply to answer questions and hold customers' hands. They don't sell; they facilitate. As Oreck explains, sometimes a machine will belch dirt or make a funny sound. "What is the sound like?" the Telephone Sales Representative will ask. The customer will make an imitation, or, in some cases, put the receiver next to the machine and turn it on. Chances are it's a small matter that is easily fixed. In fact, Oreck claims that his machines are so simple, the average handyman can order a part and install it with ease. "This customer care center is an expensive operation," Oreck says. "But we want satisfied customers. When there's a question, we always lean in the customer's favor. And these people have the authority to make it right."

Oreck's insistence on world-class customer care extends to his retail operations as well. For example, whenever someone makes a purchase at retail, a store representative carries it to the car; if someone is bringing merchandise back for repair or return, an employee will hurry out to the parking lot to help bring it in.

The Oreck Product Line

In addition to the XL, Oreck offers a deluxe "hypo-allergenic" vacuum with a filtration system that eliminates 99.7 percent of all the irritants from the air. Other products include a variety of canister machines, car vacs, the Oreck Orbiter floor cleaner and waxer, a line of air filtration machines and a water filter.

In March 1997, David Oreck and Associates bought the Regina Corporation for cash from Philips Electronics. Founded in 1892, Regina manufactures a complete line of vacuum cleaners, steam cleaners and electric brooms. The purchase included a state-of-the-art factory of over 375,000 square feet.

More About Oreck

David Oreck learned to fly over 50 years ago, and aviation is one of the great loves of his life. He now has commercial, multi-engine and seaplane licenses and is instrument-rated. He owns three airplanes: the Waco, a T-34 military trainer built by Beech in the 1960s and a Twin Bonanza.

The Oreck Corporation sponsors the world-famous aerobatics stunt pilot Frank Ryder, who performs at air shows nationwide in one of two Oreck stunt planes. Oreck is unapologetic for plastering his logo all over the planes. ("Is Goodyear ashamed to let the world know who's flying that blimp?" he asks rhetorically.) According to Oreck, more than 28 million people attend air shows every year — more than any other event. At the shows where Ryder performs — usually those shows where the Blue Angels or the Thunderbirds are on the program — Oreck sets up a pavilion where the complete product line is demonstrated and sold, yet another channel of distribution. It's good publicity and neatly combines business with pleasure.

Oreck also runs every day. "In the past 50 years, I've run 50,000 miles and gone nowhere," he says.

In addition to flying and running, David Oreck is a "RUB" — a Rich Urban Biker. His other hobby: riding the Harley-Davidson motorcycles with straight pipes and no muffler. "Ya gotta make noise," Oreck says. "That's your protection."

"Boys and their toys," Oreck mused later. "Is it true the one to die with most toys wins?"

Surrounding the Country

What makes the Oreck marketing effort so extraordinary is that conflict between Oreck and its distributors, syndicators and licensees is nonexistent. As Oreck explains it:

> When American Express does a mailing, a tiny percentage of cardmembers order. Many prefer to get their hands on the product before they buy. Many of our licensees and independent retailers ask when the next American Express mailing will go out, because they see an immediate surge in business.

All of Oreck's marketing efforts — print, broadcast and direct mail — include a toll-free 800 number.

"If the customer wants to buy then and there, we sell," Oreck says "On the other hand, if she wants to see it and try it, we direct her to the nearest store. We never try to take a sale away from a dealer. We do not engage in any kind of predatory practices."

What David Oreck has done is combine general advertising with direct marketing. He is blitzing the marketplace with messages that create awareness; at the same time — unlike traditional advertisers — he makes it possible to order on the spot.

It's an elegant concept, but workable only if six inviolate criteria are met. They are:

(1) A product that literally every consumer and business of any substance in America must have.

(2) A $300+ product.

(3) Plenty of margin.

(4) A strong after-market

(5) Easy payment options.

(6) A high-profile, utterly believable, likable and trustworthy spokesperson.

In effect, David Oreck is surrounding the country. Anywhere you look or listen, you find David Oreck's smiling face or classic radio voice making you an irresistible, no-risk offer; and you can order on the spot if not this time, next time.

This will not work with a $10 product or a $1,000 product; it won't work with vertical products such as kitchenware (no need for it in offices) or fax machines (no need for them at home); it will not work with a product that has no after-market. For example, Oreck has a housefile of a million names (which he will rent selectively) to whom he can sell bags, parts and other products on an ongoing basis.

In fact, I can't think of another product for which Oreck's unique marketing structure could work.

Can you?

Points for Marketers to Consider

1.

Running a vacuum cleaner is not anyone's favorite occupation. You can't make it glamorous. It's not fun. It's a boring product, right up there with toilets and Jockey underwear. But you gotta have one, or the quality of your life will suffer.

David Oreck's approach to acquiring customers is to get inside the head of the homeowner or business decisionmaker and figure out all the possible objections to buying a new vacuum cleaner.

What are the drawbacks to the typical vacuum cleaner? It's heavy; it's noisy; it's cumbersome; it spews dust; it never seems to do a complete job. Let's face it, vacuuming is a pain in the ass.

When I first started in direct marketing at Grolier Enterprises, my boss, Lew Smith, sat me down and gave me a half-hour lecture on direct mail. His words are still etched in memory. At one point he pulled out a column from the old *Saturday Review* by radio personality Goodman Ace who had assembled the 12 most powerful and evocative words in the English Language:

You - Save - Money - Easy - Guarantee - Health
Proven - Safety - Discovery - New - Love - Results

I typed up this list and pasted it on the lamp on every desk I ever had; the logic: if these are the most powerful and evocative words, direct mail copy should be laced with them.

To these 12, I added one more. In the words of Dick Benson, "Free' is a magic word."

In his appeals, David Oreck uses — or implies — every one of these words. The *health* and *safety* comes from the built-in dust protector. He *guarantees* his product and, if for any reason you're not satisfied with it, you can return it for full refund. It's a *proven* product, because over 1 million of them have been sold. He offers a *free* hand vac when you buy the 8-pound Oreck-XL.

2.

Virtually every book on copywriting urges the writer to figure out the USP — the Unique Selling Proposition of a product, the one thing that makes it different and desirable. Oreck has articulated at least seven. His machine is light, powerful, dust-free, easy to use, fully guaranteed, cleans dust left by other machines, and you get a wonderful premium to boot.

What is your unique selling proposition? Do you not have several of them? Are you articulating *all* of them to your prospective customers?

3.

Many companies hire celebrities to hawk their products. Is that smart, really? Yes, in effect a famous person is tacitly endorsing the product. At the same time, you have to stop and say, "Hey, that's James Earl Jones or Charlton Heston or Larry King or Charles Osgood!" Don't their personae get in the way of your benefits and your message?

An example. All my life I was a fan of TV personality Dennis James. Long before *The Price Is Right*, James used to announce professional wrestling. His trademark was a bone-crackling device; when one of the big bozos on screen got, say, a hammerlock on the other and began applying pressure, James would squeeze his bone cracker and it made the event deliciously excruciating. James's other hallmark: The Mystery Hold of the Week. I remember one huge Hulk Hogan-type spinning another huge Hulk Hogan-type over his head, round and round, before slamming him and jumping on him for the win. As they were spinning, James yelled into the microphone: "Okay, mother, that's the mystery hold of the week. The first 50 postcards that correctly identify the Mystery Hold of the Week win a box of Whitman chocolates!"

About three years ago I saw James do an insurance commercial on TV. I remember yelling up to Peggy, "Holy smoke! That's Dennis James! He looks great!"

I had loved James. And here he was selling insurance. I saw him a number of times, but I absolutely cannot tell what the insurance was. Something mutual — maybe Mutual of Omaha or Physician's Mutual.

What is fascinating is that after Dennis James died, the commercial was replicated by an unknown actor *exactly* — the script, the intonations, the gestures and mannerisms. Guess what. Results were exactly the same, but with one major difference: Since the insurance company wasn't paying big bucks to Dennis James, the cost per order was far less and the commercial far more profitable!

With David Oreck acting as his own spokesman, he not only communicates decency and believability, but it is clear he is *passionate* about his product and its value. That passion shines through, which can never happen with celebrity spokespersons who are paid big bucks to say nice things about a product or service.

4.

Oreck's offer is powerful. Take the 15-Day Challenge. Let me send you my 8-Pound Oreck-XL. Then vacuum your floor with your current machine, and then go over what you just vacuumed with an Oreck. You will find dust in the bag, guaranteed. Or your money back. No questions asked. What's more, you'll get a free machine.

In the words of the great 1920s advertising practitioner, Claude Hopkins:

> The right offer should be so attractive that only a lunatic would say 'no.'

20

American Express, MCI, Reader's Digest, et al.:

The Catch-22 of Privacy

In 1993, my wife, Peggy, and I bought an 1817 house in center city Philadelphia. I asked Mary Brooke, our wonderfully capable real estate agent, how to get a mortgage.

"Call Fred Winter," she said immediately.

We called Fred Winter and the following Saturday morning, Winter, on the way to a golf game, showed up at our rented flat to receive a chicken sandwich and dispense a mortgage. Peggy and I answered questions and Winter wrote.

Winter asked for bank statements and financial records, which we provided. Two weeks later we had a mortgage — 15 years at a low 6-1/2 percent.

It was that easy.

In late March of that year, I was in Columbus, Ohio, for a speaking engagement at an isolated Radisson motel, no car and low on cash. I walked up the midway around the corner from the motel, shoved a piece of plastic into a machine and instantly had $300 cash; what's more the receipt also printed my bank account balance 800 miles away in Pennsylvania.

In my wallet are three credit cards: American Express Platinum and two Visa. Added together, I have a mind-blowing $40,000 worth of credit in my hip pocket! Such a thing was unthinkable when I was working at my first job as a page boy at NBC in the late 1950s making $40 a week.

How is it that I can command these lordly sums of cash practically on demand?

Quite simply, Peggy and I have kept our noses clean, paid our bills and been generally responsible citizens. As a result, a lot of data about us has been built up in computers around the country.

Because of this data, we are able to function with relative ease in the fast track of city life and constant business travel. And . . . the icing on the cake: A dizzying array of mail order offers and catalogs to satisfy my every wish and whim — all from mailers who want me for a customer and who will save me hours of battling crowds, polluting the atmosphere with my car exhaust and, above all, save me money.

My old boss and mentor Lew Smith used to say: "Happiness is having options."

The system gives me options.

Hooray for the system.

The System Turns Ugly

Several years ago in California some nut looked up the address of sitcom actress Rebecca Schaefer at the state motor vehicle bureau, rang her doorbell and killed her.

California authorities went ballistic and passed a bill making it illegal to release data on drivers without their prior consent. The outcry led to a bill introduced in the U.S. Senate by California Senator Barbara Boxer to limit access to motor vehicle data nationwide.

The question: Is this a good thing or a kneejerk reaction by a bunch of politicians trying to look good to a nervous and fearful electorate by jumping on an isolated tragedy and flailing it into the public's consciousness with the ferocity of a Singapore caning? In other words, should personal information be strictly limited and very difficult to obtain without prior consent.

Liberals would answer "yes!" Civil libertarians would respond, "Wait a minute, what does the Constitution say?" List and data compilers would say, "No!"

Until March 13, 1994, the terms of the debate were very clear cut.

From attorney John H. Awerdick of Stryker, Tams & Dill in Newark, N.J., came the following letter regarding a $1 million award to the parents of two murder victims:

> *The Orlando Sentinel* of March 13, 1994, reported a jury verdict against Rainbow International Carpet Cleaning and Dyeing Company. Its employee, Alan Robert Davis, murdered Carla McKishnie and Eleanor Ann Grace. He got access to their apart-

ment as an employee of the carpet cleaning company. That company had not done a background check. Had they accessed a database, they would have found that he had prior criminal convictions and, presumably, would not have hired him . . . .

My point: Information is benign. It can be used for good purposes. It can be used for bad purposes. Most of the time it is used for innocuous purposes. Laws should not be written based on isolated horror stories.

What have we there? Three murders. One the result of someone accessing personal information in a database and two the result of someone *not* accessing personal information in a database.

Catch-22.

Privacy in the Age of Data Rape

Logic dictates that if someone does business with you, you have every right in the world to add that person to your database, keep track of every transaction and make just about any offer you believe will be responded to.

Right?

WRONG!

This is a true story of a marketing scheme by one of the major airlines — I don't remember which one.

Prior to the era of frequent-flyer miles, the airline's agency came up with the idea to take advantage of the revolutionary new technique of computer personalization — of creating personalized letters to include not only the person's name, address and personalized salutation ("Dear Mr. & Mrs. Sample"), but also adding information about that person in the body of the letter as a reminder of the relationship to show how much the airline cared.

Why not write a letter to all recent passengers thanking them for flying with the airline and include a temporary membership card for admission to the airline club room at the local airport? the agency reasoned. This might generate some club memberships and some travel business. The airline marketing department liked the idea and gave the green light.

The personalized letter went something like this:

Dear Mr. & Mrs. Sample,
     We were delighted that you chose (name of airline) for your recent trip to Las Vegas . . .

One small problem existed.

In a number of instances, the "Mrs. Sample" who flew with Mr. Sample, was NOT Mr. Sample's wife, but another lady.

When the letter arrived in homes across the country, the real Mrs. Samples opened it (remember, it was addressed to Mr. & Mrs. Sample).

Instead of database wizardry, a marketing catastrophe ensued.

Divorces.

Law suits.

Ugly. Ugly.

So, yes, you own your customers.

But you have to be damn careful how you treat them.

Nobody at the agency — nor the airline marketing department — was a Method Marketer. Nobody thought through all the potential scenarios.

Here's another fiasco.

How the Operations People of a Major New York Bank Very Nearly Put It Out of Business

In the late 1960s, one of New York City's biggest banks undertook a massive upgrade of its computer system. One of the benefits: the disparate accounts of individual depositors could be consolidated. In the past, a depositor with a passbook savings account, a CD, a checking account and a mortgage would receive a separate statement in the mail for each. If these reports and canceled checks could be combined into a single monthly statement, the bank operations people reasoned, the savings in First Class postage and paper would be huge — amounting to tens of millions of dollars a year. What's more, the marketing people believed it represented tremendous time saving for the customer whose entire finances would be conveniently printed on a single sheet of paper.

     Right?

     WRONG!

The new system was instituted on a bankwide basis (no testing), whereupon the egg hit the fan.

Instead of huge savings, the bank suffered huge losses.

What happened?

It turns out the lion's share of the bank's small depositors were blue collar workers who worked for hourly wages — teamsters, construction workers, subway motormen, longshoremen. These workers received not one weekly check from their employer, but two — one check for regular salary and a second check for overtime.

The routine in virtually every one of these households was for the husband to dutifully turn over his regular paycheck to the wife and keep the overtime check for beer and walking-around money.

The vast majority of wives had *no idea* about the second check — until the new consolidated statement from the bank came through.

As with the airline marketing department writing letters to Mr. & "Mrs." Sample, the bank wound up with thousands of angry customers, some divorces and a number of lawsuits.

It took years for the bank to recover.

Could the bank have foreseen this disaster?

Probably not.

One of basic rules of marketing is to learn everything you can about your customers and create wants accordingly. In this case, even the most sophisticated survey or focus group could not possibly discern the little financial hocus-pocus game played by hourly workers with their wives. For example, any survey by the bank would presumably be opened by the wife who would wholeheartedly endorse the idea of a single, consolidated survey. No focus group of the hourly workers themselves would be possible; time off from work would mean a loss of income.

And hardly would one of the little yuppie MBA bankers with the sphincter-tight smile be able to go beer drinking with a teamster to figure out his lifestyle and how to create new and better wants. Most white-collar MBAs leave the house, climb into the car, drive to work, park in the company lot and go into the office where they spend the day with other MBAs just like themselves.

They have missed interacting with the people to whom they are marketing. How in the world can they become Method Marketers — get inside the heads and under the skins of their prospects and customers — when they operate in the elitist ivory towers of home, office and country club? Maybe they rub elbows Saturday mornings at the mall, and, once a year, mix socially with the folks in the mail room at the office Christmas party.

But to be successful in marketing, you have to become the person you are marketing to.

To become someone, you have to know all about that person intimately.

This is the basis of the great privacy debate.

The Old, Original Way of Marketing by Mail

Once upon a time, if a marketer wanted to make an offer, the mailing was created and a list was rented. In the 1960s, legendary freelance copywriter Ed McLean was hired to write a direct mail subscription letter for *Newsweek*. At the time he wrote it, McLean was new to the business and became fascinated with the whole concept of list selection while sitting in on meetings with Pat Gardner (later circulation director of the now-defunct Family Media) and the late Red Dembner, then *Newsweek*'s circulation director. McLean's letter began:

> Dear Reader,
>   If the list upon which I found your name is any indication, this is not the first — nor will it be the last — subscription letter you receive. Quite frankly, your education and income set you apart from the general population and make you a highly rated prospect for everything from magazines to mutual funds.

It was an offbeat approach — one that both flattered the reader and, at the same time, let prospects in on how they came to receive the solicitation.

Many people wrote in to ask what list they were on. A few complained. Many more responded by subscribing to the magazine. It was control for many years and was mailed in the hundreds of millions.

Today, McLean's mailing would never fly. In fact, McLean's rule is:

> You've got to dumb-down what you know.

In other words, you may know a lot about the person you are writing to, but you cannot reel off information about a person that you got from someplace else. It is eerie. It is creepy. It is disrespectful.

Example: Letters from insurance companies to me that say,

Dear Mr. Hatch,
  Congratulations on your upcoming 63rd birthday.

I never told them I was 63. I don't like being reminded I am 63. These guys have been prowling around other people's information and spying on me, and it makes me damned angry.
  What could they have said?

Dear Mr. Hatch,
  If you are in your early sixties — or perhaps have a parent or loved one who has reached that point in life — it's important to know . . . ..

Of course, they know I'm about to be 63. *But I don't know they know.* In other words, the writer's specific knowledge about me is *operating behind the copy.* He has dumbed-down what he knows.

To create a mailing back in the days of Ed McLean and *Newsweek,* you looked for a likely list and ordered 5,000 names for a test. If the test worked, you confirmed the test by mailing an additional 25,000 names. From there you would reconfirm with bigger test of, say, 150,000 names. If results held up, you could move into big numbers.

When the Postal Service mandated the use of 5-digit Zip Codes in 1960s, many in the list business (not known as a group of conceptual thinkers) predicted it would be the end of direct mail marketing as it was then known; the cost of converting all the names would be prohibitively expensive.

In fact, Zip Codes were the seeds that allowed direct marketing to grow, flourish and become the most precise and sophisticated marketing system in the world today.

In simple terms, using Zip Code analysis, a marketer could analyze sales and bad debts area-by-area across the country.

The Book Club's Gaffe

In the early days of Zip analysis, one of the big book clubs was running its regular weekly full-page and double-page ads in the *New York Times Book Review.* Legend has it that a reader in the Bedford-Stuyvesant section — the area in Brooklyn made up of a predominantly poor minority population — filled out the coupon to join and mailed it in. After several months with no acknowledgment of the order and no books, the reader called the club and inquired about the order. The customer service clerk who took the call wrote down all the information — the customer's name, address and Zip Code — and put the caller on hold. Several minutes later, the clerk came on the line.

"We're not filling any orders in that Zip code," she said.

Yet another case of the egg hitting the fan.

Michigan Bulb's Goof

Michael Fishman of the list management firm The SpeciaLists moved to a new house. The family that moves to a new home is a prime candidate for direct marketers. One reason: the new neighborhood may be unfamiliar to them and it's start time for all the regular support systems: new pharmacy, new physician, new garden supplier, new clothiers, new bank, new car registration and insurance. So, to save time, they turn to their favorite catalogers and mail order suppliers.

However, Standard Class (bulk) Mail is seldom forwarded, so no regular catalogs will arrive at the new home for some time. For that reason, the first offers to appear in the new homeowner's mailbox strike gold.

In the 1990s, Michigan Bulb sent its garden catalog to new homeowners — an obvious and beneficial offer. After all, when people buy a new home, chances are good they'll welcome the opportunity to beautify the outside.

Michael Fishman of The SpeciaLists, Ltd., sent me the catalog he had received; the address read:

```
CAR-RT SORT        **CRO2
Prizewinner's Claim check

034346627 2FC* HS-97


     Michael F. Fishman
     [Street Address]
     Columbia Savings
     [City, State, Zip]
```

Fishman wrote to me:

> Check the addressing on this Michigan Bulb mailing to my home address. The third line is the name of the bank with which I have my mortgage for a home purchased in August 1990. The compiler who supplied the names for this campaign captured the bank name from town records and used it to create the list, including the name and address data.
>
> If mine is not an isolated case — and tens of thousands of records are prepared this way — the compiler is fanning the flames of the privacy wars. Even the casual consumer uninformed in the intricacies of our business could decipher the source of this addressing anomaly.

Actually, an outsider would not figure this out, because it appears on the face of it that the bank probably rented its list of mortgage holders to Michigan Bulb. To the consumer, the bank is very likely the bad guy. No doubt bankers all over the country had to do some fancy verbal footwork to deal with confused mortgage customers.

When this example was used in a slide show during a presentation I gave, it generated a hot letter from Michigan Bulb's lawyer, my friend John H. Awerdick:

> [Michigan Bulb] was as disturbed as Mr. Fishman by the information revealed by the compiler. Perhaps strict quality control by Michigan Bulb might have caught the mistake. They have instituted tighter controls since the incident, but they do not guarantee freedom from glitches. Privacy insensitivity by the compiler was the real problem.
>
> Frankly, I believe that the [*Who's Mailing What!*] article was more balanced than your talk. It left me as a listener with the impression that Michigan Bulb rather than the list compiler was the data rapist. I hope in future talks you will find an example other than Michigan Bulb or that you will use it anonymously. At least I trust you will note that the incident occurred years ago, was the compiler's fault and led to corrective action.

My reply to John Awerdick:

> Regarding Michigan Bulb, I made very sure to put that in the category of inadvertent data rape. It was an error. It was sloppy work. It was dumb. The fault was not with the list compiler. The list compiler gets the information — including the name of the bank and the amount of the mortgage — and sells

that information to mortgage insurance companies. Michigan Bulb wanted part of that information for another purpose.

Michigan Bulb either gave the wrong specs when ordering the list or it was a glitch by the list compiler.

Either way, Michigan Bulb did not have a knowledgeable person eyeball the list before the mailing went out. Michigan Bulb was the mailer. Its name was all over that envelope and catalog. The buck stops there . . ."

MCI as Data Rapist

Below is copy from a mailing I received from MCI:

YOU'RE INVITED

```
(203) 329-1996
Bonus Code SH12    700/H15
Mr. Denison Hatch
210 Red Fox Rd.
Stamford, CT 06903
```

(Please make any necessary corrections)

Mr. Gordon Grossman
HAS INVITED YOU TO JOIN MCI® AND FRIENDS & FAMILY[SM] SO YOU CAN BOTH SAVE 20% ON YOUR MOST IMPORTANT LONG DISTANCE CALLS.

I had known and worked with DMA Hall of Fame Circulation Director Gordon Grossman for many years. He would not release my name to MCI for a promotion. I called him and asked if he could possibly have given MCI permission to contact me. Grossman was incensed and dug into the case like a dog going for a bone.

He wrote in *Who's Mailing What!*:

> The editor of this newsletter has written several times about examples of what he called "Data Rape" — involving a direct marketer's misuse of his database. I have accused him of exaggeration. Now that I've been well and truly data raped myself, I no longer do.
>
> . . . On April 17, a rogue telephone rep working for MCI entered an order for Friends & Family in my name and listed (at least) Denny Hatch and (at least) one other person as members of my Calling Circle. The rep took their names from my MCI records as people I called most often using MCI long-distance service.

In the ensuing article, Grossman outlined the five basic steps MCI failed to take in order to insure the authenticity of the offer and the protection of personal call record data. He concluded:

> Many thoughtful members of the direct marketing community have reminded us in recent months that the issue of "privacy" is likely to be one of the biggest threats to our continued prosperity, and even existence, in the next decade.
>
> I agree. I fear the Naders and their ilk. But even more than our sworn enemies, I fear our "friends" . . . the direct marketing businesses that give our enemies the ammunition they need.

From Christine Seelig of MCI to Denny Hatch on November 17, 1992:

> I understand that you were contacted by MCI informing you that Mr. Grossman included you in his MCI Friends & Family Calling Circle and inviting you to join MCI. Mr. Grossman's Calling Circle was established in error. He did not provide your number as one of those he frequently calls, and was not aware MCI would attempt to contact you and ask you to join MCI. I apologized to Mr. Grossman for contacting you, as this was not his intent.

The idea that MCI's security was so lax that any little sales rep could access the calling records of its customers is appalling.

The American Express Mess

The Direct Marketing Association and privacy advocates give American Express high marks for respecting cardmembers' privacy and for the full disclosure of how it collects information and what it does with that information.

But do consumers fully understand the implications? If they did, wouldn't this give them the creepy-crawlies?

Here's what American Express sends to its new cardmembers:

> *At American Express, we want you to understand all that the Card affords you, including the offers you receive through the mail and by telephone.*

These offers come directly from us, from our affiliates, from establishments that accept the Card, or from other well-established companies. Each offer is carefully developed to ensure that it meets our standards. Additionally, we try to make sure that these offers reach only those Cardmembers most likely to take advantage of them.

To do this, we develop lists for use by us and our affiliates based on information you provided on your initial application and in surveys, information derived from how you use the Card that may indicate purchasing preferences and lifestyles, as well as information available from external sources including consumer reports.

We may also use that information, along with non-credit information from external sources, to develop lists which are used by the companies with whom we work.

These lists are developed under strict conditions designed to safeguard the privacy of Cardmember information.

Notice to New Cardmembers: Your name and address will be suppressed from marketing mailing lists used by non-American Express companies for four weeks after you have been accepted for Cardmembership to give you the opportunity to elect not to receive marketing mailings in accordance with this notice.

Many Cardmembers tell us they appreciate these offers, as well as information on Cardmember benefits. However, if you no longer wish to receive these offers and information about benefits, please choose one or more of the following options:

❑ Please exclude me from American Express mailings, including new benefits and American Express Merchandise Services catalogs.

❑ Please exclude me from mailings by other companies, including offers in cooperation with American Express provided by establishments that accept the Card.

❑ Please exclude me from lists used for telemarketing.

Okay. But . . . what if a cardmember buys a lot of medicine . . . or frequents gay bars . . . or sends bunches of flowers to a lady who is not his wife . . . or flies to Las Vegas when he told his family he was in Detroit in business . . . or pays a huge auto repair bill . . . or pays a malpractice lawyer a fat fee . . . doesn't the list go on and on?

Frankly, is this anybody's business but that of the cardmember and the payee? Isn't it only tangentially the business of American Express?

For all the kudos American Express gets from the privacy advocates, nowhere on this form is the cardmember given the opportunity to stop American Express from creating a massive, electronic, individual dossier and using it for other purposes. The only choice offered: not to receive mailings or telephone calls.

Where, for example, is the American Express guarantee that it won't sell this transactional lifestyle information as a do-not-mail file to, say, insurance companies or HMOs?

From a July 30, 1995, story about American Express CEO Harvey Golub in *The New York Times Magazine.*

"A Northern Italian restaurant opens in midtown Manhattan," Golub says by way of example. "We know from the spending of card members which of them have eaten in Northern Italian restaurants in New York, whether they live in New York or Los Angeles. We make an offer of a free or discounted meal available only to those card members. The offers are now more relevant."

What Are the Ethics Here?

This raises the question: Who owns the data?

True, Northern Italian restaurants in Manhattan that accept the American Express card are Golub's customers.

But aren't the patrons who frequent those restaurants — first and foremost — the restaurants' own customers? Is it ethical of American Express — a third party — to use transactional data to raid the good customers of one restaurant and urge them to try a competitor? Isn't this a naked betrayal of the merchants who trustingly offer the American Express charge option and pay a transaction fee far higher than what they pay Visa or MasterCard?

In late May 1996, I receive a letter from Kate Paxton of Kratz & Company that said:

> For ten years, the Platinum Card team has tracked and ana-
> lyzed the spending habits of America's most successful individuals
> and has amassed a wealth of valuable information about this in-
> fluential demographic group. Executives at the Platinum Card
> would like to share with you some insights into the most success-
> ful techniques they have found for marketing to this influential
> and growing group of consumers.

I am an American Express Platinum Cardmember. How do I feel about Kate Paxton's offer? Read on.

A front-page story in *The Wall Street Journal* of February 24, 1995, describing the Philip Morris Companies' $10 billion libel suit against ABC was titled "American Express Sends a Statement That's Quite Wrong."

> So in October of last year, Philip Morris resorted to an ex-
> treme measure: It sent out subpoenas to 13 companies including
> Citicorp's Citibank, AT&T Corp., Hertz Corp. and American
> Express seeking travel and telephone records of the two ABC pro-
> ducers who worked on the story . . .
> Vivian Wilkerson, the American Express clerk who
> answered the call, informed Philip Morris's lawyers at the
> New York firm of Wachtell, Lipton, Rosen & Katz that she had
> the documents ready and that they could be picked up by mes-
> senger . . . .
> What Philip Morris's lawyers got from American Express
> was far more than they had requested. The tobacco giant had

sought just one month's corporate card records for producer Walt Bodnanich and associate producer Keith Summa. The narrow search covered the period — January 1994 — during which Philip Morris believed a meeting with the source had occurred.

But Ms. Wilkerson instead turned over roughly seven years of the producers' receipts. And included in these records were corporate-card receipts of at least a half-dozen journalists with no involvement at all in the ABC matter, including reporters at *The Wall Street Journal* between 1984 and 1992.

How could this have happened? American Express says that, somehow, it goofed.

The Data Warehouse

In the July 31, 1995, issue of *ComputerWorld*, Kim Nash wrote:

> Not only has MasterCard International, Inc., started to build one of the world's biggest data warehouses, but the credit-card company last week said it plans to gradually open the system to its 22,000 bank, retailer, restaurant and other partners . . .
>
> Up to 30,000 user PCs, workstations and other client devices will ultimately have access to the warehouse, which will contain data on the company's 8.5 million daily credit- and debit-card transactions, MasterCard officials said.

Aren't marketers playing fast and loose with highly sensitive, intensely private data? Once fully understood by government and consumers alike, aren't marketers heading for a cataclysmic juggernaut with the regulators who could legislate us all back to the Stone Age of database technology?

Poaching on the King's Preserves

Freelancer Malcolm Decker put it this way:

> The consumer is king (or queen, where appropriate). We exist, professionally, at his pleasure. So it's not smart to annoy the king.
>
> And if you want his custom, you not only avoid abrasive encounters, you do your damnedest to serve, cultivate, nurture and even anticipate the king's needs and desires.

Does that mean you say "God bless you!" before the king sneezes — or bill him and ship him an unordered year 2000 diary in July of '99? Or, in the service of the king, do you use spies, wiretaps, privileged information and a high-powered telescope to pry open his private life in an effort to better anticipate his needs?

That might be annoying. The hangman's loop says you'd better not.

We're overwhelmed by the enormous amount of data we generate. They demand to be used. Brash managers on the horns of their P&Ls are sorely tempted — but they better not cross over into the king's preserve — not without his informed consent.

From a purely pragmatic, long-term view, data poaching carries other penalties. It tells the monarchs you know too much for your own good and makes them wonder how you got the information.

Data poaching creates distrust exactly at the time you want to build confidence. It shows up, in anemic Recency-Frequency-Monetary [RFM] figures and poor list performance. Ultimately, even licensed hunters in the direct marketing community are regarded with suspicion.

The basic answer to the privacy question, I believe, is inherent in the golden rule. Treat prospects as well as customers with respect, enter their private worlds only at their invitation, and when you leave, take with you only what they knowingly gave you. And if it's given to you exclusively, hold it in confidence.

Rather than data poaching, let's focus on consumer benefits and dedicate our resources to creating and selling these benefits.

Life After Privacy Laws

From database whiz and agency owner James Morris-Lee with the following scrawled across it in handwriting, "This scares the hell out of me!":

Starting this fall, *Reader's Digest* plans to send millions of people with high blood pressure, high cholesterol and other conditions something extra with their magazine: a booklet filled with articles and prescription-drug ads, all about the very ailment each subscriber has.

What the subscribers may not realize is that the booklet stems from an aggressive new tactic in a race by marketers to collect and use sensitive, personal data to target customers. It also marks a new frontier in magazine publishers' increasingly cozy relations with advertisers.

— Sally Beatty, Staff Reporter
The Wall Street Journal, April 17, 1998

On January 26, 1998, *The Toronto Globe & Mail* reported that privacy legislation was about to be introduced by the government of Canada.

The law will try to ensure that personal data collected by businesses for one purpose will not be used for other purposes without the consent of the individual.

The 28 words above represent the guts of privacy legislation as it affects marketers. With some 80 privacy bills pending in Congress and more than 2,000 in the state legislatures, and equivalent laws in force in a number of countries overseas, some contingency planning might be in order. How will we cope?

Ultimately, the customer acquisition side of direct marketing will be affected. After all, paying customers expect marketers to be knowledgeable about their wants by maintaining data and creating more wants. Here's what I see:

(1) Direct marketers will band together to crate a giant PR campaign to persuade consumers that direct marketing is wonderful and the more information they let us have, the better and more relevant offers they will receive and the better lifestyle they will enjoy.

(2) Like Europe and Asia (and, soon, Canada), the business of customer acquisition in the U.S. will center on nontraditional media — Direct Response Television, off-the-page advertising, take-ones, etc. The initial cost of media will be cheaper than the $500/M cost of solo mail. Marketers will expend a great deal more expertise, energy and money in converting leads to sales and sales into lifetime customers.

(3) If this be the scenario, look for a spike in magazine and newspaper advertising, and the list rental and database businesses to take something of a hit.

Beyond that, status quo ante bellum.

21

Cochran & Co.

Lessons from the O. J. Verdict

"Who do you think was most responsible on the defense for the acquittal?" asked Larry King that night on the air.

"Jo-Ellen Dimitrius," replied Gus.

— Dominick Dunne
Another City, Not My Own

Jo-Ellen Dimitrius was the jury consultant. She took a random list of juror candidates, selected the right ones and then worked with the defense team on crafting the message. In direct marketing, that's called great list work.

Prosecutor Marcia Clark, on the other hand, was so convinced the DNA evidence would slam-dunk prove O.J. Simpson guilty of murdering his ex-wife and model Ron Goldman that she paid little heed to the makeup of the jury.

"Lists are the most important ingredient of direct mail," the late guru Dick Benson said. "I know of no mailer who spends enough time on lists." Where Marcia Clark thought of the jury as simply a list to be manipulated, Johnnie Cochran and Dimitrius & Co. treated the jury *as people* and played them like a fine violin. Nick Dunne writes:

> "I've begun to think that the DNA isn't going to have any effect in the long run," said Gus, shaking his head. "It's too difficult to understand. I figure that if I can't get it, they're not getting it in the jury box, either. The more information you give a jury, the more you confuse them. My take on Barry Scheck's strategy on DNA, about which he knows a great deal, is that he talks brilliantly over the heads of the jurors, knowing they're not understanding what he's talking about, so that in the long run, they'll dismiss the importance of it."

I watched a lot of the O.J. trial and agree with Dunne. The DNA presentations bored me to stupefication. What do I remember? Barry Scheck's trashing of the L.A.P.D.'s Dennis Fung for his inept collection of evidence. The Mark Fuhrman brouhaha over the use of the "N" word. The words, "contamination of evidence." And Johnnie Cochran's doggerel, "If the glove don't fit, you gotta acquit."

If the O.J. trial were direct mail, the prosecution intellectualized the message with the DNA evidence, using the equivalent of a circular only. The defense team went for the gut and put the L.A.P.D. on trial — the equivalent of a highly emotional letter. Everybody knows a mailing with a letter will outpull a mailing with no letter and only a circular every time.

In other words, with good list work and a highly emotional appeal, you'll kick butt every time. As guru John J. Flieder has said:

> When emotion and reason come into conflict, emotion always wins!

22

Who's Mailing What!

My Day in Court:
(The Royal Courts of Justice, Chancery Division, That Is)

*Taking Method Marketing techniques
into another arena in another country*

He that goes to law holds a wolf between the ears.
— Robert Burton, *Anatomy of Melancholy*

Aside from marketing, success in one other profession is totally dependent on the practitioner getting inside the heads and under the skin of others to think how they think and feel what they feel.

That profession is the law.

The litigator who does not get inside the heads of the jury at every point in a trial, with every witness, with every direct- and cross-examination, with every exchange with the judge — and see precisely what the jury sees — will lose.

I once found myself in a sticky situation which called on all my knowledge of Method Marketing.

In March 1995, I flew to England to exhibit at a trade fair in Wembley Park outside London.

At 10:30 a.m. on the opening day, Jeremy Ridgway walked up to my booth at the Wembley convention hall. Wearing a light colored double-breasted suit, he was tallish, maybe forty, with a pasty white face, high forehead, glasses and short reddish hair that was greased down. He held up his business card.

"There's a hearing today at two o'clock," he said, his tone smug and mean, his lips tight. "I'm giving you this as a courtesy. The court will be issuing an injunction, and we'll be marching over to shut you down. You can't exhibit here."

Pointing to the back of the card, he added: "If you want to attend, here's a phone number you can call — the judge's clerk." He pronounced "clerk" as "clark."

He turned on his heel and walked off.

The nightmare of every world traveler is to wind up as a defendant in the court of a foreign land. I had no connections in the UK. No way of getting a lawyer. No idea where the hearing was to be.

Let's say my mind was awhirl.

The Background

My business is direct mail . . . advertising mail . . . some refer to it unkindly as junk mail. Since 1984 my wife Peggy and I had been proprietors of a newsletter and library service called *WHO'S MAILING WHAT!* We had a network of correspondents around the country who forwarded their mail and catalogs to me and I analyzed it, cataloged it and wrote about it — some 3,000 to 4,000 pieces a month. By subscribing to my service, advertising professionals could read about successful direct mail (and poor direct mail) and order copies of other people's mailings to see what the competition was doing and, in the words of one practitioner, "steal smart."

For nearly 10 years, Peggy and I ran the newsletter and library service from our family room in Stamford, Connecticut. At one point we had 1,700 subscribers — almost entirely in the United States — but had picked up a few subscribers in the UK as well as Germany, France, Canada and the Pacific Rim.

On September 25, 1989, *The Wall Street Journal* ran a front-page story titled, "You Call It Junk, But Denison Hatch Sees Gold in It." Reporter Cynthia Crossen's lead sentence:

STAMFORD, Conn. - Imagine a guy who sits in his basement 12 hours a day, poring over junk mail the way Frank Purdue scrutinizes chickens. That's Denison Hatch.

It was my 15 minutes of fame; suddenly our cranky little enterprise was known all over the world.

Denny Hatch in front of The Royal Courts of Justice, about to go on trial and scared to death.

Early in 1992 I had several meetings with Richard Dorsett, a fortyish British marketer with a pudgy face, crew cut and a build rather like a miniature NFL linebacker. Our intent: to set up a corporation in the U.K. to offer my American *WHO'S MAILING WHAT!* service to British direct marketers.

Why would foreigners be interested in American direct mail advertising? Quite simply, American direct mail is the best in the world. It's not because we're smarter or more creative. We have 100 million households, 11 million businesses — all reachable using any of 20,400 lists. By comparison, there are only 5,000 lists in all of Europe and the U.K. combined. Americans can test, retest, and test again. No other country in the world has numbers like ours. My library of 50,000 mailings in over 200 categories is a veritable treasure trove of invaluable marketing information. I can save people a fortune in unnecessary testing. Since people are people everywhere, American direct mail translates and travels well; American mailings — with appropriate translations and cultural changes — work with killer precision overseas.

When Richard Dorsett tried to register *WHO'S MAILING WHAT!* in the U.K. and form a corporation, Jeremy Ridgway surfaced.

A British statistician, Ridgway had founded a company in 1991 called Market Movements. One of his products was a service like mine that collected direct mail, annotated it and sold his reports for a lot of money.

The name of Ridgway's service: *Who's Mailing What?*

At the hint of Dorsett's and my entering the U.K. market, Ridgway went ballistic, claiming he had been using the name and was well established; if we attempted to set up shop there, he would shut us down under the law of "Passing Off." (I would be "passing off" my *WHO'S MAILING WHAT!* for his *Who's Mailing What?*) Under British law, Ridgway was allowed to steal my title, operate with impunity and keep me out of the U.K. — even though I had already been in business for seven years . . . even though *WHO'S MAILING WHAT!* was a registered U.S. Trademark . . . even though my entire business was American direct mail advertising, whereas his was exclusively devoted to mail in the U.K . . . and even though I had a few U.K. subscribers.

What is passing off in the U.K. would be legalized censorship and commercial piracy anywhere else in the world.

At the time I thought of the famous line in *Oliver Twist:*

> "If the law supposes that," said Mr. Bumble, "the law is a ass,
> a idiot."

Almost incidentally, Ridgway wanted to know in the middle of all this ugliness, if I would be interested in making available my American direct mail for him to distribute to his customers in the UK.

After legal skirmishes and lots of lawyer's bills on both sides of the Atlantic, Dorsett and I decided to back off.

Later that year, our little corporation was acquired by North American Publishing Company. Peggy and I moved to Philadelphia to run *WHO'S MAILING WHAT!* and take over the editorial helm of the direct marketing magazine *Target Marketing*.

Fast forward. March 13, 1995. London.

I had more or less forgotten about Ridgway when I flew to Great Britain to exhibit at the London Direct Marketing Fair at Wembley. Would the Brits be interested in seeing samples of American direct mail? I wanted to know. Would they subscribe to an American newsletter on the subject?

I arrived to set up the booth on Monday afternoon. A messenger appeared and told me to sign for a letter, which I did. Inside the plain white envelope were two letters, both dated that day; both were from Ridgway's law firm threatening me with perdition if I exhibited. I set up anyway and went back to the hotel where I called Peggy at the office. She had received a copy of the letters by fax. What was I planning to do? I didn't know, but I asked her to make copies of the cover pages of my first two issues of *WHO'S MAILING WHAT!* — both of which were dated — and fax them to me; whatever happened, I would clearly be able to prove I had been in business since October, 1984.

I hung up and went to the theatre.

The following morning at 10:30 a.m., Jeremy Ridgway showed up to tell me about the upcoming hearing at two that afternoon. As he was walking away, I studied what he had written on the back of his business card; the phone number was tiny, almost illegible and in pinched and angry handwriting.

I found a telephone in the crowded lobby, inserted 10 pence and dialed the number. A man answered and I asked about the hearing. He told me to wait and he would look it up. I waited and waited, whereupon the phone hiccupped and went dead. I inserted another 10 pence and dialed again. "Still looking," he said. "After a moment, he came back on and started to talk, but the phone hiccupped and went dead. In desperation, I inserted a brass pound coin and got the man for the third time. The hearing was to be in the High Court, Court 40. What High Court? Where?

"The Royal Courts of Justice. The Chancery Division."

"Where?"

"At the Royal Courts of Justice."

"What address?"

"Fleet Street and The Strand."

We hung up.

I tried to think the thing through.

If I did not make an appearance, Ridgway would win by default; the injunction would be issued, and I would be shut out of the show. I could show my wares today — have one full day at the show which would answer my questions about possible British interest in American direct mail; however, I would be out of business tomorrow and Thursday. I envisioned constables, Bobbies and Scotland Yard men in trench coats cordoning off my booth and ordering me to pack up and leave.

Humiliating.

On the other hand, if I did appear and won, I would have two full days at the show plus my good name intact.

If I appeared and lost, at least I would have fought the good fight; I would be bloodied but unbowed.

What the hell. I decided to to do it.

Besides, I thought, what a kick! How many American citizens have ever had a chance to argue a case in the High Court of Justice?

But then would I be able to argue at all? Or would the British legal establishment sandbag me the way Ridgway did? And the ultimate question: By representing myself, would I have a fool for a client? That point was moot; I had no connections in the UK and didn't begin to know how to find a lawyer.

As I was leaving the convention hall, I saw my old colleague Richard Dorsett, whose stand was next to the main entrance. "Ridgway is furious," I said.

"He's exhibiting here, you know."

"I know. And he's threatening to shut me down."

"Are we going to have a bit of a punch-up?" Dorsett asked gleefully.

I shrugged and left for the Wembley Park station.

On the train , I studied a map of London and found The Royal Courts of Justice. The nearest underground stop was Holborn.

Trying to imagine the upcoming scenario, I glanced momentarily down at my stomach. Looking back at me with a silly, mischievous grin was the upside down face of Mickey Mouse in front of a screaming red background punctuated with large white polka dots. Jesus, my favorite convention necktie! Hardly appropriate for an appearance in the High Court of Justice!

I fished out my 1911 *Baedeker* to see if I could get as sense of the place I would be going to. I take perverse pleasure in traveling with old *Baedekers*; they still contain the greatest travel information ever published. What's more, anything built after 1911 isn't worth spending time with. Prince Charles says it's so. Karl Baedeker:

> Immediately to the E. of Clement's Inn, on the N. side of the Strand, rise the **Royal Courts of Justice**, opened in 1882, a vast and magnificent Gothic pile, forming a whole block of buildings, with a frontage toward the Strand of about 500 ft . . . The principal internal feature is the large central hall, 138 ft. long, 48 ft. wide, and 80 ft. high, with fine mosaic flooring . . . The building contains in all 19 court-rooms and about 1100 apartments of all kinds, but a large addition is being built on the W. side.

I put the faded red leather book away and stared mutely out the window at the gray world of London suburbia racing by.

The Royal Courts of Justice . . .

The Chancery Division . . .

What is Chancery?

Suddenly my mind rocketed back a half century, to the D'Oyly Carte Production of Gilbert & Sullivan's *Iolanthe* at the Century Theatre in New York City, where I was taken as a boy. The incomparable Martyn Greene was the Lord Chancellor. That Christmas, I was given the record album, a collection of 78s that I played constantly, to the point where I could recite all the lyrics by heart. The vision of a randy old man cavorting about the stage in robe and wig played MTV-like in my head:

> The constitutional guardian I
> Of pretty young Wards in Chancery,
> All very agreeable girls — and none
> Are over the age of twenty-one,
> A pleasant occupation for
> A rather susceptible Chancellor!
> But though the compliment implied
> Inflates me with legitimate pride,

It nevertheless can't be denied
That it has its inconvenient side.
For I'm not so old, and not so plain,
And I'm quite prepared to marry again,
But there'd be the deuce to pay in the Lords
If I fell in love with one of my Wards!
   Which rather tries my temper, for
I'm ***such*** a susceptible Chancellor!

At the Holborn station I rode the escalator up into the sunlight on Kingsway, a wide, busy street choked with traffic. Standing at the entrance to the underground was a wizened little Munchkin of a man with a short white beard, his stained polo coat down to his ankles. "Where can I find The High Courts of Justice?" I asked.

"I can get you to the Courts," he said in cockney. "I can't promise you justice."

He pointed the way and asked for the price of a cup of coffee; I gave him a quid.

The first order of business was a new necktie, which I found in a low-end haberdashery shop — muted blue and green flowered pattern for five pounds. I changed ties on the fly, stopped at a stationery store to buy a small notebook and pressed on.

Ten minutes later I found the "vast and magnificent Gothic pile" — a sprawling, cupcakey gray-brown stone structure with turrets, conical roofs, spires, leaded windows and seemingly endless pointed arches of every height and width. High up on either side of the main entrance were the emblems of Justice and, in huge shiny black Gothic type:

The

Royal

Courts

of

Justice

It was Lifeboat Day. All over London that day ladies held out plastic piggy banks in the shape of a boat's hull collecting money for The Royal Lifeboat Institution. I offered the Lifeboat lady in front of the courts a pound if she would take my picture. She agreed, handing me a sticker for my lapel. I held her red lifeboat piggy bank and posed; she snapped; I went inside where my briefcase and I were X-rayed in the airportlike security system.

The main hall was everything *Baedeker* said it was; easily it could

Royal National Lifeboat Institution

The Lifeboat Day lapel sticker
Denny Hatch wore to court.

have been mistaken for the nave aisle of a great cathedral. At the information desk, I was told Court 40 was in the Queen's Building at the far end of the hall and to the left.

I went through a low arcade of stone columns and brick-vaulted ceiling out into the sunlight of an open courtyard, where a sign showed the way to the Queen's Building, a drab modern structure that resembled a 1950s version of Ellis Island. I found Courtroom 40. A glassed-in bulletin board proclaimed:

COURT 40
Before Mr. Justice Rattee
Tuesday, 14th March, 1995
At half past 10

Motions

1. Sleipner UK Ltd. & anr v Martin
2. The Institute of Charted Accountants in England and Wales v Malkin
3. Osprey Belt Co Ltd. v. Revel Shoes Ltd.
4. Combined Mercantile Securities Ltd v TS Bank pk & ors

Standing around was a small gaggle of officious young men wearing black suits and white biblike ties, the kind you associate with Quaker or Lutheran ministers. These were barristers — lawyers who presented cases in court (as opposed to solicitors who do the gritty-gray work of researching and preparing cases and writing ugly letters).

I walked into Courtroom 40, a smallish room with 1960's wooden wainscoting and light tan walls. Chiseled into the front wall over where the judge would sit two levels up was a large gilded crest of England. At the back of the room were wooden benches, not unlike church pews; down front, a single long table with a wooden lectern in the middle and bench with a blue Naugahyde cushion. On the left side of the room were two more pews. In all, I guessed the court could hold 70 persons.

Sitting at the table on a dais higher than ground level but below where the judge would sit was a gentleman of medium height, wearing tinted glasses and blue suit. (Every man I had seen wore either a blue or black suit or a black robe.) We introduced ourselves; he was Albert Collins, usher of Mr. Justice Rattee's court. Yes, this was the place.

Would I be able to answer charges and address the court, I asked.

"If you are a litigant here in person, you may speak, of course," he replied. Collins was gracious; I liked him immediately.

"Where do I sit?"

"You're a litigant appearing in person. Why, you sit here," he said pointing to the bench in front of the pews. Nothing between me and the judge.

"And when can I speak?"

"The justice will tell you when."

"How do I address the judge?"

"Always as 'My Lord.'"

"My Lord," I repeated.

I wrote the words "MY LORD" in huge letters on the file folder I had on the table. I didn't want to embarrass myself by calling him "Your Honor," "Your Grace," "My Liege," "Your Worship" or even "Sir."

"My Lord . . . " I said to myself. I thought with disgust, "Didn't this class-sick society learn any kind of lesson from the American Revolution?"

"Will the judge be wearing a wig?" I asked.

"Oh, yes, sir."

"The shoulder-length model or the short one."

"The short one, Sir. Come outside the courtroom and I'll have the justice's clark have a few words with you."

In the dark hall outside, several knots of people were holding last-minute conferences. One group consisted of an untidy young man and woman in dark overcoats, a barrister and an older gentleman in blue suit. The older man, Albert Collins said, was the justice's clark. Wearing a blue suit with red-and-black rep tie, he was white haired with a small, neat white mustache, glasses and a protruding tummy. When the clark was free, Albert Collins took me over to meet him. I mentioned Ridgway and Market Movements.

The barrister overheard our conversation and said that he was on the case. This was Guy Tritton, six feet tall with horn-rimmed glasses and obviously very full of himself; except for Tritton's mop of curls, he was a ringer for the English comic actor Ian Carmichael who was so hysterically funny in *I'm All Right, Jack* and *Brothers in Law*, where he played a barrister.

Tritton wore a blue suit and a white shirt with narrow red stripes, most of which was covered with his white bib thing. I watched fascinated as he struggled to get his short white wig over his ample curls.

In Court 40 I took my seat. I was alone in the front row as we waited for the judge. Seated at a table facing me was a round-faced man in a black robe — a dead ringer for the character actor Franklin Pangborn. He had very black mustache, and he, too, wore a wig. I learned later this was the clark of the court who took notes and created the official record of the proceedings. No court reporter was present, so presumably no transcript would be available. The justice's clark joined the court clark seated at a table in front facing me.

"Mr. Hatch," came a booming voice from behind. I turned. Barrister Tritton handed me a sheaf of documents. I read through them: complaints . . . old correspondence between lawyers from 1992 . . . photocopied articles about direct mail . . . Ridgway's current P&L . . . Programmes from the Direct Marketing Fair . . . Ridgway's Affidavit . . . and a Notice of Motion to shut me down.

Above me at the front of the room, Albert Collins — now clad in a black robe — opened the door next to the judge's bench. We all rose. Enter a bewigged and berobed Mr. Justice Rattee.

The Law is the true embodiment
Of everything that's excellent,
It has no kind of fault or flaw,
And I, my lords, embody the law.

Mr. Justice Rattee took his seat and we all took ours. He was late forties with a square jaw, rimless half glasses — a ringer for E.G. Marshall. All the players were from Central Casting, with the exception of myself, a balding, pear-shaped American businessman of sixty.

Albert Collins took an empty chair next to the judge's clerk. Four men were arrayed opposite me: Collins, the justice's clerk and the court clark seated with their chairs at eye level; presiding over the proceedings from his perch high above was Mr. Justice Rattee.

The first case dealt with a Sicilian restaurateur whom the tax authorities were trying to shut down because he was thousands of pounds in arrears in VAT tax payments. A plain, pudgy woman barrister haltingly pleaded to allow the restaurant to remain open; otherwise the owner would have no income and would never be able to pay his back taxes. After twenty minutes of argument, the motion was denied and that contingent left the room.

Things looked bleak. Mr. Justice Rattee was not Mr. Nice Guy. Our turn.

The Hearing

I kept my eyes front. Guy Tritton rose behind me. In a booming voice filled with unctuous self-confidence he began. He was the quintessentially overbearing young British barrister; I decided he was not Ian Carmichael but rather John Cleese in curls and horn-rimmed glasses.

God, how I wanted to win this thing!

TRITTON: My Lord, this is about advertising and about direct mail. This is a classic case of Passing Off.

He pronounced direct as dy-rect, and passing as possing.

My Lord, you have before you a series of documents which I would like to take His Lordship through.

MR. JUSTICE RATTEE: None of these is sworn.

TRITTON: No, My Lord. The time pressures were such that we could not do it. There is a direct marketing fair going on in Wembley. It will last two more days and it is imperative that an injunction be issued today, or irreparable harm will be caused my client. May I take you through the documents?

MR. JUSTICE RATTEE: By all means.

Tritton then recited the contents of the documents, ending up with the motion.

TRITTON: Now, My Lord, would you take a moment to read the affidavit?

MR. JUSTICE RATTEE: Of course.

You could cut the silence with a knife as Mr. Justice Rattee read through the document. At length he said, "All right, I've read it."

Tritton explained that his client had a substantial sum invested in the name *Who's Mailing What?* and that this American company had come over to the Fair and was creating deliberate confusion between the two companies. Already irreparable damage had occurred as people came up to the defendant's booth believing it to be his client's booth. Tritton painted me as an interloper and a thief and said in no uncertain terms that I was the villain of the piece.

As he droned on, I began feeling worse and worse. With two solicitors, a barrister, reams of photocopied material, Ridgway was spending a small fortune to extricate me from the show.

I remembered the current brouhaha in my own country where a junkyard dog named Newt was extolling the English legal system because the loser pays all court costs, thus, supposedly, reducing frivolous litigation.

How would this caper look on my expense account?

Tritton said that the court had authority to shut me down under Rule 65, Section 4 on page 1184. Mr. Justice Rattee pulled a white-covered book from the corner of his desk and turned to page 1184.

I began to get gloomier and gloomier as Tritton and the judge joined forces to rewrite the *ex parte* injunction to shut me down. For Tritton and his prosecutorial team, this appeared to be a slam-dunk. I had about a hundred pounds cash and no check. Would the court take Visa?

Suddenly my visions of being F. Lee Bailey were turning to Old Bailey.

I suffered what is known in the medical profession as a klong — a sudden rush of shit to the heart.

I could always run out the door, stop at my hotel where I would pack quickly and head for the airport. My room was on the ground floor; if they followed, I could go out the window.

When Tritton and the judge had finished agreeing on the wording, Tritton said, "Now, My Lord, there seems to be a Mr. Hatch here. I don't know who he is, why he's here or whom he represents."

I raised my hand feebly.

MR. JUSTICE RATTEE: Mr. Hatch, who are you and why are you here?

I rose, weak in the knees. I could feel many pairs of eyes boring into me front and back. The only way I could win in this court would be for the judge to see me as the beleaguered victim from another country. For that reason, I kept my accent very American — with the flat a's and hard r's you hear in Chicago or Minneapolis.

HATCH: My Lord, I am the world's foremost authority on direct mail . . .

MR. JUSTICE RATTEE: But why are you here? Do you own the company? Whom do you represent?

In his tone of voice I detected a combination of sarcasm, condescension and not a little touch of anger. I sensed immediately what he was about; if I were some grandstanding American wacko out to disrupt this proceeding, he wanted to quash me quick.

HATCH: My Lord, I do not own the company. I am the editor and founder of *WHO'S MAILING WHAT!* Three hours ago when I was at my booth at the Wembley Fair, Mr. Ridgway came up and handed me a card saying that this hearing would be taking place at two o'clock. It all happened today. I thought I should be here.

MR. JUSTICE RATTEE: Umph . . .

HATCH: May I continue?

MR. JUSTICE RATTEE: Go on.

HATCH: My Lord, in 1984 my wife and I started a newsletter and library service called WHO'S MAILING WHAT! I apologize to the court this all happened so suddenly that I was unable to get a solicitor or barrister. I did call my office and they faxed me the cover pages of my first two issues with the dates clearly showing as October and November 1984. It has been continuously published up to the present time.

At the time we started, I tried to get the name *WHO'S MAILING WHAT!* trademarked. I do not know UK trademark law, but in the US a trademark cannot be issued for a name that says what a thing is. However, after five consecutive years of publishing and using the name, I applied for a trademark. There were no objections, so I now have a trademark on WHO'S MAILING WHAT! in the U.S.

As I said, I started my *WHO'S MAILING WHAT!* in 1984. Mr. Tritton's client started his business and started using my title, *Who's Mailing What?* in 1991.

I monitor American direct mail; Mr. Tritton's client monitors British direct mail.

In 1992, my company was acquired by North American Publishing Company in Philadelphia, which publishes 14 business magazines. My wife and I moved to Philadelphia where we continue to run *WHO'S MAILING WHAT!* and the magazine *Target Marketing.*

I came to London to see if any British advertising people would be interested in American direct mail. I am not in competition with Mr. Ridgway. His entire business is devoted to direct mail in the U.K. Mine is entirely about American direct mail.

I do not see any confusion. If anyone comes to my booth looking for information about direct mail in Britain, I send them to Mr. Ridgway's booth. Thank you, My Lord.

I sat down.

MR. JUSTICE RATTEE: Thank you, Mr. Hatch.

The judge thought a moment. "I am not convinced this is a case of possing off," the judge said. "And I am not convinced I have the power to make an order until I am shown that it is a matter of law."

Tritton replied: "My Lord, this all happened very quickly. I wasn't able to be fully prepared. I must request a recess to look up the law."

"You may have forty minutes," the justice said. "no more."

Gilbert's lyric swirled in my brain.

Ere I go to court I will read my brief through
(Said I to myself — said I.)
And I'll never take work I'm unable to do,
(Said I to myself — said I!)
My learned profession I'll never disgrace
By taking a fee with a grin on my face,
When I haven't been there to attend to the case,
(Said I to myself — said I.)

Albert Collins came down from his chair and told me to be back in court at twenty of four.

As I was leaving, it was apparent Guy Tritton and the two lawyers were unnerved. Were things beginning to shift my way? Did I have a chance? Was I inside the judge's head?

I walked around the Royal Courts of Justice. It was eleven in the morning in Philadelphia, and I had an overpowering urge to call Peggy at the office in Philadelphia to tell her I was arguing the case in the High Court of Justice. But the pay phone did not take credit cards and I didn't know the AT&T access number.

Back in court, Tritton nervously handed me six photocopied pages and sent a set up to Mr. Justice Rattee's desk. We all stood as the judge reentered the room. I raised my hand and asked to speak. The judge nodded.

I rose and told the story of a woman in the Netherlands five years ago who subscribed to my newsletter and then kept calling me with questions.

HATCH: Finally during one of her calls, she announced she was going to start a service like mine in the Benelux countries and she was going to call it *Who's Mailing What* just like me. "I would prefer you didn't call it *Who's Mailing What*," I said. 'That's my name and people will be confused.' So she called it *Vie Mailt Vat!* which is Dutch for Who's Mailing What. And for the last five years, we have lived in peaceful coexistence. Thank you, My Lord.

This brought a smile to Mr. Justice Rattee's face. "Thank you, Mr. Hatch."

Tritton was on his feet behind me at once. "My Lord, I cite here the Law of Possing Off, by Christian Wadleigh; Wadleigh is the leading authority. As you can see on page 3, the operative case here is Lord Diplock in *Advocat* and Lord Parker in *Spaulding v. Gamage.* Lord Diplock sets up five categories."

Tritton read the five categories, and he and the judge skirmished over the wording of the law.

TRITTON: This is fraudulent use of my client's name, My Lord. Not fraud in the criminal sense, you understand. But false. Misleading.

MR. JUSTICE RATTEE: What is misleading? The American *Who's Mailing What* talks about American direct mail, isn't that correct?

TRITTON: Misrepresentation, My Lord.

MR. JUSTICE RATTEE: Misrepresentation of *what?*

The Justice seemed to be growing impatient.

MR. JUSTICE RATTEE: Mr. Hatch, you cover only American direct mail, is that right?

I rose and held up the current issue of *Who's Mailing What!*

HATCH: My Lord, the subtitle of my *WHO'S MAILING WHAT!* is: "The only newsletter, analysis and record of direct mail in America."

MR. JUSTICE RATTEE: And, Mr. Tritton, your client covers direct mail in the U.K., isn't that right?

TRITTON: But, My Lord . . .

MR. JUSTICE RATTEE: Isn't that right, Mr. Tritton?

TRITTON: Yes, My Lord, but . . .

MR. JUSTICE RATTEE: Then these are two completely different products.

Taradiddle, taradiddle, tol lol lay!

TRITTON: It's a matter of logic, My Lord. Let's say I found a business and start doing business as "A" . . . and someone comes along and started doing the same business under the name of "A." That would be a diversion.

MR. JUSTICE RATTEE: How can there be a diversion when you have different products? No one is going to buy yours rather than his, because they are different products. One deals with the U.S. and the other deals with the U.K.

TRITTON: My Lord, damage occurs . . .

MR. JUSTICE RATTEE: You say damage occurs. This conference in Wembley is a one-day affair. What damage will your client suffer?

Tritton's voice took on a hard edge.

TRITTON: My Lord, what if Mr. Hatch exhibits some kind of objectionable behaviour that causes embarrassment to the other *Who's Mailing What?*

Objectionable behaviour? I sat demurely in my blue suit, Custom Shop shirt, brand new muted blue-and-green flowered tie. The Lifeboat Sticker on my lapel proved I was a kind and generous citizen of the world.

Objectionable behaviour? Could Mr. Justice Rattee imagine me falling-down drunk and lurching up the stairs to the balcony of the exhibit hall where I would whip out my nasty and urinate all over the exhibitors below? He would know better. Such a scenario was not possible, given the niggardly, thimble-sized shots served everywhere in the U.K.

MR. JUSTICE RATTEE: What sort of objectionable behaviour, Mr. Tritton?

TRITTON: Uh . . . Uh . . . Supposing he fails to follow up on leads!

Taradiddle, taradiddle, tol lol lay!

TRITTON: Or if he fails to make known the distinction. There has already been confusion. People have come to one booth thinking it was the other.

HATCH: My Lord, I am not interested in tricking anybody into thinking that I cover British direct mail.

TRITTON: But, My Lord, this is clearly a classic case of Possing Off!

MR. JUSTICE RATTEE: Are the products different?

HATCH: Yes, My Lord. One is the U.S.; the other is the U.K.

MR. JUSTICE RATTEE: Mr. Tritton, *are these not different products?*

TRITTON: Well, yes, My Lord, but . . .

MR. JUSTICE RATTEE: Then they are not in competition. I will not grant the *ex parte* injunction.

Mr. Justice Rattee stood up and walked out of the room.
I sat stunned.
I had won.
I had argued a case in my own behalf in the High Court of Justice *and won!*

I looked up. The faces of Albert Collins, the justice's clerk, and the court clerk were wreathed in smiles. I went up to Collins, shook his hand and thanked him for his courtesy and hospitality. After exchanging a few words with the clerk of the court, I walked out, passing Guy Tritton and his duo of untidy little solicitors in worried conversation. In London, you walk. I don't know where I walked to. But I walked. It was 4:30 in the afternoon. Beginning of rush hour. The streets were jammed with cars and people. I kept walking. On air! What an incredible high!

> *Bow, bow, ye lower middle classes!*
> *Bow, bow, ye tradesmen, bow ye masses!*
> *Blow the trumpets, bang the brasses!*
>   *Tantantara! Tzing! Boom!*

Only after I had climbed into a taxi and was riding back to my hotel did the awful truth of what had really happened come crashing down on my head.

God Herself had played the cruelest of practical jokes on me.

It was as though I had gone out on the golf course totally alone and hit a hole in one.

IN THE HIGH COURT OF JUSTICE

CHANCERY DIVISION

MR JUSTICE RATTEE

TUESDAY THE 14TH DAY OF MARCH 1995

IN THE MATTER OF AN INTENDED ACTION

BETWEEN

JEREMY RIDGWAY (trading as MARKET MOVEMENTS)
                                        Intended Plaintiff

              and

TARGET MARKETING INC..
                              Intended Defendant

UPON MOTION made ex parte by Counsel for the Intended Plaintiff (hereinafter referred to as "the Plaintiff")

AND Mr Hatch of the Intended Defendant company attending

AND UPON READING the documents recorded on the Court File as having been read

AND the Plaintiff by his Counsel undertaking forthwith to issue a Writ of Summons claiming relief in the form of that mentioned to the Court this day

THE COURT DOES NOT THINK FIT to make any Order on the said Motion save

(1)   that the Plaintiff be at liberty to issue a concurrent Writ of Summons and a Notice of Motion and to serve

       (i) the said Writ of Summons

(ii) a Notice of Motion and

(iii) this Order

upon the Intended Defendant (hereinafter referred to as "the Defendant") out

of the jurisdiction of this Court at 401 North Broad Street Philadelphia PA

19108 or elsewhere in the United States of America

(2)   that the time within which the Defendant is to acknowledge service is to be

within 22 days after service

Appendix
Some Basic Definitions

Advocate: The ultimate achievement of a marketer — a repeat customer who not only spends money with you but who also urges friends and neighbors to do likewise.

Buyer/Subscriber: A person who has said "yes" to your offer but may not have yet paid the bill.

Control: An advertisement or mailing package against which the results of all other tests and efforts are measured.

Cheshire Label: A simple paper label containing a name, address and source key that is affixed to an order card.

Conversion: A magazine circulation term for a subscriber who renewed for the first time; also a first-time repeat buyer or donor.

Direct Marketing/Database Marketing: Manipulating people from a distance, keeping careful track of what they buy, creating more and more wants and continually delighting them with your products and service.

Donor: A contributor to a charity.

Dry Test: Offering for sale a product that does not yet exist to see if the market will respond.

Effort: Any advertisement, direct response TV commercial or direct mail package that goes out with the intention of generating response.

Focus Group: Assembling a group of consumers or prospects and leading them in a discussion of a product category as a whole or your product in particular.

General Advertising: Using broadcast, space, skywriting, hiring kids with sandwich boards to stand on street corners, etc., to create *awareness* about your product or service.

Hotline: Hotline names are recent buyers or donors and, therefore, very desirable to reach and more expensive to rent.

Johnson Box: The headline of a direct mail letter that appears above the salutation; reputedly invented by freelancer Frank Johnson.

Lift Letter (Lift Piece): An extra element in a mailing designed to "lift" response.

Magalog: A self-mailer (nonenvelope mailing) that is a cross between a catalog and a magazine.

Marketer: A customer manager — as opposed to a product manager — who creates wants rather than servicing needs.

Marketing: Finding and acquiring new customers and keeping them in a state of perpetual delight.

Market Research: Surveying a potential audience to find out whether a product has a chance and surveying the competition to learn what you are up against in terms of product and price.

Mother-in-Law Research: Asking a friend or family member for an opinion about what you propose to offer.

Multi-Buyer: One who buys more than one product from you or donates to your cause more than once a year.

Package Goods: What you see in supermarkets outside the deli, produce, dairy and meat departments.

Paid Buyer/Subscriber/Donor: A paying customer.

Promotion: Hyping your product or service by sampling or making an offer in the form of discount coupons, but not maintaining the individual customer records.

Product Manager: Usually associated with the package goods industry — a person responsible for seeing to it that a specific product is on the shelves, the pipeline is open and consumers know about the product.

Prospect: Someone who has indicated interest in what you have to offer or whose demographics and/or psychographics make him or her a likely customer.

Renewal: A magazine term for a regular subscriber who has renewed more than once. (See Conversion)

Retailing: The most demanding profession in the world.

RFM: Recency-Frequency-Monetary Value — the basic measurement of the quality of a customer.

Rollout: Cashing in on the proprietary information gathered from a test and using it to successfully market to a much wider universe.

Sales: Persuading prospects, customers and donors to spend money with you.

Sampling: Giving away (or sending) an actual sample of your product.

Suspect: A person who might do business with you.

Test: Trying out a promotion on a small scale to see what happens.

TSR: Telephone Sales Representative — an outbound or inbound tele-marketer.

Wet Test: The next step after a dry test. In a dry test, the audience indi-cated interest. With a wet test, the product exists, allowing the marketer to gauge retention and customer satisfaction.

INDEX

ABOUT DENNY HATCH . . .

Denison Hatch — freelance direct mail copywriter, designer and consultant — is contributing editor of *Target Marketing* magazine serving the direct marketing community. In addition, he is founder of the newsletter *Who's Mailing What!*, the only publication that covers American direct mail for direct matters.

In past lives he has been a book salesman, an advertising salesman, run book clubs, been a copywriter for a direct mail agency.

In 1984, with his wife Peggy, he launched the newsletter, *Who's Mailing What!* out of their home in Stamford, CT; it was based on his massive library of direct mail samples. In 1992, his company was acquired by North American Publishing Company in Philadelphia where he continued to publish the newsletter, as well as editing *Targeting Marketing* and the *Directory of Major Mailers and What They Mail*.

To create the newsletter, Denny would read 3,000 to 4,000 direct mail packages a month in more than 200 categories—business, consumer, non-profit and catalogs—and presided over a library of over 200,000 direct mail samples; for a fee subscribers can get copies of any of these mailing packages.

In 1989 he was featured in a front-page article in *The Wall Street Journal*, has been quoted in *Time, Newsweek, Forbes* and has appeared on NBC's Today program. Denny is a frequent speaker at direct marketing seminars and conferences in the U.S. and the Far East. He is the author of three published novels. His book, *Million Dollar Mailing$*, was published in 1993. *2,239 Tested Secrets for Direct Marketing Success*, co-authored with Don Jackson, was published in December 1997, by NTC Contemporary Books, Lincolnwood, IL.

Denny can be reached at dennyhatch@aol.com